Transcultural Poetics and the Concept of the Poet

> Ranjan Ghosh poses a series of challenging questions about poetry, its methods and its manners, drawing on a striking range of intellectual and spiritual contexts, both eastern and western, and moving with enviable fluency between many of the greatest figures of the English literary tradition. A ranging and inclusive writer, Ghosh exemplifies in a highly individual way the imagination he singles out for notice in Coleridge—'a syncopation of contrary elements.'
>
> —*Seamus Perry, University of Oxford*

A preface has been supplied by Professor Haun Saussy.

Haun Saussy is University Professor in the Departments of Comparative Literature and East Asian Languages & Literatures and the Committee on Social Thought at the University of Chicago. His books include *The Problem of a Chinese Aesthetic* and *The Ethnography of Rhythm*.

Critiquing the politics and dynamics of the transcultural poetics of reading literature, this book demonstrates an ambitious understanding of the concept of the poet across a wide range of traditions—Anglo-American, German, French, Arabic, Chinese, Sanskrit, Bengali, Urdu—and philosophies of creativity that are rarely studied side by side. Ghosh carves out unexplored spaces of negotiation and intersections between literature, aesthetics and philosophy. The book demonstrates an original method of 'global comparison' that displaces the relatively staid and historicist categories that have underpinned comparative literature approaches so far, since they rarely dare stray beyond issues of influence and schools, or new 'world literature' approaches that affirm cosmopolitanism and transnationalism as overarching themes. Going beyond comparatism and reformulating the chronological patterns of reading, this bold book introduces new methodologies of reading literature to configure the concept of the poet from Philip Sidney to T. S. Eliot, reading the notion of the poet through completely new theoretical and epistemic triggers. Commonly known texts and sometimes well-circulated ideas are subjected to refreshing reading in what the author calls the 'transcultural now' and (in) fusionised transpoetical matrices. By moving between theories of poetry and literature that come from widely separated times, contexts, and cultures, this book shows the relevance of canonical texts to a theory of the future as marked by post-global concerns.

Ranjan Ghosh teaches in the department of English, University of North Bengal, India. To know more about him please visit his website: http://www.ranjanghosh.com/

Routledge Interdisciplinary Perspectives on Literature

For a full list of titles in this series, please visit www.routledge.com.

63 **Transnational Narratives from the Caribbean**
    Diasporic Literature and the Human Experience
    Elvira Pulitano

64 **Cartographies of Exile**
    A New Spatial Literacy
    Edited by Karen Elizabeth Bishop

65 **The Contemporary Literature-Music Relationship**
    Intermedia, Voice, Technology, Cross-Cultural Exchange
    Hazel Smith

66 **Post-Conflict Literature**
    Human Rights, Peace, Justice
    Edited by Chris Andrews and Matt McGuire

67 **Landscape, Seascape, and the Eco-Spatial Imagination**
    Edited by Simon C. Estok, I-Chun Wang, and Jonathan White

68 **Auto/Biography across the Americas**
    Transnational Themes in Life Writing
    Edited by Ricia Anne Chansky

69 **Ecocriticism and Indigenous Studies**
    Conversations from Earth to Cosmos
    Edited by Joni Adamson and Salma Monani

70 **Representations of Anne Frank in American Literature**
    In Different Rooms
    Rachael McLennan

71 **Hospitality in American Literature and Culture**
    Spaces, Bodies, Borders
    Ana Mª Manzanas Calvo and Jesús Benito Sánchez

72 **Transcultural Poetics and the Concept of the Poet**
    From Philip Sidney to T. S. Eliot
    Ranjan Ghosh

Transcultural Poetics and the Concept of the Poet
From Philip Sidney to T. S. Eliot

Ranjan Ghosh

LONDON AND NEW YORK

First published 2017 by Routledge

2 Park Square, Milton Park, Abingdon, Oxfordshire OX14 4RN
52 Vanderbilt Avenue, New York, NY 10017

Routledge is an imprint of the Taylor & Francis Group, an informa business

First issued in paperback 2019

Copyright © 2017 Taylor & Francis

The right of Ranjan Ghosh to be identified as author of this work has been asserted by him in accordance with sections 77 and 78 of the Copyright, Designs and Patents Act 1988.

All rights reserved. No part of this book may be reprinted or reproduced or utilised in any form or by any electronic, mechanical, or other means, now known or hereafter invented, including photocopying and recording, or in any information storage or retrieval system, without permission in writing from the publishers.

Notice:
Product or corporate names may be trademarks or registered trademarks, and are used only for identification and explanation without intent to infringe.

Library of Congress Cataloging-in-Publication Data

CIP data has been applied for.

ISBN: 978-1-138-82631-1 (hbk)
ISBN: 978-0-367-87114-7 (pbk)

Typeset in Sabon
by codeMantra

Contents

Preface: Forces of Habit vii
Acknowledgements xi

1 Trans-habit   1
2 Mistress-Knowledge? Abuse, Apology and After   21
3 'To you I submit my selfe, and worke. Farewell': The Poet
   and the Reader   43
4 'Launch not beyond your depth but be discreet': The Tulip Poet   62
5 'Fearful Symmetry': Quantum Creativity   90
6 'Hero as Poet': Thomas Carlyle and 'Future Poetry'   108
7 'O life unlike to ours!': Matthew Arnold as an Indian Sage?   126
8 The 'Platinum' Poet and the Trans-Habitual Making of a Poem   147

Bibliography 177
Index 193

Preface
Forces of Habit

Haun Saussy

> I was cleaning a room and, meandering about, approached the divan and couldn't remember whether or not I had dusted it. Since these movements are habitual and unconscious, I could not remember and felt that it was impossible to remember—so that if I had dusted it and forgot—that is, had acted unconsciously, then it was the same as if I had not. If some conscious person had been watching, then the fact could be established. If, however, no one was looking, or looking on unconsciously, if the whole complex lives of many people go on unconsciously, then such lives are as if they had never been.
> —Tolstoy, diary entry cited in Viktor Shklovsky, "Art as Device"

"What is an author"? Michel Foucault's way of raising this question, in 1969, unsettled a stultifying consensus around the institutions of literacy. The publishing, reading, teaching, citing, debating, translating, classifying, buying and selling of books call at every moment on a figure known as "the author" (indeed, I have just repeated that gesture in alluding to Michel Foucault, 1926–1984, author of "What is an Author?"). Identifying the author, creating a profile or personality that guides interpretation, excluding forgeries from the author's corpus and misunderstandings from the author's reception, are indispensable gestures. But Foucault unsettled the habitual practises that center on the author by asking how this figure had come to be constituted through history, and to what our investment in authorship pointed. What, in short, is "the author-function"? For some practises of knowledge in the modern era, Foucault argued, authorship was irrelevant or anecdotal at best. The theory of evolution by natural selection does not depend for its fruitfulness on the personality of Charles Darwin; biology is a collective practise set in motion by discoveries and hypotheses that biologists adopt and use to make further discoveries, some of which may contradict theories and observations made by Darwin. Science, says Foucault, is a non-authorial discourse because its method of validation is impersonal. Literary writing, on the other hand, depends on authors for its validation. A newly discovered poem from the early seventeenth century will make a far stronger claim on our attention if it can be plausibly assigned to Shakespeare; the poetry of Baudelaire is inseparable from the life of Baudelaire, the readership he created for himself, the standards of beauty and ugliness he devised. And by way of showing the contingency of this division of the field of knowledge into author-dependent and author-independent practises (roughly parallel to the division between the humanities and the sciences), Foucault asserts that in a pre-modern medieval world, in the absence of a culture of experiment and public verification of results, the knowledge we would call scientific was highly author-dependent: a statement about medicine carried authority if it was attributed to Aristotle or Galen. And under this medieval dispensation, a love song or a knightly romance could circulate anonymously or under a variety of names, or be adapted and rewritten dozens of times, because aesthetic merit did not hinge on identifying the person whose work it was. Moreover, in our time, the goal of many of our most significant artists and writers has been to make creation anonymous again, like Cage composing through chance operations: to reduce the author-function to zero or thereabouts, and thereby to open the field of possible interpretations.

Foucault's purpose was to make us think about authorship rather than invoking it automatically, habitually. He succeeded, of course: the essay is cited hundreds of times in a wide range of disciplines. But the fable it offers has a certain provincial character. It is a tale told about the Western world, about the emergence of distinct, indeed highly contrasted disciplines of science and humanities, about the cultivation of individuality and its deliberate mortification (in literature, at least since Mallarmé, though this may be only a supplementary form of individuality). These bold categories—science/literature, premodern/modern, author/non-author—permit a disturbance of the consensus, but cannot take us far enough toward a satisfying answer to the question, "what is an author?" So let us ask again: what, across the broadest range of cultures and periods that we can muster, have authors been, how have they functioned, why has it been important or unimportant to know anything about them? We should learn, in short, to ask Foucault's question rather than let him ask it for us. What is an author in pre-imperial China? What is an author in the last century before Muhammad? What is an author in fifteenth-century Mexico? What, generally speaking, are the imaginary resources that ideas of authorship unlock?

This is the plane on which Ranjan Ghosh's *Transcultural Poetics and the Concept of the Poet* frames its questions. The matter of its discourse is, first, a series of English-language authors, all canonical, all possessing the attributes of fully recognised authorship (they attract dozens of entries in each year's *MLA Bibliography*, they are influential, they have shaped the language, and so forth). But though Ghosh starts from that condition of authorship, he does not leave his subjects there. Probing the conditions of poetic speech in the case of Sidney, Jonson, Carlyle, Arnold and many another writer, he finds that the terms of poetics pioneered in Sanskrit, classical Chinese, Arabic, Persian, or modern Bengali do more to indicate the powers of authorship than do the words and concepts that would have been familiar to these post-Renaissance English writers. It is not "the mind of Europe" that he sees recapitulated in their self-reflection, but something bigger and other.

A word about Ghosh's method of proceeding. Unlike many researchers in cross-cultural poetics or psychology, he does not waste time finding equivalences. The terms familiar to Tagore or to al-Farabi are sufficient unto themselves. Moreover, his cross-cultural investigation does not seek to proffer universal answers. The book is structured like a spiderweb, hazarding hundreds of filament-like connections between passages of books that often have only a little history in common. The "impassioned discontinuous continuity" that Ghosh finds in Coleridge sets out the structure and ethos of this book. It shows that "meaningful communication" across cultures does not have to be a matter of common denominators and agreed-upon terms. Ghosh seeks "the way and mechanism to overcome the blinkered, absolutist, nonpluralist relativism that incommensurability legitimizes." He finds it in something he calls "trans-habit."

Habit has a poor reputation in aesthetic theory. Viktor Shklovsky's "Art as Device" (1913), practically the manifesto of modernism, denounces the "automatization" that deadens our perception of life, causes us to perform habitual actions so unthinkingly that we are not even conscious of having performed them. To break these reflex arcs, to make the stone stony, is the mission of art according to Shklovsky. Ghosh, more alert to the acquired nature of cultural characteristics, seeks to enact a similar "estrangement" to Shkovsky's by warping habit away from its usual path. He chooses to interrupt English or European reception by putting it under the light of theories and explanations from elsewhere. This he calls trans-habit. "Trans-habit is the provocation to stop being deceived by the beauty of customs and mores and being confronted instead by the sublime of self-exceeding that reconsiders our threshold factors of existence."

Among the habits Ghosh disrupts is one that anyone engaged in cross-cultural work will have noticed. It is all very well to acquire expertise in and appreciation for Japanese historical narrative, let us say, or Malay poetry. But on the way to sharing this appreciation with a wider public, the theoretical vocabulary we use is almost always drawn from the usual Greek, Latin and European sources. And when we describe a poem as a lyric, a novel as autobiographical, or a story as self-referential, the history and cultural specificity of such terms do not come to mind; their application is automatic. Only once in a great while does a term come the other way, as when *rasa* or *qi* had begun to be adopted as technical terms in general poetics. The habit of assuming the identity between the modern Western norm and the universal cannot really be broken by protesting ethnocentrism, or by instituting committees for the reform of critical vocabulary; it is broken by the "trans-habit" of doing the opposite thing, of not hesitating a moment before elucidating Sidney's poetics with *takhyil, iltidhadh* and *sha'ara*. Readers may cry out, "But these are barbarous and unkempt terms never introduced to us before, blank cheques drawn on mysterious banks!"

I advise not asking for an advance hermeneutic, but staying with Ghosh to see what happens. Spiderweb, after all, is stronger than an equal volume of steel—and the measure of this book is not its "solidity" (a term that seeks to reward predictability; "solid" often means "boring") but its tensile strength.

The question trans-habit asks is, after all, whether it is possible for us to go beyond the horizon of our known and accepted references, whether we are free to change ourselves. This might be the core question of liberal democracy, but one unspoken and untheorised by those who take the person as the basis and center of rights, duties and will. Trans-habit has to do rather with the constitution and reconstitution of persons in circuits of behavior (including linguistic behavior). Its "inevitable momentum" is about changing the terms of knowledge. No one book can do that conclusively; but this book offers a proof of concept and an adventure, an experiment in changing families of thought.

Acknowledgements

After more than a decade of writing and research, when I see this book taking off for readerly reception, I associate myself with this transition through distance and desire, recognition and recalcitrance, access and accessibility, foundations and perspectivism—experiences in history, aesthetics and culture that I have tried to establish as my long standing 'trans-(in)fusion-now' position. My first endeavour to develop a trans-(in)fusionist theory of reading literature came through as *Thinking Literature across Continents*, co-authored with J. Hillis Miller from Duke University Press (2016); and then trans-(in)fusionist understanding of educational theory and philosophy gave rise to *Aesthetics, Politics, Pedagogy, Tagore: Towards a Transcultural Philosophy of Education* (Palgrave, 2016). This book establishes my trans-(in)fusionist position on comparative aesthetics—a book that does not trace the trajectory of the notion of the poet from the Renaissance to the Modern period but tries to work out a fresh method of 'global comparison', something that displaces the relatively staid and historicist categories that have underpinned comparative literature approaches because they rarely dare stray beyond issues of influence and schools, or new 'world literature' approaches that affirm cosmopolitanism and transnationalism as overarching themes. My encounters with the poets/thinkers and their aesthetics were events in pure contamination. I lost the book many a time through these long years of reading and writing; but, the losing was not about loss.

The 'losing' owes to some excellent scholars who have inspired my research interests in many ways: for my readings in Arabic and Persian poetics and criticism, Justine Landau, Rebecca Gould, Muhsin Jassim al-Musawi, Huda J. Fakhreddine and Geert Jan van Gelder stand out among many others; for Chinese poetics and philosophy, I owe a lot to Wan Keping, Zhang Longxi, Zong-qi Cai, Haun Saussy, Michael A. Fuller and Ming Dong Gu; on theoretical journeys and detours, in readings and provocations, the list is inexhaustively long: J. Hillis Miller, Laurent Dubreil, Daniel O' Hara, Ulrich Tim Kragh, Ethan Kleinberg, Claire Colebrook, Jean Michel Rabate, Susan Friedman, Robert Gordon, Simon Morgan Wortham, Karl Simms, Rachel Galvin, Tim Clark, Ian Almond, Sidney Homan, Christopher Perricone, Graham Harman and many others.

Some of my thoughts had already found a print life before getting into this book: 'Ben Jonson and His Reader: An Aesthetics of Antagonism', *The Comparatist*, Vol. 37, May, 2013, 138–155; 'A Reading in Comparative Aesthetics: Arnold as Indian Sage?' *Nineteenth Century Prose*, Vol. 34, Nos. 1/2 Spring/Fall 2007, 257–282; 'Carlyle's Hero as Poet and Sri Aurobindo's poetic theory: Reconfiguring few dimensions of Creativity', *Angelaki: Journal of Theoretical Humanities*, 11.1, 2006, 35–44.

My persistent and persuasive projects in the incorporealities of transphilosophical studies continue through my forthcoming books where the eros of tradition, the submarine potential of concepts and paradigms, and liminal habitations at the cross-roads of the sciences and humanities leave me perturbed and peregrinative. Someone said that being everywhere is being nowhere. For me, true thinking begins when one finds the character and potential of 'nowhere': finding a 'place' when one has lost his places. Reflections and meditations from 'nowhere' produce the atopic shock that knowledge regimes need to experience—the potency of trans where thinking can only begin from an 'entangled island' and critical understanding from the realisation that the power of a room or a pitcher is always in its emptiness.

1   Trans-habit

> Accident is the omission of act in self & the hindering of act in another; This is Vice, but all Act is Virtue. To hinder another is not an act; it is the contrary; it is a restraint on action both in ourselves & in the person hinder'd, for he who hinders another omits his own duty at the same time.
>
> —William Blake[1]

> "Do you really think," inquired the patient Diotima of the polemical Socrates, "that if a thing isn't beautiful it's therefore bound to be ugly?. ... And that what isn't learned must be ignorant? Have you never heard of something which comes between the two?" Plato[2]

> Within the rhythms of life, the swinging gateway opens and novelty emerges spontaneously to revitalize the world, tempering whatever has moved to an extreme, and reclaiming whatever has strayed from the path. Whatever is most enduring is ultimately overtaken in the ceaseless transformation of things.[3]

Can habit, with its repetition, a uniformity of happening, and comfort-generation have a conative property to trouble and stir? A certain habit of doing or performing repeated over a time generates an indulgence for a change, albeit transient. But the transience is a habitation for experiencing a performative alternative which might be disruptive in a positive way. What that means is that the 'alternative' can be re-creative resulting in habit-shedding; consequently, it espouses a new act which, again, in its repetitive fervour, can surface as a new habit. If getting positioned over is a habit, abandoning oneself for the 'random' is a habit too. A habit dies hard but it can have the simmer beneath the supposed encrustation, graduating from a deadened status to a 'staging', from an establishment to enfranchisement. Habit then is not a polarity, rather, is reason; it is also difficult to reason why something becomes a habit. Habit is will and intelligence locked in a tricky combination. Going out of habit—the trans-habit—is a way of seeing and performing the *flanuer* in all of us. Michel Serres's glorious evocativeness is worth our attention:

> Method passes through the forest considering the trees of no account; it crosses the wide sea. Thus the farmer ploughs the field to kill all plants and roots and to coax it so that a single plant may flourish without rivals; he despises as a savage the woodsman who is expert in

trees and vines, in the places and times of each, finding his way in the forest with no paths or compass, by means of markers so ingrained that they become instinctive. Taking the straight path out of the woods without seeing anything is equivalent to liberating oneself from savagery or wilderness. These two relationships to places and space are still the distinguishing mark today of the distance between the man of science and the man who is called, disparagingly, a literary man or poet—wild—the distance between the landscape and the panorama.[4]

Here lies the profound antagonism between the science of habit with the poetics of habit. Rabindranath Tagore points out how the habit of rhythm of the universe is a trick, a mystery, a panorama and a labyrinth. Our living, thinking and modes of expression in art and life are impatient with the wry and insipid forms of habit. Habit operates to challenge our conditions of existence and thought; its potency is in outlawing the most conceivable curves where 'adventures begin with shipwreck'.[5] The poet is the sailor is the rambler. Habit is in revisiting habit wherein the story stays embosomed.

Jim Garrison rightly notes:

> to say customs form habits is a pragmatic naturalist's way of agreeing with Gadamer that culture has us before we have it, and that our task is to become reflectively aware of our habits to discriminate those that enable us to understand from those that do not. We all live lives prescripted for us by cultural texts; for example, ideas like "Free Will," "the Bible," or "Enlightenment ideals of Rationality" condition our understandings, including feelings, about ourselves and others even as we strive to edit and emendate the story of our lives. To acknowledge oneself as controlled by habits and conditioned by prior social customs is simply to recognize that one's values, beliefs, interests, perceptions, and so on are primordially predetermined by the social context, including dominant cultural texts, of a given historical epoch. We cannot eliminate social conditioning or the prejudices that result; we can only deceive ourselves into believing that we have. Socially conditioned habits constitute our self-identities.[6]

Habits determine our experience, our precincts of knowledge, through familiarity bred thereof. So Thomas Carlyle lets us see through his *Sartor Resartus* how customs 'has hoodwinked us, from the first; we do everything by Custom, even Believe by it; that our very Axioms, let us boast of Free-thinking as we may, are oftenest simply such Beliefs as we have never heard questioned'.[7] Trans-habit challenges our customs of thinking and thought, leaving inherited habitual attitude under scrutiny. This is not to discredit all forms of thought and knowledge that habits establish and generate. Carlyle is right to observe that 'habit is the deepest law of human nature. It is our supreme strength: if also, in certain circumstances, our miserablest weakness'.[8] Habit then builds the fire of opposition under it and trans-habit intensifies and diversifies that inherent opposition further. The repetitiveness of habit and consciousness against being dulled by its iterative torpor can result in moral virtues and a separate vein of emotion[9]; habit in its seriality can be physiological in nature and origin too.[10] Habit insensitivises us to its own operations; we are habituated into losing our consciousness of habit. The authority of habit deauthorises us.

Powered by an inward principle, habit, as a 'blind giant', conceals, as Ralph Waldo Emerson notes, our power of improvement. Contradicting Emerson, I would like to argue by saying that describing habits is not always about describing ourselves, for if habit straps a law it also exposes man to 'another law'. Habit is inviolately regulative and yet self-reflexive (a Carlylean unconscious). Emerson's observations, however, implicate this hypostasizing and yet transforming power of habit:

> [...] I desire to warn you against the smallest taint of evil existing in you, because, there are such things as habits. I beseech you to consider that every action you do is either the beginning of a habit, or is part of a habit already existing. And the terror of this consideration lies in this fact, that we are not one thing, and our habits another, but that we are formed by them, and changed by them.[11]

Trans-habit is a complicated game of authority positions: changing baton of power, intent, will and creativity. It produces the power and dynamics of 'listening'.

The rhythm of life and our ways of seeing are habits caught in *hexis* and *praxis*—emerging from the verb *ekhein* which is about having a state and disposition.[12] Felix Ravaisson looks into an active agency that habit is capable of concealing: disposition transforming into a potential (*dunamis*) that can trigger change and counter-change (*hexeos*). Potential is acquired for mutable disposition and stay possessed for more actualization (*energeia*). Clare Carlisle and Mark Sinclair explain Ravaisson's understanding of active force in habit as a drive or tendency which comes close to Leibniz's interpretation of the law of inertia: 'if *hexis* signifies a "way of being", it is a way of being of the body, which is not the mere mechanism or material thing envisaged by Descartes and Kant, but intrinsically active and dynamic. If, through habit, "the idea becomes being", this is a process that involves the body and its movements'.[13] Will and instinct are complicit in habit manifestation or abilities of habit which although stays as apparent antipodes are yet not incommensurable opposites: 'habit is the dividing line, or the middle term, between will and nature; but it is a moving middle term, a dividing line that is always moving, and which advances by an imperceptible progress from one extremity to the other'.[14] Habits come with beliefs and embodied habits come with emotions, as John Dewey tells us. There cannot be much disagreement with Dewey when he observes that all habits are affection and instrumental in constituting the self, bearing a 'projectile power'.[15] Habit works with the force of will and also with a sense acquired through a commitment to a repetition. It orders and systemises our actions and, strangely, in its benumbingly customised and socialised monotony, bears the worm of a manifestation which can be transitive and refigurative in nature. The understanding and affection that habit builds are, hence, thrown into crises, brought under violence, resulting in an unpeace which becomes a potential trigger for greater manifestations. Interruption in the continuity of habit becomes an inception in thought. Habit *thinks* when habit is denied. Ruptures in habits do not simply come from rational interrogation into the legitimacy and validity of its continuity; they come from impulses also—the sudden power to break free from routine codes of acts and thoughts, a release of energy that solicits imagination and indulgences. Trans-habit is the provocation to stop being deceived by the beauty of customs and mores and being confronted instead by the sublime of self-exceeding that reconsiders our threshold factors of existence. This generates 'active listening'.

I

T. S. Eliot's brief but deep habitation in Immanuel Kant resulted in four essays in the early part of his career. He believed that Kant spent a lifetime in the 'pursuit of categories, fixed only which he believed, rightly or wrongly, to be permanent, and overlooked or neglected the fact that these are only the more stable of a vast system of categories in perpetual change'.[16] One may argue saying that this fixing of categories is tantamount to habit formation: habit of aesthetics, etymologically meaning perceiving. However, trans-habit implicates categories under revision and change resulting in, to refer to Eliot again, ideas and flux—'each is the other' because 'idea and flux are … relative to each other, but … also to our point of view; from which there are inevitably degrees of reality, leading up to the Idea of the Good, which is, however, identical with all the other degrees, being at once a goal and an immanent concrete universal'.[17] Habits of thinking without being independent and irreducible categories explore the relation of the one to the many where interpretation mediates between the domains of being and becoming to evolve a coherence that is not permanent. This lends an ant*agon*istic rhythm to trans-habit—its witful investment in debate and the inevitable incidence of opposition because 'what makes a real world is difference of opinion'.[18] In Sanskrit philosophy, there are the *vada* and *dwandhyas*—the logic and dynamics of counter or opposition. Trans-habit initiates what in the Buddhist, Hindu and the Jaina tradition is called *tarka*. This pattern of negotiation or dialogue does not always require resolution or expire in agreement. *Tarka* on or about a habit leads to revisionary premises, pushing the frontiers of possibility. It can work diffractively—foregrounding a premise where *vada*, *vivada* (counter argument), *pramana* (evidence, reason), non-*pramana*, *pratyaksa* (perception), *anuman* (inference) do not work in a pattern that is neither and conclusive nor inconclusive, not always in an inflexible soundness of judgement but diffractively, in interference and transposition. *Tarka* in trans-habit does not become generalization but is, sometimes, theory whose premises of argument can be under the anxiety of revision or reformulation. It changes *pratyaksa* and makes us rethink *pramana*. Trans-habit is the recurrent knock on the doors of perception, piercing through the 'heavy curtain'[19] of habit. In the Tibetan Buddhist theory of argumentation, we encounter a 'proper opponent (*phyi rgol yang dag*) whose dialectical understanding is not an aggressive overcoming of the other but an effort to know through a cooperative proponent (*sngargol*)'. The habit of communication is not confined to understanding; inference and interference mark certain habituality of conversations into occasions of knowledge of the unknown. Proper opponent constitutes both in mediation and meditation. Hiroshi Nemoto points out that it is not in refutation that a proper opponent is constructed; it builds on the habit of a dialectic conversation that does not require a referee.[20] Nemoto observes:

> Phywa pa considers the roles of a proponent and an opponent within the framework of "inference for others." He conceives of a dialectic conversation which can be described as educational. In his system, an opponent plays the role of a good student who seeks to gain an inferential knowledge on the basis of a probative argument presented by a proponent who is a capable teacher….Phywa pa depicts this typology [the typology of the opponents] to show how a proponent can lead various types of opponents to obtain an inferential knowledge.[21]

As a compulsive insider to trans-habit, the demon of opposition makes us see two kinds of changes: successions or s-changes and Cambridge or C-changes. Nico Strobach writes:

> An *s-change* always takes place between two positive states, e.g. between rest and motion, on and off, alive and dead, green and red or c sharp and a flat (these states following immediately upon one another) and *C-changes* do not take place between positive states. Instead, they consist in the beginning or ending of one positive state which is reflected by the fact that we might answer the question "Is this red?" by saying "yes" at one time and by saying "no" at another, while acting vice versa when confronted with the question: "Is it false that this is red?".[22]

Strobach further notes that every s-change will have two C-changes in it: 'the ending of the old and beginning of the new state', the change between rest and non-rest, non-motion and motion. Change then is a happening not mere in alteration but obtained through a simultaneity inscribed in a contradiction—the opposition of two states of existence. So border-thinking haunts the question about whether paradigms and dimensions of thought system are really at rest, reified by accepted modes of reception or in motion all the time? If in motion, how can they be considered as reified and established? If being in rest is being in motion, we encounter consequences that become contradictious because the instant of rest and motion seem to function in simultaneity. Contradictions define habit as much as habit conceals the contrariety of the instant of motion with the instant of rest or the tangle of limiting instants—the 'both-state' option.

This option in trans-habitual thinking calls on singular historicity where Walter Benjamin's idea of 'interruption' [*Unterbrechung*] makes allowance for form-giving and generates its own efficacy for *trans*-formation. Interruption provides the form that does not function like a container that, as Samuel Weber explains, 'separates and opposes "inside" from "outside," immanence from transcendence, order from chaos. Rather, interruption as the enabling limit of form links it to what it must exclude in order to establish its own immanence. But since that outside—like the Saussurean 'milieu' of signifiers—is never to be exhaustively determined, the alterity involved is not a form of dialectical negativity'. It involves, as Weber argues, a relationship that stays qualified as 'ambivalent'.[23] Talking about attention and habit, Benjamin points out that 'all attentiveness has to flow into habit, if it is not to blow human beings apart, and all habit must be disrupted by attentiveness if it is not to paralyse the human being. To note something and to accustom oneself to it, to take offense, and to put up with a thing—these are the peaks and troughs of the waves on the sea of the soul. But this sea has moments of calm'.[24] This calm is the point of torment. Concentrated attention and barely noticeable distraction form a troublous combination for the development of habit. Benjamin observes that habit has its complement and we 'cross its threshold in sleep. For what comes to us when we dream is a new and unprecedented attentiveness that struggles to emerge from the womb of habit'.[25] Habit, thus, has a barely 'perceptible noise' in it—an 'insect humming or flying'—which carries our attention to separate levels of concentration and efficacy. Trans-habit distracts habit with a 'dream' which includes the peaks and the lows and the rhythm of calm that embosoms both the troughs and crests of expression. So trans-habit in its interruption refuses, on most occasions, to exist as the exhaustible container because the latency of opposition singularises the formations. It brings me to see how Georg Simmel's 'stranger'[26] through his habit of engagement, estrangement and detachment comes to invest the notion of interruption further. Trans-habit generates the politics and the aesthetics of the stranger: a figure who is distant and meddlesome, curious, inquisitive and outlandish and outsider. The stranger is the figure who 'wanders' combining both liberation and fixation—not the 'wanderer who comes today and goes tomorrow, but, rather, as the person who comes today and stays tomorrow. He is, so to speak, the potential wanderer; although he has not moved on, he has not quite overcome the freedom of coming and going'.[27] *Trans* creates the stranger as a kind oddness, some freedom from conventions and not much restricted by 'habits, piety and precedent'.[28] Trans-habit for me generates a strangerhood which is not just flippant and facetious, but has an objectivity that, as Simmel observes, 'does not simply involve passivity and detachment; it is a particular structure composed of distance and nearness, indifference and involvement'.[29] This calls for a fresh interrogation into the rhythm of alterity and contrariety which remains a recurrent motif in this book. Trans-habit's stranger-ness lies in believing that meaning is in the mask; it imports 'foreignness' to our community of meaning formation. So trans-habit gets one to invade a variety of communities of thoughts and traditions, creating possibilities of new relationships between the host and the target conceptual domains. But such relationships are never seized to the point of exhaustion resulting in trans-habit keeping up its strangerhood which, again, is the interruption. Trans-habit plays up on the dynamics of nearness and farness of ideas and ideologies to generate the circulation of the host, visitor, guest, transit, travel, affiliation, membership, ambiguity, outsider and so on.

I am tempted to see such a space—radical negativity—as Massimo Caciarri's 'metropolis' that

> shows the impossibility of synthesis, the impossibility of the city as synthesis where conflicts would disappear or be hidden or preventively repressed. The Metropolis defeats any community mentality: the conservative or regressive attitudes, from family life to the image of people coming home from work to "cultivate their kitchen gardens," as well as the progressive ones, from the image of technological comfort and individual freedom to the dream of mass liberation and to the vision of Venice as unique city in the world.[30]

This calls for a productive space, a positive habit of creativity. Underlining the complexity involved in game and habit, rules and combinations, Cacciari writes in 'Loos and His Angel':

> The deeper one's participation in a game, the more these 'openings' issue from practice itself, from "habit." The truly present has deep roots—it needs the 'games' of the 'old masters,' the languages of the posthumous. Hence, the tradition of which we are speaking here does not unfold from book to book, drawing to drawing, "line" to "line," but follows the long detours, the waits, the labyrinths of the games among the languages, of linguistic practices.[31]

But trans-habit, true to Cacciari's spirit which clearly is not in line with post-modern luridness, is indulging a 'stroll': the stroll in the mode of 'seeing, thinking, and writing that confronts the limits, not knowing what can be anticipated, not wanting to reach a conclusion'—architexture that hesitates to provide a transcendent solution and reductive finality. This is not refusal but a hesitancy that looks into stroll as a habit in nostalgia and deliverance. Like the way Simmel's stranger cannot be a marginal figure, trans-habit cannot be an action in isolation, vindicating a change or revision of habit through estrangement from others. Marginality is no approach to creativity. Trans-habit is engagement, an art to negotiate beyond oneself, not underground but aboveground.

What fate does trans-habit encounter in being complex, in its embeddedness in 'complexity'? 'The notion of complexity', explains Michel Alhadeff-Jones,

> refers to the quality or condition of being complex. Adapted from the Latin expression "complexus" (14th century) and adopted from the modern French, the term derives from "cum" and "plectere", meaning surrounding, encompassing, encircling, embracing, comprehending, comprising. Originally denoting "embracing or comprehending several elements", its use in English tended to be akin to the sense of "plaited together, interwoven". Referring to things or ideas "consisting of or comprehending various parts united or connected together" or "formed by combination of different elements", "complex" is often understood as a synonym either for composite and compound, or complicated, involved and intricate.[32]

No idea is simple, for all simple ideas are inscribed in a complex system of thoughts and experiences, rather, in the complexities of *trans*. Habits indeed are formed in complexity. We scarcely realise how they are formed on the edge of chaos. Trans-habit builds on incommensurability, like the acrasiales amoebas that know their ways to connect and sustain even in case of its immediate environment getting depleted of essential resources. Keith Morrison notes that 'they collect together and form a "foot" containing about a third of the aggregated cells and spores. These migrate in search of a new environment that is suitable to sustain life, forming a new colony of amoebas....The organism is responding to the environment by reconfiguring itself and metamorphosing in order to survive: it is an open system responding to its environment. The process involves self-organization, and the slime mould, reinvigorated, is capable of survival; the whole process is dynamic'.[33] Trans-habit is autocatalytic, knowing ways of emergence and revelation. Lack of sustaining nutrients in an aesthetic-cultural context is no impediment to further patterns of survival and sustenance. Forms of creativity owe its living substantially to autopoesis—self-generative and self-perpetuating. This speaks of a complexity which feeds on others and finds its life in co-evolution where connection is not compliance always— blasé commensurability—but entangled dynamics of unpredictability and constellation.

II

Trans-habit informs my conceptualisation of the poet in this book with the principles of distance and desire. The habit of distance here is chronological, contextual, geographical and cultural which, in its restrictive order and structural definitiveness, provokes the ingress of the stranger, the moment of the alien. So the intersubjective motor in habit creates its own reflexivity. Trans-habit as a Badiouan event makes us speak outside the acknowledged universals of routine. It challenges the *habitus* of transcultural habit of reading, intensifying our understanding of subjects through an intricate and unexpected understanding of travel and trajectories. This can also function like Erich Auerbach's conception of the *Ansatzpunkt*: the starting point, rather a 'good point of departure' that may enable a rich compass of cultural-epistemic variety, 'concreteness and precision on one hand and, on the other, 'its potential for centrifugal radiation'.[34] Taking off the Auerbach highlane, I see such translocomotory operations as the 'comparative dystopic unease', an intra-active world-wideness, which I have argued elaborately elsewhere, as 'intra-active transculturality'.[35] This calls for reimagining our links with literary history and poetics, changing, as Birgit Kaiser argues, the 'footing on which texts meet each other: no longer as objects of national (or regional) descent, pre-existing their encounters in a comparison, but as "relata" whose qualities and effects are specified by way of relating while specifying the "apparatus" (the texts, the reading and the reader) at the same time'.[36] Culture, as Derrida points out, 'never has a single origin' but decentered to get exposed to divergence, the uncanny presence of other: the necessity

> to make ourselves the guardians of an idea of Europe, of a difference of Europe, but of a Europe that consists precisely in not closing itself off in its own identity and in advancing itself in an exemplary way toward what it is not, toward the other heading or the heading of the other, indeed—and this is perhaps something else altogether—toward the other of the heading, which would be the beyond of this modern tradition, another border structure, another shore.[37]

The 'shoring' is worlding, world formation, something that Jean-Luc Nancy would like to qualify as worldwideization. On this axis of elaboration, trans-habit is a 'thinking', an *Auseinandersetzung* with the other, *Gelassenheit* which is about responsive and responsible opening and, also, Heidegger's equivocality (*Mehrdeutigkeit*).

Distances bred by trans-habit, hence, are relational, calling for a vivacity of critical thinking, a force that presents us differently to ourselves. But does distance disturb us? Isn't it proximity, hence, familiarity, that keeps us in habituated ease, and does the breaking down or narrowing the gap with the unfamiliar spark the consternation? David Hume points out that

> men are principally concern'd about those objects, which are not much remov'd either in space or time. ... Talk to a man of his condition thirty years hence, and he will not regard you. Speak of what is to happen tomorrow and he will lend you attention. The breaking of a mirror gives us more concern when at home, than the burning of a house, when abroad, and some hundred leagues distant.[38]

The tyranny of habits secures itself through *intimacy* with objects and events producing a life world which does not encourage shock and entail risk—the tension between thinking close-up and in long shots. Habits fail to note the movement and momentum that gets imperceptivity built around it; it has a peculiar *indifference* to the formations that mere living out of habits generates. This is the indifference of a world outside the habit-domain of one's existence. Trans-habit effectively becomes the effort to connect with this indifference.

Habits then are *integrative* and ontologically negotiatory which, as Mary Parker Follet reminds us, is individual and simultaneously collective—a co-existence that contributes to the understanding of the world. Trans-habit comes close to such 'progressive integrations' and 'ceaseless interweavings' with unlike-me paradigms of understanding and knowledge.[39] So, in the context of my arguments in the book, a British poet is always a 'plus' to the situations he works in and interacts with—his independence is signatured with an *integration* with others, a reconstruction in being lost-found-missed-imprisoned-exiled. Trans-habit builds on a relational poetics of doing and experiencing. Relationality is ingrained in a leverage, both dispositional and organismic, that trans-habitual encounters provide. This generates the 'taking in' that involves reconstruction through a dismantling of set-pieces of thinking—'the experience of discordant feelings'.[40] 'Taking in' is the dynamics and poetics of encounters with cultural and literary conditions that are external and, yet, intrinsically revisionary. This points to the experiences that decimate a polarised ego to 'transfuse one another while being each its own identity'.[41] So trans-habit declares an existence which is always a part of a wider happening and event, quivering 'along various radii like the wind-rose on a compass, and the actual in it is continuously one with possibles not yet in our present sight'.[42] The possibles come through resemblance which is an intricate circuit of connections that are not facile equivalences. Eric Hayot notes that 'every philosophical and literary modernism is itself subject to an internal, undermining comparative action, in which the "foreign" always and in advance inhabits the "native" national paradigm'.[43] The acts of comparison or resemblance are riddled and spooked by the foreign, the strange, the uncanny: the provincial, the national, the European, the hegemonic, the traditional go under the anvil to realise its own in the other, its locomotion in the travel it makes with the others. Trans-habit is also about 'decreation'[44], a sort of destruction enabling an escape into the configured—habit murders habit, knowing habit is about killing habit. But in such decreations we encounter the principle of resemblance and antagonism—principles I have made significant use of in understanding the notion of the poet in this book. In 'Three Academic Pieces', Wallace Stevens writes:

> Take, for example, a beach extending as far as the eye can reach, bordered, on the one hand, by trees and, on the other, by the sea. The sky is cloudless and the sun is red. In what sense do the objects in this scene resemble each other? There is enough green in the sea to relate it to the palms. There is enough of the sky reflected in the water to create a resemblance, in some sense, between them. The sand is yellow between the green and the blue. In short, the light alone creates a unity not only in the recedings of distance, where differences become invisible, but also in the contacts of closer sight…. So, too, sufficiently generalized, each man resembles all other men, each woman resembles all other women, this year resembles last year.[45]

Trans-habituality encourages resemblances that are delicate, antagonistic and magnetic. Resemblance then is explanatory and controversial, a desire and contrariety; it is both intensification and reinforcement.

III

The aesthetic problem of trans-habit is about enabling the 'insertion of art into everyday life'—a fresh pattern of thinking that inspires one to create.[46] A trans-habitual performance, rather performativity, is the event (from Latin *venire*, meaning an 'out-come' or 'coming out', *e-ventum*)[47] where, as Deleuze would qualify,

> there is indeed the present moment of its actualization, the moment in which the event is embodied in a state of affairs, an individual, or a person, the moment we designate by saying "here, the moment has come." The future and the past of the event are only evaluated with respect to this definitive present. On the other hand, there is the future and past of the event, considered in itself, sidestepping each present, being free of the limitations of a state of affairs, impersonal, pre-individual, neutral.[48]

So trans-habit has its inseparable connection with habit and the invincible acceleration to withdraw from habitual modes of thought; for instance, as Chapter Seven demonstrates how the event of habitually constituting a poet within Matthew Arnold's theory of poetry withdraws but, again, does not *break* from its own familiar premise to reformulate an alien habit of reading. This is not breaking away from a transcendent point of origin or repetition—surely not the multiplicity born from the One. Akin to

A. N. Whitehead's 'cell-theory of actuality', trans-habit proclaims inseparability from the actualities that birth it into being and, also, innovations and improvisionality that cannot be analysed into 'components with equivalent completeness of actuality'.[49] When Nietzsche argues that destruction is the fate of the person who at once strays from tradition ('sacrifice to the extraordinary') and remains in it (a slave)[50], we are made to inhabit an order that adventurises upon the play of chaos and discipline, norm and scandal, the authoritative and abyss. This order is not a unification of multiplicities but a creative event—a poetics of relationality. Discounting habitual experience and the character of matter, Whitehead sees a splash, a disturbance in transcending a normative given: 'if we consent to apply to the apparently steady undifferentiated endurance of matter the same principles as those now accepted for sound and light', that is, 'vibration'.[51] Trans-habit is inscribed in vibration, rather, synonymous with such an effect. Certain forms or apparatus of arrangement are prehended; others, develop like the stone dropped into a still pond of water.[52] This is not to misconstrue trans-habit as a revolution always in a ceaseless acceleration. On several occasions, its epistemology is methodological, its mattering is settled and becomes a conservative manifestation without the acknowledgement of the other; this constructs occasions when interference builds, the process of 'concrescence' is at play, patterns are reformulated without relata and retrospection. Haun Saussy rightly suggests a rethinking of our organising principles—'the national filing system for authors and works, and the habit of referring to nations interchangeably with languages'. Implicating trans-habit, he notes that 'the politics of comparison today would not concern nations, races, parties, or classes, but conditions—elusively omnipresent—which subtend these, and which all of us help to create. To hold them in our attention might precipitate discoveries'.[53] Can trans-habit then build on a concept of missed totality? Habits of reading lead to surrationality that unmarks the familiar territories. This is a counter-conceptualising of habit-abilities through the anxieties of incommensurabilities that thinking breeds and imports. Habits are built through an escape from habit; they are monadic and nomadic at the same time.

Trans-habit in the Agambenian way looks through paradigmatic understanding (*para-deigma*, that which is shown alongside)[54] into the zone beyond strict classificatory sense-making (*para*, next to). This ensures an exposure to intelligibility playing on the suffix, '-ability' which Agamben intones as both possibility and potentiality. Trans-habit brings the 'alien' into our understanding, demanding a negotiation with the *atopon* (the strange), the challenging cheer to work as apparent misfit. Gadamer has rightly observed that 'there would be no speaker and no art of speaking if understanding and consent were not in question, were not underlying elements; there would be no hermeneutical task if there were no mutual understanding that has been disturbed and that those in a conversation must search for and find again together'.[55] Disturbance is a way to re-accord, find ways to problematise what one has and what one finds in the other—nonreducible to each other, a dismantling of the Socratic subsumation into the One. This note of disturbance tempts me to see trans-habit as owing to a Muse whom Nancy, pursuing its Latin roots, would qualify as ardour, 'the quick tempered tension that leaps out in impatience, desire, or anger, the sort of tension that aches to know and to do'.[56] It has the restiveness and circulation of the *mens* (spirit or soul) where habits arouse excitement and displacement like the fluid movement in the body of a woman that happens habitually every month and yet without a precise prediction and poignancy. The poet configured through this book evokes Muses, not the ceremonial obligation to a single muse in time and history and certainly not to the endowments that an omnipotent and transcendental Muse delivers. Trans-habit invokes a breadth of sentimentality and ardour for enraptured submission to singularity—the singular plural potency and latency of acts and moves. This welcomes chance (*le hasard*), an active arbitrariness in creation, an accident which inscribes the habits of creation to dismantle the organising principles with a textual and theoretical tease.[57] Avoidance of aesthetic exhaustion is worlding a presence of sense 'of what appears in light: rather than the *phanein*, it is the *phaos* itself, light, and not the light that appears (lumen) by clinging to surfaces, but the light that flashes (lux) and that causes to appear, itself nonapparent as such. Lux without fiat, having neither creator, subject, nor source, being the source but in itself refracted, in itself radiant, exploding, broken'.[58] Trans-habit creates its own moments of reflection and, then again, transfigures our understanding of relationships among things and thoughts, our perceptions of the world. Trans-habitual understanding of the concept of the poet builds on principles of inheritance, a heritage of thought, institutional knowledge and a labour to establish a new order of reading.

This book has a deep and problematic investment in the monumentalist notions of heritage that inhere a particular line of vision or critical sight. Complex understandings deprivilege the gravitas of inherited habits of interpretation, leading us to the realm of intangible heritage of thinking.[59] So Ben Jonson's idea of the reader intangibly inherits *sahridaya* or Carlyle's concept of the Poet bears enmeshed inheritance with Sri Aurobindo's thinking on poetic creativity as part of a challenge to the 'heritage gaze'. Such habit-induced disinheritances are 'nonlinear, but not chaotic; nomadic, yet accountable and committed; creative but also cognitively valid; discursive and also materially embedded—it is coherent without falling into instrumental rationality'.[60] Trans-habit, thus, makes interesting transpositions: can Matthew Arnold's notion of the poet (in)fusionise into certain paradigms of Sanskrit poetics? How diffractive and intra-active is the romantic notion of creativity? Trans(pro)positions, therefore, have shock, purpose, efficacy, allurement and entertainment, adding to our interest.[61] This constructs a separate reservoir of feeling: certain actualities preclude possibilities whereas certain trans-habitual actualities promise becomings. Trans-habit is the 'occurent', the taking place, a sort of activism within which I have tried to perspectivise the notion of the poet across a wide alternative of *trembling*. The book is as much about forming habits as being surprised by habits—more in the nature of conjunctive relations. Brian Massumi, with leanings on William James, explains that

> conjunctive relation is how the before and after of a threshold passed mutually include each other in the same event, as "pulses" of the same change. Conjunctive and disjunctive relations both concern change. For radical empiricism, they are both real and immediately experienced. Disjunctive relations are felt as a self-distancing coming out of an initial condition of participation in the quasi-chaotic something-doing that is the general condition of activity in the world. Conjunctive relations are felt as a "tendency" or "striving" that continues across thresholds often marked by resistances and obstacles.[62]

Trans-habitual reading of the concept of the poet cannot ignore either of the relations and, indeed, constellates within 'compenetrate' consequences. Activist philosophy of reading plumbs quasi-chaotic domains of re-search which include investigations within a particular history and context (my thinking on Sidney and neoclassical poetics), the event of co-emergence (on Carlyle's Hero as Poet), poetics of occurrence (in my reading of Ben Jonson and Eliot) and a germinal growth through the reading of Arnold's poetics.

IV

In the operative ways of the world, Rabindranath Tagore sees a continuous inhaling and exhaling, a state of sleep and waking, a rhythm of acclivity and declivity and a halting and a restart.[63] In absence and presence, in dark and light, in concealment and manifestation such a rhythm gets maintained. This speaks of a continuity—the yes and the no, the positive and the negative, the attraction and repulsion which become a part of the creative rhythm essential to our understanding of historical situatedness, our ever-rhythmic connections with past and present. Tagore observes that 'perfect balance in these opposing forces would lead to deadlock in creation. Life moves in the cadence of constant adjustment of opposites; it is a perpetual process of reconciliation of contradictions'.[64] Historical consciousness builds on the rhythm of opposition, in adjustments between polarities, not through a linear onrush of energy but a circularity which keeps the rhythm of life going. Linearity is not the character of life, writes Tagore.[65] Energy and force constructed in singular unifocal velocity are destined to create division; it becomes bare, barren and banal with no music, creativity and play. However, when opposite forces meet and multiple forces come together, the rhythm of creation constructs its own steps and stages, forms its own unique habit. The observations of Ford Madox Ford catch the 'rhythm of habit' that informs our existence and complements Tagore's idea appreciably well:

in the arena of Triumphant Principle pendulums swing backwards and forwards: the undisputed right of to-day becoming the open question of to-morrow, and the unquestioned wrong of the immediate future. This is a platitude because it is one of the indisputable verities. In the country they say that large clocks when they tick solemnly and slowly, thud out the words: "Alive – Dead; Alive – Dead"—because in this world at every second a child is born, a man dies. But, in London, a listener to the larger clock which ticks off the spirits of successive ages, seems to hear above the roar of the traffic, the slow reverberation: "Never – Again; Never – Again," as principles rise and die, and rise and die again. … Arts rise and die again, systems rise and die again, faiths are born only to die and to rise once more; the only thing constant and undying is the human crowd.[66]

Habit is a rhythm and a rupture of rhythm; trans-habit as rhythm is both a method and a non-method—a consciousness we try to formalise and pin to a methodological rigour but which, fortunately, is always a bit out of our fold, out of our step. It owes to our horizontal and transversal understanding of culture, vertical encounters with values and background and contexts of human and non-human conditions of existence. George Bataille sees human existence as paradoxical and human life as composed of two 'heterogenous parts' that cannot blend: 'One part is purposeful, given significance by utilitarian and therefore secondary ends; this part is the one we are aware of. The other is primary and sovereign … it evades the grasp of our aware intelligence'.[67] Trans-habit seeks the hell, the transgression, the 'summit' that leaps out in energy bearing an 'instinctive tendency towards divine intoxication which the rational world of calculation cannot bear'.[68] It is dangerous because we are urged to test and rethink the law, encouraging a communication where two people risk themselves 'each lacerated and suspended, perched atop a common nothingness'.[69]

Trans-habit, thus, hides an archive of affect: entering into a trans-experience is reentering into an already existing one. This calls for a temporary dislocation of the subjectivity—a 'shudder'—a moment of moving away from what one was settled in, the effect of returning to the self aware of its finitude and situatedness. Jonathan Flatley working on Adorno's notion of 'shudder' points out that this shudder is about limitedness and historicity of one's affective life. It triggers a contact with the other, being 'touched by the other'.[70] The shudder leaves trans-habit in a circulation of contacts, both realisable, 'affective collectivity', and immanent—'aesthetic comportment' that is communicative and intra-active at the same time. Trans-habit is the 'law of good neighbours' (the Warburg principle) where thinking is acting and an urge to connect, allowing the connective potential as much a measure of itself as generating surprise and passivity. Here, I am tempted to read my theorisation of trans-habit within Giorgio Agamben's *festina lente*—the haste in slowness—that urges on explorative study to continue yet patiently, at times passively, by being with others and dwelling in individuation, in own modes of action involving studium understood in the sense of shock. Trans-habit builds its rhythm of study, the *festina lente*, a 'shuttling between bewilderment and lucidity, discovery and loss, between agent and patient'.[71] It has its own problematic encounters with impotentiality—the 'cannot' negotiating with the 'enabling'. Habits are *doing* as well as something one cannot do without. The inability to forsake habit speaks of a potentiality which is the articulation of an impotentiality—habit's struggle to habitualise the 'out of habit'. Trans-habit does not declare a necessity of change, not always a standardization of normed thinking and a widely agreed sovereign decision. The power of potentiality or potential thinking of trans-habit is a pointer to a remainder—the ambiguity of potential[72]—where attention is directed to our incapacities, habit's potential for the 'cannot'. This throws us into the dynamics of 'stupidity', something that Avitor Ronell calls "foolsophy". But how does one know stupidity when it exists as an unknowable quotient? Ronell perceptively notes that 'as long as I don't know what stupidity is, what I know about knowing, remains uncertain, even forbidding'.[73] So every habit comes with an uncertainty of accomplishment—an act stands humbled by stupidity. Knowing stupidity then is increasing and realising our habit-capital—its acts of exposure. The stupefaction of the 'cannot' and hence, the stupidity of the bounds of potentiality are interesting threads that work into the whole dynamics of trans-habit. Stupidity is not the antonym of knowledge rather, the blindness towards the indistinguishable topography of the potential and the impotential.

This finally brings us to what Henri Lefebvre calls 'rhythmanalysis', where our habits of reading are scarcely mastered and possessed, rather, repeated where each repetition comes with a difference. Lefebvre rightly complains that since we confuse rhythm with movement [*mouvement*] a mechanical overtone is ascribed to rhythms 'brushing aside the organic aspect of rhythmed movements'. His observations are worth a patient visit:

> Musicians, who deal directly with rhythms, because they produce them, often reduce them to the counting of beats [*desmesures*]: 'One-two-three-one-two-three'. Historians and economists speak of rhythms: of the rapidity or slowness of periods, of eras, of cycles; they tend only to see the effects of impersonal laws, without coherent relations with actors, ideas, realities. Those who teach gymnastics see in rhythms only successions of movements [*gestes*] setting in motion certain muscles, certain physiological energies, etc. Is the origin of the procedure that starts with generalities found in abstractions? No! In the field of rhythm, certain very broad concepts nonetheless have specificity: let us immediately cite repetition. No rhythm without repetition in time and in space, without reprises, without returns, in short without measure [*mesure*]. But there is no identical absolute repetition, indefinitely. Whence the relation between repetition and difference. When it

concerns the everyday, rites, ceremonies, fêtes, rules and laws, there is always something new and unforeseen that introduces itself into the repetitive: difference.[74]

The rhythmanalysis of trans-habit denies absolute repetition; it prefers to work on the gap between beats—the 'grey gap between black beats: the tender interval'.[75] Habit is both a fore-having of understanding and refiguration of reason. So trans-habitual rhythm *presences*. Meaning presences when habits are exhausted, habits have gone past habitualities. As I have argued elsewhere in transcultural reading of literature, presence is about mediation, negotiation and eventual transformation. Morphogenetically, there is a continuity of presence—the presence-continuous—that keeps aesthetic experiences tense. For me, presence is in the making and unmaking of the habit of present, in flitting in and out of the chambers of the defined, formed and constituted bounced off against the irrepressible, hard-to-define and the ever-constituting.[76] Working on the hiatus that the figured and the figural produce, 'presencing' opens a distance between the fixed moments of representation and the disappearance of habits—the uncanny interlocking of acts of awakening and remembering which Rancière points out as modernity not being contemporaneous with itself and hence, 'deprived of the categories of its own understanding'.[77] This investigation into the concept of the poet then cannot ignore the rhythm of the uncanny—apprehensions of presence of thoughts and vibrations that could be understood as relational without being institutionalised and authorised. Trans-habit often thrives in 'unbelongingness' where meaning is caught in the twilight of fearful symmetries. The rhythm of literature or the *taal* of the literary, as this book tries to demonstrate and realise, is, then, the complexity of the second hand of the clock.

Notes

1. Geoffrey Keynes (ed.) *Poetry and Prose of William Blake* (London, 1948), 735.
2. Plato, *Symposium* in *Collected Dialogues* (New York, 1961), 554.
3. Roger T. Ames & David L. Hall (trans.) *Daodejing: Making This Life Significant* (New York: Ballantine Books, 2003), 83.
4. Michel Serres, *The Five Senses*, (trans.) Margaret Sankey and Peter Cowley (London: Continuum, 2008), 270.
5. Ibid., 278.
6. Jim Garrison, 'A Deweyan Theory of Democratic Listening', *Educational Theory* 46, no. 4 (1996), 430.
7. See Kristie M. Allen, *Second Nature: The Discourse of Habit in Nineteenth-Century British Realist Fiction*, A Dissertation submitted to the Graduate School-New Brunswick Rutgers, The State University of New Jersey in partial fulfilment of the requirements for the degree of Doctor of Introduction, 23.
8. See *Past and Present* Vol. 10 (1843; New York: Charles Scribner's Sons, 1904) Book II, chap. xvii.

9. See Alexander Bain, *Emotions and the Will* (1859; 4th ed. 1899) chap. 9, "Moral Habits," 440.
10. See George Henry Lewes's *Problems of Life and Mind* (1880).
11. Allen, *Second Nature*, 36.
12. See Aristotle's *Nichomachean Ethics* (translated with introduction) Terence Irwin (Indiana: Hackett Publishing Company, 1999).
13. Félix Ravaisson, *Of Habit* (Translation, Introduction and Commentary) Clare Carlisle and Mark Sinclair (London: Continuum, 2008), 14–15.
14. Ibid., 59.
15. John Dewey, *Human Nature and Conduct* (New York: Dover Publications Inc., 2002), 25.
16. See M. A. R. Habib, 'The Prayers of Childhood: T. S. Eliot's Manuscripts on Kant', *Journal of the History of Ideas*, 51, no. 1 (Jan.–Mar. 1990), 93.
17. Ibid., 98. Also see M. A. R. Habib, *The Early T. S. Eliot and Western Philosophy* (Cambridge: Cambridge University Press, 1999).
18. T. S. Eliot, *Knowledge and Experience in the Philosophy of F. H. Bradley* (London: Faber and Faber, 1964), 148.
19. See Marcel Proust, *The Captive/The Fugitive*, Vol 5 of *In Search of Lost Time*, trans. C. K. Scott Moncrieff and Terence Kilmartin (London: Vintage, 1996), 621.
20. Hiroshi Nemoto, 'Who is a Proper Opponent? The Tibetan Buddhist Concept of phyi rgol yang dag', *Journal of Indian Philosophy*, 41, no. 2 (April 2013), 151–165. Also see the Jaina theory of argumentation put forward by Vādi Devasūri, who lays out various types of debate; Devasūri clearly talks about a debate which takes place between a teacher (*guru*) and a student (*śiṣya*).
21. Nemoto, 'Who is a Proper Opponent?' 162.
22. Nico Strobach, *The Moment of Change: A Systematic History in the Philosophy of Space and Time* (Dordrecht: Springer, 1998), 3.
23. Samuel Weber, 'The Singular Historicity of Literary Understanding: "Still Ending …"' *MLN*, 125, no. 3 (April 2010), 636.
24. See Steinberg, *Walter Benjamin: Selected Writings 1931–34* Vol 2 (Cambridge, Mass: Harvard University Press, 1999), 592.
25. Ibid.
26. Nedim Karakayali points out that the word 'strangeness' is a standard translation of the German word *Fremdsein*: 'in Simmel's usage, *Fremdsein* does not so much mean "being strange" but it refers to a "form of interaction" or the condition of being involved in such an interaction. While the term might also be used for referring to a "quality" of an object (e.g., the strangeness of…), given Simmel's radically relational approach, there is no such thing as "being strange" without being involved in a stranger-relation. Nedim Karakayali, 'The Uses of the Stranger: Circulation, Arbitration, Secrecy, and Dirt' *Sociological Theory*, 24, no. 4 (Dec. 2006), 314.
27. See 'The Stranger', in Kurt H. Wolff (trans.) *The Sociology of Georg Simmel* (Glencoe, Ill.: The Free Press, 1950), 402.
28. Ibid., 405.
29. Mark Salber Phillips, *On Historical Distance* (New Haven: Yale University Press, 2013), 11.
30. Massimo Caciarri, *Architecture and Nihilism: On the Philosophy of Modern Architecture* (trans.) Stephen Sartarelli (introduction) Patrizia Lombardo (New

Haven: Yale University Press, 1993), 21. Trans-habit has a Venice like orientation to it: moving in and out of structures of thought and traditions, a compelling architecture. 'In Venice one can see realized the duplicity of life ...Double is the sense of these squares, that, because of the lack of vehicles and the narrowness of streets, look like rooms. Double is the sense of meeting, pushing, and touching of people in the *calli* ... Double is the sense of life in this city-now a crossing of streets, now a crossing of canals, so that it belongs neither to the earth nor to .the water: and we are always seduced by what appears behind the Proteic shape of Venice, as if it were its real body. ... Venice has the equivocal beauty of adventure which rootless floats into life, as a torn flower floats into the sea. That Venice has been and will be the *city of adventure* is just the most perceptible expression of the deepest destiny of its image: it cannot be a home for our soul, cannot be anything but adventure'. Georg Simmel, 'Roma, Firenze, e Venezia,' in Cacciari, *Metropolis*, 197.
31. Caciarri, *Architecture and Nihilism*, xlviii.
32. Michel Alhadeff-Jones, 'Three Generations of Complexity Theories: Nuances and ambiguities', *Educational Philosophy and Theory*, 40, no. 1 (2008), 68.
33. Keith Morrison, 'Educational Philosophy and the Challenge of Complexity Theory', *Educational Philosophy and Theory*, 40, no. 1 (2008), 21.
34. Erich Auerbach, 'Philology and Weltliteratur,' (trans.) Marie and Edward Said, *Centennial Review*, 13, no. 1 (Winter 1969), 15.
35. See my Chapter Five 'More than Global' in *Thinking Literature across Continents* (Durham, London: Duke University Press, 2016, co-authored with J Hillis Miller).
36. Birgit Mara Kaiser, 'Worlding CompLit: Diffractive Reading with Barad, Glissant and Nancy', *Parallax*, 20, no. 3 (2014), 276.
37. See Steven Burik, *The End of Comparative Philosophy and the Task of Comparative Thinking Heidegger, Derrida, and Daoism* (Albany: State University of New York Press, 2009), 75.
38. Phillips, *On Historical Distance*, 14.
39. Mary Parker Follet, *Creative Experience* (New York: Peter Smith, 1951), 134.
40. Alfred North Whitehead, *Adventures of Ideas* (New York: Free Press, 1967), 258.
41. Mary Parker Follet, *The New State: Group Organization the Solution of Popular Government* (New York: Longmans, Green and Co., 1918), 77.
42. *A Pluralistic Universe* (1977) in *The Works of William James* (ed.) Frederick H. Burkhardt, Fredson Bowers & Ignas K. Skrupskelis (Cambridge, Mass., London, England: Harvard University Press, 1975–1988), 131.
43. Eric Hayot, 'Bertrand Russell's Chinese Eyes' Modernisms' *Chinese Literature and Culture* 18, no. 1 (2006), 149.
44. Simone Weil's *La Pesanteur et la grace*, Pocket (12 février 1993).
45. Stevens, 'Three Academic Pieces,' in *The Necessary Angel: Essays on Reality and the Imagination* (New York, 1951), 71–72.
46. Gilles Deleuze, *Difference and Repetition* (New York: Routledge, 1994), 293.
47. See Rob Pope, *Creativity: Theory, History, Practice* (London: Routledge, 2006), 65.
48. Gilles Deleuze, *The Logic of Sense* (New York: Columbia University Press, 1990), 151.
49. Alfred North Whitehead, *Process and Reality: An Essay in Cosmology* (ed.) D. R. Griffin and D. W. Sherburne (New York: Free Press, 1978), 256.
50. Friedrich Nietzsche, *Human All Too Human* (trans.) Marion Faber (Lincoln: University of Nebraska Press, 1984), 283.

51. Alfred North Whitehead, *Science and the Modern World* (New York: The Free Press, 1967), 35.
52. 'For we should conceive the ripples as effective in the creation of the plunge of the stone into the water. The ripples release the thought, and the thought augments and distorts the ripples'. Alfred North Whitehead, *Modes of Thought*, 36.
53. See Haun Saussy, 'Axes of Comparison', in *Comparison: Theories, Approaches, Uses* (ed.) Rita Felski & Susan Stanford Friedman (Baltimore: Johns Hopkins University Press, 2013), 73–74.
54. G. Agamben, *The Coming Community* (trans. M. Hardt) (Minneapolis: University of Minnesota Press, 1993), 9.
55. Hans-Georg Gadamer, *Philosophical Hermeneutics* (trans. & ed.) David E. Linge (Berkeley: University of California Press, 1977), 25.
56. Jean-Luc Nancy, *The Muses* (trans.) Peggy Kamuf (Stanford: Stanford University Press, 1996), 1.
57. Gayle A Levy, *Refiguring the Muse. Currents in Comparative Romance Languages and Literatures* (New York: Peter Lang, 1999), 112–124.
58. Kalliopi Nikolopoulou, '"L'Art et les gens": Jean-Luc Nancy's Genealogical Aesthetics' *College Literature*, 30, no. 2 (Spring 2003), 179.
59. I have appropriated the idea of intangible heritage from Laurajane Smith's *Uses of Heritage* (London: Routledge, 2006).
60. Braidotti, *Transposition*, 6.
61. Alfred North Whitehead, *Process and Reality*, 259.
62. Brian Massumi, *Semblance and Event: Activist Philosophy and the Occurrent Arts* (Cambridge, Mass.: MIT Press, 2011), 5.
63. Rabindranath Tagore, 'Bharatvarsher itihaser dhara' (The Tradition of Indian History), in *Rabindra Rachanavali* Vol 13 (Kolkata: Government of West Bengal, 1990), 491. Translations are mine.
64. Tagore, *A Vision of India's History* (Calcutta: Visva Bharati Bookshop, 1951), 13.
65. Tagore, 'Bharatvarsher itihaser dhara', 491.
66. See Louise Blakeney Williams, *Modernism and the Ideology of History: Literature, Politics and the Past* (Cambridge: Cambridge University Press, 2002), 106.
67. G. Bataille, *Eroticism*, (trans.) M. Dalwood (London, 1987), 192.
68. Bataille, *Literature and Evil*, (trans.) A. Hamilton (London, 1985), 22.
69. Bataille, *Visions of Excess*, (trans.) A. Stoekl (Minneapolis, 1985), 119.
70. See Jonathan Flatley, *Affective Mapping: Melancholia and the Politics of Modernism* (Cambridge, Mass.: Harvard University Press, 2008), 83.
71. G. Agamben, *Idea of Prose*, (trans.) M. Sullivan & S. Whitsitt (Albany: State University of New York Press, 1995), 64.
72. Agamben, *Potentialities: Collected Essays in Philosophy* (ed. & trans.) D. Heller-Roazen (Stanford, Calif.: Stanford University Press, 1999), 254.
73. Ronell, *Stupidity* (Urbana: University of Illinois Press, 2002), 4.
74. *Rhythmanalysis: Space, Time and Everyday Life* (trans.) Stuart Elden & Gerald Moore (London: Continuum, 2004), 5–6.
75. Vladimir Nabokov, *Ada, or Ardor: A Family Chronicle* (New York: McGraw-Hill, 1969), 572.
76. See my 'Presence Continuous' in *Presence* (ed). Ranjan Ghosh and Ethan Kleinberg (Ithaca, NY: Cornell University Press, 2013), 187.
77. J. Rancière, 'The Archaeomodern Turn', in M. P. Steinberg (ed.) *Walter Benjamin and the Demands of History* (Ithaca, NY: Cornell University Press, 1996), 28.

2 Mistress-Knowledge? Abuse, Apology and After

> One day when him high courage did emmoue,
> As wont ye knights to seeke aduentures wilde,
> He pricked forth, his puissant force to proue,
> Me then he left enwombed of this child.
>
> —Edmund Spenser[1]

> It hath beene thought an honour to the learnedest of the Fathers, to have been the Author of a good Poem.
>
> —John Donne[2]

'The words "poetry," "poet," and "poem" have entered English and many European languages from ancient Greek, but not from very old Greek,' writes Andrew Ford. He observes:

> Before the fifth century, the general Greek term for what we call poets was *aoidoi*, "singers," which did not differentiate composers from performers. To speak of a "song" when no specific kind was in view, words like *humnos* or melos ("tune") served, or the more general *aoidē*, "singing" as an activity rather than an object, a "poem." Apart from these words, capable of a more or less general usage, the archaic lexicon lacked a unitary term comprehending them any individual forms of singing that were attached to specific contexts. The recognized kinds of song were defined not as parts of a realm of discourse to be distinguished from something like "prose," but as familiar activities connected with particular social and religious occasions. To change the terms by which song is designated may imply different definitions of the activity and its place in the social world, and so it is worth noting that it is first in texts of the fifth century that we find those who composed songs called "makers" or "poets" (*poiētai*) and clearly distinguished from the "singers" (*aoidoi*) who performed them; instead of "singing" (*aeidein*, *aoidē*), they are said to be engaged in "making" or "poetry" (*poiēsis*, from the verb *poiein*); finally, what they produce may be called a *poiēma* or "made thing."[3]

Philip Sidney's poet is no different: a maker-poet deeply inscribed in transhabitual ways of creativity. Harvesting on a trans-habit, Sidney's poet is almost a cosmopolitan who travels with rigour and purposefulness through a contrastive terrain involving Aristotle and Plato on one end and the Psalter, Italian poetics, classical Greek and Latin poetic theory and contemporary English literary criticism on the other to produce an idea of the poet. However, a significant body of criticism around Sidney centres on his alleged unoriginality as a thinker, who is said to have qualified beyond being an imitator of Aristotle and Italian Renaissance poeticians.[4] But borrowings were fairly common in the Renaissance period and Sidney dug into many sources without inept replication but through revision and insight. This spoke of questioning the prevalent habit of poetic creativity and merit and promised an appropriative process that had its own distinctive understanding and acumen to it—a skill that made Sidney draw on 'earlier teaching, selecting, adapting and fusing together ideas gathered from many sources, in order to set forth ultimately his own conception of poetry, independently arrived at'.[5] So confining the *Apology* to a polemical demonstration of personal commitment to poetry and a programmatic enterprise on Renaissance literary theory declares many missed encounters with Sidney's deep investments in poetic configuration, process and experience. The *Apology* builds its own habits of understanding and poetic evaluation and is fed out of the habits of its times and inherited circulation of thought and epistemes—independently dependent, a multiplex (*plex*, in the sense of the folding) of past and present.

I

For Sidney, the poet is the 'first light-giver to ignorance'[6], the deliverer of knowledge, the father of learning, the first bringer-in of civility, the right popular philosopher, and monarch of all learning (17). The poet is also a teacher of virtue, the kindler of courage and is envisaged to play a role in the religious life of a nation. He is gifted with an extraordinary ability without forgetting to look 'in an unflattering glass of reason' (35). The noblest sort is termed *Vates*; the second kind, he remarks: 'whether they properly be Poets or no let Gramarians dispute'; the third are 'indeed right Poets'. In an astute reengagement with the habitual premises of the functions of the poet and creativity, Sidney contours the 'right poet' supervening on the nature of imitation, purpose, afflatus and the telos of poetry. The right poet works within the 'Zodiack of his owne wit' and is 'lifted up with the vigor of his owne invention' to *make* new things by falling on a divine aid, the enabling creative authority of the holy spirit—the echoes of *Genesis* are clearly heard in the *narratio* of the *Apology*. He has the ability to read the Scripture rightly, translating, as Michael Raiger argues,

> divine command into poetic form, leading the soul to virtue by the delightfulness of its appearance. Human possibility (freedom) and divine command (grace) here find a meeting place in the intersection of Scripture (text) and Spirit (will). The hermeneutic of "right" poetry is linked with reading Scripture literally and tropologically (morally), but entirely

severed from the two other Thomistic tropes of interpretation—the allegorical (symbolic) and anagogical (referring to the divine life of God and our participation in it). Informed by Scripture, it does not translate into a hermeneutic of reading nature symbolically, since it is Scripture itself which has interpreted nature according to the light of revelation.[7]

Raiger shows us that in line with a Reformation approach to reading Scripture, Sidney's right poet becomes didactic without being unlimited by the revelatory borders of Scripture. Christ's parabolic method of instruction becomes the literary form of the right poet, which is why Sidney sees 'many mysteries' as embosomed in poetry with the purpose to prevent 'profane wits' from abusing them. Raiger sees Sidney's right poet as reversing the atrophic effects of sin 'in the poetic representation of the perfection ordained from creation' and this facilitates our understanding of the analogical connection between God and poet as *maker*.[8] Despite the controversy over the nature of creativity associated with the right poet, the divine nature of poetic inspiration cannot be wholly metaphorical and poetic art is not a whole scale human act. Poetic creativity, as Sidney made evident on occasions, has a divine breath and 'calleth the sweet Muses to inspire into him a good invention'. Roger Moore is right to observe that

> unlike many of his contemporaries, for whom a claim of divine inspiration was often simply a nod to the classical past or mere rhetorical ornamentation, Sidney seems to have made a more sustained investment in prophecy. He does not consider divine poetry a feature of the dim past nor does he regard it as residing only in the Bible or in works (such as Du Bartas's *Sepmaines*) that retold biblical stories. His notion of the Spirit is more fluid and potentially more dangerous. For him, prophetic inspiration "bloweth where it listeth" (John 3:8) and appears in unlikely places, even in the works of "right" poets who trade in fictions. By insisting upon the quasi-divine capabilities of contemporary poets who rely on the divine breath to encourage virtuous behavior, Sidney approaches theologically radical territory and comes close to defending the spiritual freedom also claimed by contemporary sectarians and some moderate evangelical prophets.[9]

At the end of the *Apology*, Sidney finds many mysteries in poetry and, indeed, prophets always 'spoke in an oblique, puzzling fashion, and by invoking the terminology of esoteric "mysteries" available only to a few'. The *Apology* itself being an elaborate prophecy whose inspired messages and arguments, Sidney admits, will be understood and legitimised by few.[10] Scaliger's calling the poet 'another god' with the power to 'create (*condere*)' reinstalls the Platonic epistemic foundations within a Christian god without impugnment. So from a firm philological standpoint, Scaliger refuses to restrict the term maker or another god to 'candle makers' and, resuscitating the original usage of the learned Greeks the term is applied to both the God and the poet.[11] The poetic spirit in the Psalms forms a close transpoetical parallel here. There is no denying a 'sharp and clear mind' and a prophetic spirit, an obvious poetic inspiration and poetic utterance that verge on a discovery of the divine-human relationship. In the Qumran document of the Psalms, we have the reference to David as being wise, intelligent and irreproachable before God and before mankind in all its ways. Close to Sidney's poet-prophet we find in the Psalms vigorous emotion, life-sense and profundity of thought—the art of 'new song'.[12] The right poet and the Psalmic poet work on a 'structural intention', a lovely recognition for 'design', a faith in inquiring spirit and subtilised intellect. There is vindication for visioned will, life-spirit where 'my heart overflows with a goodly theme'/ I address my verses to the king;/ my tongue is like the pen of a ready scribe' (Psalm 45). The right poet appropriates the ready scribe in that both exhibit thought-power and combine the best of the philosopher, the prophet and the singer, avoiding 'dialectical contradiction'[13], cryptogram and enigma.

Sidney's penchant for abstraction and beauty in poetry emphasises the faculty of 'seeing' in the poet; this, again, is psalmic in nature. Beauty and virtue are the *res ipsae* for Sidney and poetic creation must have the virtuous strain in it. The right poet's habits of creativity are locked in a comparative agon with moral philosophy and history. The moral philosopher provides 'learned definition[s]' of virtue the reality of which remains in the dark until the 'imaginative and judging power' of poesy comes into effective play. It is through the 'speaking picture of poesy' that virtue stands to be illuminated and figured forth. Sidney and his Italian counterpart Scaliger inform their aesthetic of creativity with a connection built around art and nature. At variance with the moral philosopher who deals with abstractions, the poet depicts facts and situations in such a way that they conform to the law of probability or necessity. Truth is accessible only in terms of 'probabilities' or 'conjectured likelihood' (15). The imaginative truth is said to triumph over historical truth. In a transpoetic web of connection, Tagore's observations are insightful:

> Here comes in the difference between the truth of nature and the truth of literature. On the one hand, a mother's grief is so obvious, its circumstances of pose and gestures, of voice and tears, of surroundings and concomitant events, are so convincing, that our sympathy is evoked without further ado. On the other hand, the bereaved mother in real life is neither in a fit state, nor has she power, to express her feelings in their fullness. So the mother does not weep in literature as she weeps in nature, but that does not make her grief in the former case any less true.[14]

So the truth of literature is said to be higher than the truth of actuality. Artistic truth scores over naturalistic truth in its aesthetic delight that is not ordinary pleasure but something much finer and disinterested. Tagore, in his poem "Balmiki," says that the poet's imagination is truer than Ayodhya (here Ayodhya is the representative of external reality). The poet, for Sidney, shows things as they ought to be rather than as they are. David Daiches points out that 'Sidney has changed Aristotle's probable "should" to moral "should"'.[15] Sidney deviates from Aristotle's 'should' of probability to the 'oughtness' of a world that is fundamentally moral in character and, thus, more edifying than the real world. The poet's skill serves better than the mathematician, dealing with ethical and not geometric proportions. He, as Beach argues, is involved in trying to balance the 'highest point of man's intelligence' with the 'efficacy of Nature' and the 'right honour of the heavenly Maker'. So 'the healthy imagination delivers ideas which relate immediate ends to more encompassing functions: a man to his part; an art to the commonwealth; the commonwealth to nature; and nature to providence; the soldier, as we will see, to love. And since his ideas have an extraordinary power to motivate, the poet approaches the "ending end"'.[16] The moral philosopher or theologian can teach virtue only in the abstract but the poet paints images of ideal characters and makes virtue appear attractive by example. It is with the poet that we get poetic justice. The poet's feigning serves the purpose of moral instruction far better than the facts of the historian.

> For indeed Poetry ever setteth virtue so out in her best colours, making Fortune her well-waiting handmaid, that one must needs be enamoured of her.... And, of the contrary part, if evil men come to the stage, they ever go out... so manacled as they little animate folks to follow them. (16)

Working on the dialectic of the poet and the historian in Renaissance literature, Blair Worden shows us that in the sixteenth century, 'poetry and history alike made new claims and subjected themselves to new tests'. Through the advocacy of Sidney, the poet became an inventor or maker but many historians tried to sift the 'myth from the verifiable' and, in the process, as Worden notes, triggered a decline of the myth much endeared by the poets.[17] Although Sidney's *Apology* elevated poetry and scorned history, it did not meet with any 'counter-blast from the historians'. Worden observes further that

> when history and poetry did quarrel, the disputes were those of what a recent account fittingly calls an "intense sibling rivalry." In the Elizabethan and Jacobean age, that time of extraordinary accomplishment in both poetry and history, the siblings came of age. The intimacy of the relationship is hidden by our sense of teleology: by our alertness to, and concentration on, distinctions of genre and thought that anticipate our own mental landscape.

Poetry and history were 'capacious and fluid' disciplines and, in Sidney's *Apology*, 'poetry includes both verse and fiction, while history includes both mindless antiquarianism and the use of the past for rhetorical persuasion and for application to the present. In order to oppose poetry and history to each other, Sidney makes light both of the overlap between them and of the varieties within them'.[18] Here, in a trans-habitual momentum, Giovanni Pontano's way of seeing the 'coming together' of poetry and history deserves a brief mention. Pontano believed, as Ernesto Grassi points out, that 'poetry and history have a common aim, to clarify why and by what means man left the forest and built up a human world and community in freedom. They both show how man strove to be like the gods, how the laws arose, and how man came to investigate nature. History and poetry recall past events full of dignity (*rerum vetustarum ac remotarum repititiones*), and describe places, peoples, nations. They both report the sudden changes of fate, the plans men make to develop the future'.[19] The historian in his commitment to objectivity needs to avoid subjective emotions but the truth that he investigates cannot be rational truth independent of time and place. His language is formed through his choice of words which includes ornaments and not necessarily logical inferential discourse. How would the historian record, for instance, the yelling and cries, the storms, the commotion of the sailors and soldiers, the fear and bolting among elephants when Hannibal crossed the Rhone? What objectivity can the historian bring to his account of Hannibal's military march across Rhone? The language of the historian and the sensibility of the poet are called into synergy, making the truth of a situation—a historical event—shine in its gravitas of objectivity and the strength of imagination and insight.

On the strength of adjudging the 'philosophical and divine' Virgil as his favourite poet, Scaliger considered history as *poesis historica* where the poet 'practices the right reasoning of philosophy by teaching moral precepts in ways that move men to action'. The power of poetry to teach and delight associates it with either perdition or beatitude.[20] As over the dialectics and negotiation of poetry with history, Sidney settles on the side of poetry rediscovering Aristotle in the *Poetics*. David Quint observes that 'Sidney adapts his Aristotelian defence of poetry to the pedagogical concerns shared by the humanist educators, and his argument exploits the division in their thought which followed the Erasmian rejection of secular history from the moral curriculum'. Citing the example of a historical reading of Alexander, Quint points out that historical depiction blends virtue and vice and precludes the construction of an absolute model for the students to follow. Rather, the 'absolute model that the Erasmians found in the imitation of Christ Sidney posits in the "perfect pattern" of the poetic hero'.[21] In fact, history for Elizabethans was meant for both documented and 'feigned' matter. George Puttenham observes:

> ... the good and exemplarie things and actions of the former ages were reserved only to the historicall reportes of wise and grave men. ... These

historical men nevertheless used not the matter so precisely to wish that al they wrote should be accounted true, for that was not needeful nor expedient to the purpose, namely to be used either for example or for pleasure: considering that many times it is seen ea fained matter or altogether fabulous, besides that it maketh more mirth than any other, works no lesse good conclusions for example then the most true and veritable, but often times more, because the Poet hath the handling of them to fashion at his pleasure, but not so of th'other, which must go acoording to their veritie, and none otherwise, without the writers great blame. Againe, as ye know, mo and more excellent examples may be fained in one day by a good wit then many ages through mans frailtie are able to put in use; which made the learned and wittie men of those times to devise many historicall matters of no veritie at all, but with purpose to do good and no hurt, as using them for a maner of discipline and president of commendable life.[22]

Puttenham sees poets devising many historical matters for the purpose of doing good and not causing hurt towards a 'commendable life'. Sidney sees philosophers providing precept, the historian recording example but the poet as giving in his fictitious example 'a perfect picture of whatever the philosopher saith should be done'. The poet alone is capable of integrating an example with precept and Sidney's *Apology* demonstrates poetry's power to move through allegory and illustrative examples wherein the imaginative and the ethical are conjoined. Sidney here comes close to Tasso who finds the poet—distinguished from the historian who considers the truth of particulars and the philosopher that of universals—as seeking a perfect form that emphasised the truth of the universals more than the particulars.[23]

George Gascoigne, one of Sidney's contemporaries, in *The Adventures of Master*, was troubled by the vexed relationship that literature had with truth where history in a story is deflected towards the story-telling activity of the narrator. He could not accept the privileging of history over fiction, for readers might 'go away full fraught with falsehood' if historical truths in the form of reports, interpretations and conjectures were considered as determinant of narratives framed as actual events. Susan Staub points out that like 'the fiction-writer, the historian constructs an artifice, and his claim to truth is as problematic as that of the poet. History, too, is feigned history. Instead, Gascoigne posits that there is a truth greater than that of history'. This truth comes from imaginative literature and poetic invention. The poet and the historian get active on the same terrain which involves discovering hidden documents, relying on expert testimony and falling on witnesses 'to lend credence to his-story'. Staub shows us that Gascoigne

> uses the term to mean more than just the finding out of proper subjects and metaphors; when he speaks of "fayn[ing] a Fable by invention", Gascoigne interchanges inventing with fiction-making. Always

anticipating the criticism such a definition might evoke, however, Gascoigne insists that even in the "most feyned fables and imaginations" poets "metaphorically set forth unto us the right rewardes of vertues, and the due punishments for vices". Gascoigne expresses great confidence in the poetic endeavor.[24]

So, in contrast with historians trying to describe virtue in men and ways, the poet becomes a poetical historian who takes over historical action and beautifies such action for further teaching and delight. The poet invents 'perfect patterns' which historians cannot produce, in that Cyrus, Aeneas and Ulysses become character patterns, rather topos of things to be followed or delightfully appreciated for. The poet combines the Greek maker with the Roman prophet—poetic art in a Democritus way has Nature for his principal object. Poetry fails when the scale of life and nature are misappreciated. The poet imitates and combines his aesthetic projection into a form which is both constructed and ethically set and valued. Sidney, as Robert Strozier notes,

> explicitly embraces nature as the progenitor of art and consequently assumes the existent thing as prior to idealization of it in the poet's mind. This is implied in his comparison of the historian and poet, where the poet may improve history for "further teaching", and in Sidney's further claim that the poet invents the complete expression of virtue. The poet's experience, in other words, begins in phenomena and ends in art.[25]

Staying close to Sidney's allegiance to Aristotle, one can argue that mimesis is concerned with the presentation and exploration of some idea of a 'possible'. With the knowledge that correctness in poetry is not identical with correctness in politics, the poet transforms the singulars in the process and partly completes what nature cannot bring to a finish—the transition to the golden.[26] What we find in *On the Parts of Animals* (IV, 10) and *On the Generation of Animals* (I, 4)—nature makes the best of the materials it has at her disposal and works with a thrust toward the ideal—come to attain a better thing or higher reality (*beltion*).

II

Sidney defines poetry as

> an art of imitation, for so Aristotle termeth it in his word *Mimesis*, that is to say, a representing, counterfeiting or figuring forth; to speak metaphorically, a speaking picture, with this end to teach and delight. (7)

He transforms the concept of imitation into one of creation or ideal imitation according to which, the poet imitates not the actualities but the *ideal reality* behind the actual. The concept of the right poet owes to the Neoplatonic tradition that considers the 'imitation' of the reality formed in the poet's mind as a potent source of poetic creativity. The art of imitation negotiates aesthetically with the reality formed in the mind of the poet beyond the world or nature that we interact with physical directness. The veracity of poetic imitation and consequent representation cannot be the true measure of poetic art. There is a necessity to secure some freedom from nature: going *beyond* nature than *following* nature can ensure creativity of high merit. In fact, Sidney's concept of the poet has the idealising strain with its foundation in Renaissance Platonism. Turning the tables on Plato, it focuses on the poet's access to the ideal with the thumping obliteration of the negative potential of role-models.

How does the poet 'feign'? How does he plot? Explaining two divisions of imitation—icastic and phantastic—the stranger in *Sophist* points out that likeness-making is one of the kinds which produces a copy by being faithful to the 'proportions of the original, similar in length and breadth and depth, each thing receiving also its appropriate colour'.[27] Sidney's Idea points to a vein of creativity which sounds more mysterious than the 'ideal and sensible qualities depicted by Shakespeare or Spenser'. Maynard Mack insightfully observes that 'it is not difficult to see how Sidney's theory of poetic making through the "Idea or fore-conceit" resembles Plotinus's description of the arts shooting "back up to the forming principles" because for 'Plotinus, art and nature proceed according to the same "reason principle", but art surpasses nature in its ability to "make up what is defective in things". This seems to square nicely with Sidney's view that the poet, working through his "Idea or fore-conceit" does not imitate nature but goes hand-in-hand with her, making a "golden" world which is better than the brazen one she produces on her own'.[28] In his negotiation with the material world Sidney is different from Plotinus also. The poet does not turn away from the 'too much loved earth'; instead, he endeavours to make it lovelier. Mack shows us further that

> Sidney agrees with Plotinus that art and nature are vehicles for contemplating the higher realities they figure forth; but unlike Plotinus he does not reduce their function and value to this alone. For Sidney, contemplation does not lead one to turn one's back on the work of art or on the world; it leads one rather to incarnate (another Christian concept that was anathema to Plotinus) the Idea of the work in one's own life and to redeem the world through heroic moral action in that world. For Sidney the material world and active life are both good, and art aids the perfection of both. Thus, with Plotinus as with Sidney's other predecessors, resemblance should not be taken for identity.[29]

As against phantastic art, Sidney's poetry is icastic for it re-creates the real, agreeing with Scaliger's dictum: '*At poeta et naturam alteram et fortunas plures etiam ac demum sese isthoc ipso perinde ac Deum alterum efficit*'.[30]

Falling back on the dialectic emerging from *Genesis* about man's ideal nature and sinful state—a principle that persisted through Renaissance poetics and culturalogics—Sidney sees the poet as constructing a communicative pathway between the 'erected wit' and 'our infected will'. Neoplatonically, the poet's icastic imitation, as contrasted with the phantastike, combines decorum, energia and didacticism, leading Sidney to observe:

> Only the poet disdaining to be tied to any such subjection, lifted up by the vigour of his own invention, doth grow in effect another nature, in making things either better than nature bringeth forth, or quite anew, forms such as never were in nature, as the heroes, demi-gods, Cyclops, chimeras, furies, and such like. (6)

Here, we can encourage a comparative run with J. Harington, who like Sidney answers back Agrippa's polemics against poetry.[31] The poets are charged with being 'liars'. Harington in answering to that accusation points out that the poets, on the contrary, convey truth in manifold forms. He supports his proposition with the instance of the ancient poets who encompassed myriad sense and mysteries in their poetry. With strong allegiance to the patristic and the post-classical theory, Harington explains that the poet conceals the mysterious truths of poetry to protect them from profanity that comes from abuse and misuse. The verse, as part of their art, is meant for the weaker capacities, the moral sense is directed to stronger stomachs and the allegory is meant for the conceited and the imaginative minds. He hails the mystical way of writing for the poet. To charge the poet's art as fictive would be incorrect, for Harington emphasises the oblique method of teaching by reference to Demosthenes's success in persuading the Athenians and emphasising the biblical use of many parables. He denies outright that poetry breeds error and, if one admits that poetry pleased fools, Harington hastens to add that it made the fools wise by presenting them with 'tales able to keep a child from play and old man from the chimney corner'. (18) So all forms of poetry may be read with pleasure and profit. Sidney declares, with an unmistakably Puritan emphasis on the responsible individual mind, that making poetry is essentially the discipline of an enlightened intellect; this seeks to overcome earth-bound thoughts and inclinations in an attempt to recover something of the true and perfect knowledge lost since 'the first accursed fall' (6). Imaginative treatment of life provides the opposite recipe for 'right' poetry where mimesis is not a mere imitation of the world as is seen by our imperfect eyes, but a 'figuring forth' (7) of the 'nature' of higher order and recreating in his imaginative mind the world as it may have existed in the Creator's mind (with a prominent emphasis on the Christian model of creation). The poet, in his flight 'borrow nothing of what is, hath been or shall be; but range, only reined with learned discretion, into the divine consideration of what may be, and should be' (8). It is a world present in the mind of the creator which is distorted by the phenomena of nature but well manifested by the creative endeavours of the poet. So the concept of *creation,* here, is not to be interpreted in the sixteenth-century sense of the word—not *effingere* but *creare.* John McIntyre notes:

> The Renaissance mimetic exercised the whole man in contemplation. If the poet's representation of beauty be considered ideal, his concept of man's ability to comprehend that ideal was real. For what hindered man's response to beauty was "his enemie vice, which must be destroyed, and his cumbersome servant Passion, which must be maistered." Accordingly, the "masking rayment of Poesie" moves the passions, excites the intellect, and arouses the will. This involvement of the total person is "not Gnosis but Praxis"; for the specific kind of teaching which Sidney imputes to the poet is this interior movement of soul, which delights as it directs.[32]

'Invention' then is the distinguishing character of the poet; he creates new things by drawing on his own wit. Zuccaro, in his book *L 'Idea de 'pittori, scultori et architetti,* points out that the artist is bestowed with the ability to produce an infinite number of artefacts that resembles the objects of nature and in his production he makes a new paradise appear on earth. The artist forms many ideas in himself and his representations are varied as well.[33] In fact Sidney's use of the terms 'Idea or foreconceit' or 'another nature' or 'golden' points to what Zuccaro refers as the new paradise.

> Nature never set forth the earth in so rich tapestry as divers poets have done; neither with pleasant rivers, fruitful trees, sweet-smelling flowers nor whatsoever else may make the too-much-loved earth more lovely; *her world is brazen, the poets only deliver a golden.* (6)

Sidney is making an interesting, though not an original, point here. It is not the mere exercise of his imagination, but the exercise of his imagination to create a better world—better than the real—is what justifies the poet.[34] This has obvious reference to the admiration of Zelmane (*Arcadia*) at Amphialus for the abilities of a 'maker'. The higher level of ideal imitation is the 'other nature' or Pamela's 'right heavenly nature' or 'unnatures Nature'. The poet's reason can discern the innate reason within universal nature, providing a representation that is more perfect, dearer, and agreeable than anything in nature. The lovers in fiction are 'truer' than those of the real life, the friends are more 'constant', the warriors are more 'valiant', the princess is more 'right' and the heroes are more 'excellent' in every way. For him, hence, Plato was the most poetical. If the poet teaches delight, the philosopher teaches delightfully. But 'because Sidney understands', as A.C. Hamilton notes, that the poet's entire purpose is to feign his golden world of images, he goes beyond the Horatian account of the end of poetry and emphasizes wholly its rhetorical end of "moving." This end is included, of course, by the Italian critics, and Scaliger speaks of poetry "docendi & mouendi, & delectandi."[35]

Within a humanist aesthetics, the tilt was towards 'instruction'. Tasso, the Italian poet, wrote that the goal of epic and indeed all poetry is 'to profit by delighting, that is, delight is the cause why no one fails to obtain benefit, because delight induces him to read the more gladly'.[36] For Sidney, in an inversion of the principles which is peculiarly his very own, the poet *delights* and *instructs:* 'But it is that feigning notable images of virtues, vices, or what else, with that delightful teaching, which must be the right describing note to know a poet by' (9). The delight is real and substantial, but not without the discipline. It has its own usefulness and recognises harmony, perfection, goodness and success, appealing to the principles of judgement and understanding. So delight gives to instruction the power to move. Raiger points out that 'poetry does not have its end in itself, but in the idea which it presents. Sidney's "right poet" creates images of moral goodness which are desirable, leading the soul into the realm of perfection much as Plato's beloved brings to mind the celestial vision of Beauty recalled from the spiritual realm. In this dynamic which builds on natural desire to direct the soul beyond nature, we see the cognitive (phenomenological) elements which take Sidney's notion of mimesis beyond that of Aristotle'.[37] So the moving power of poetry owes its operation not to the Aristotelian idea of the noble in tragedy but to the Platonic notion of Eros. Within a 'dynamic iconography', the poet's mimetic habit is less concerned with the representation of action and more with the speaking picture, allegorising virtue as an ideal.

The poet's utterance cannot be brought under the overarching value judgement of good or bad: 'for the poet, he nothing affirms, and therefore never lieth' (27),[38] vindicating how the poet succeeds better in fiction than in truth and also throwing up the Renaissance commonplace now most familiar from Touchstone's declaration in *As You Like It*: 'the truest poetry is the most feigning'.[39] Fulke Greville, who was a close associate of Sidney, did not see imagination as a glorious category in poetic creation. Although acknowledging, like Sidney, of the ability of imagination to create anew—to 'feign', to 'forge' or 'make'—he is suspect of the potentially reckless breadth that it can produce. Good imagination, as Sidney does not fail to admit, is governed by the rational faculty which, also, takes wise measure of irrationality as a paradigm for creation. The making and feigning power of poetic imagination must overcome the impediments of humors and passions, forbidding any appeal to what Puttenham qualifies as the 'phantasticall part of man'. Poetry can present speaking pictures through such control and prudent access, accenting thereby the right ways of enframing. Proper function of poetry, then, for Greville is pleasurable instruction. Norman Falmer clarifies the issue by pointing out that Greville's 'dominant concern is that the poet should show "Nature how to fashion/Her selfe againe, by ballancing of passion". Thus, having exercised control over his matter, having fulfilled the office of 'maker' by 'feigning' and 'imitating' under the strict control of both the rational faculties and the technical demands of his art, the poet would bring to bear upon the varied and often warring passions a positive measure of balance'.[40] In a trans-(in)fusionist move, we encounter an interesting discussion in Arabic poetics which involves the principles of sincerity, truthfulness and lie (feigning) in poetic ethics. Vicente Cantarino argues that

> the concept of the poet as a liar and poetry as a lie received acceptance in Islam on the basis of Islamic cultural Arabization and alliance with the linguistic heritage of even pre-Islamic Arabic times. The result was that the meaning had been changed, and the poetic lie no longer had moral implications. Sincerity and truthfulness, or lack of it, on the part of the poet could not be understood as the authenticity of feelings or opinions expressed.[41]

Qudama ibn Ja'far of the Abbasid period believes that a poet should not be judged by sincerity alone. In *Kitab Naqd al-shi'r* (*Book on Poetic Criticism*), he emphasises the importance of holding an idea and enframing it creditably at a particular moment. Poetic lie and truthfulness have generated a moot 'problematic' and, although Qudama identifies the relationship between poetic creativity and the art of lying, a moralising impact leads him to throw his weight behind poetic sincerity that stays inscribed in veridic experiences and discourses. Poetic 'feigning' that produces aesthetic experiences of high quality for Sidney held similar importance for Ibn'Abd Rabbih, the tenth-century Moorish poet, who in his *Al-'Iqd al-Farīd,* looks into perfection and the beauty of poetic expression and does not necessarily concentrate on the truthfulness of depiction. Sincerity, for both Sidney and Ibn 'Abd Rabbih, does not come from mere morality itself; aesthetic mimesis produces the charm and delicacy of poetic configuration where counterfeit becomes invention. The renowned tenth-century Iranian scholar Abd al-Qahir al-Jurjani comes closer to Sidney's idea of poetic feigning when he observes in *Asrar al-Balaghah* (*The Secrets of Elucidation*) that

> he who claims "the one that lies most" to be the best poetry maintains a theory that the possibilities of the art can expand and its rays spread, its field of action broaden, and its manifold aspects branch out when the poet relies on achieving a greater range and imaginative creativity, and claims that to be reality which is basically an approximation and imitation, and aims at delicate forms and interpretations.[42]

Sidney's *Shā'ir* (poet) has the *takhyil* (the imaginative creativity) and the *sha'ara* which is the art of knowing and perceiving.[43] The poetic lie is reconstruction and not distortion where the ethics of lying or feigning become a part of the dialectic of delight and instruction. This puts Sidney's idea of mimesis—delivering the golden—in meaningful communication with the ways in which Averroes and Avicenna problematise delight (*iltidhadh*) through their Aristotelian understanding of mimesis. Hazim al-Qartajanni (d. 1285) sees the right connection between *muhakah* (mimesis) and the deployment of *takhyil* (imaginative creation). Claiming that poetry differs from demonstration, argumentation and rhetoric, he writes:

> The finest poetry is that which has beautiful mimetic representation and form, whose repute or veracity is striking, and whose falsehood is hidden, but its originality is evident. And the poet's skill is credited with the ability to propagate falsehood rapidly, to misrepresent it to the human spirit, and to impel the latter to feel moved even before it examines the former to see how it really is—all this is rightly attributed to the poet and to the forcefulness of his creative imagination in producing in the speech the power of attraction of the soul, for it is not correct to assert that this is something attributable to the speech itself.[44]

Sidney's aesthetic mimesis reemphasises Ibn Rashiq's observation that a poet perceives what no other can—the 'golden' is connected with delight through 'embellishment' and 'defacement'. This does not declare a severance from reality; the evaluation of poetry need not confine itself to truth or falsehood because poetry is fundamentally a creative discourse. For Sidney and his Arabic counterparts imaginings or mimetic projections (*mukhayyil*) have their own ethics of creation, something other than *musaddiq* (objective reality). So imagination for both Sidney and Al-Farabi, the renowned ninth-century philosopher and jurist, motivates action—it evokes the poetic power to *move* us. Nabil Matar explains that

> in motivating action it [imagination] establishes a certain legitimacy for itself. As Alfarabi states in the Treatise, reason may indicate one thing, but if imagination indicates its opposite, the individual might still choose to follow what his imagination dictates; so although the imagination might project a falsity, there is a kind of suspension of belief as the individual acts in accordance with that falsity and in contradiction to reason. Such a function of imagination, however, need not set it at the polar extreme of reason/truth; rather, and because of its causative faculty, imagination should be seen to operate within the realm of sense perception and reason but with its own creative-*mukhayyil* meaning.[45]

Here, Sidney's 'golden' is *mukhayyil* that connects imaginings with action, reflection with craft.

Like Boccaccio in *De genealogia deorum gentilium*, Bruni, Poliziano, Ficino (exponents of poetic frenzy) and Fracastoro, Sidney proceeds to develop a theory of ideal imitation—the notion that the poet imitates not the mere appearances of actuality but the hidden reality behind them. It may be observed that the Florentine Academy of Marsilio Ficino which launched Platonism as the preponderating philosophical influence misread the irony in Plato's *Ion* and *Phaedrus* about the divine frenzy. So the idea of the poet as the 'possessed' creator riding the crest of a divine afflatus passed into Renaissance orthodoxy. Gábor Katona is right in observing that poetic frenzy was never an important token of poetic creativity for Sidney. So 'probing the boundaries of human knowledge, Sidney relies on the cognitive faculties of the psyche rather than on metaphysical doctrines. He rejects Plato's intellectual asceticism as well as the worldly pride of the Neoplatonists. He probably believes that literature should not only be written for a social or intellectual elite, but for an ever-widening circle of readers, too. What Sidney wanted to see established was national literature moving people to virtuous action (praxis) by delighting them in the Horatian sense. Platonists like Nicolaus of Cusa maintained that Man's ascendance to God is totally unthinkable. Sidney was the first to ignore the theories of poetic frenzy and melancholy'.[46] With this notion as the primary strand in his creative matrix, Sidney outmanoeuvres the entire issue of truth. Without much respect to the principle of divine fury which is associated with poetic creation (as exemplified in Giordano Bruno's *De Gl' Heroici Furori*), Sidney believes that the poet's 'other nature' is the product of a vigorous activity that cannot do away with judgement and right reason. A construction of a poem is not meant for religious abuse but the poet, albeit divinely inspired, is not madly possessed by *dunamis*; he is not a *manikos*. The poet for Sidney is neither a pure prophet nor an uncritical imitator; not an astronomer, grammarian and moral philosopher, rather, an inspired maker who within his own habits of creation knows the contradiction and limitations of both polarities.[47] The prophetic powers of the 'right' poet range him 'into the divine consideration of what may be and should be' (9–10); he is, thus, figured within early modern prophetic discourse.

The poet deals with, as Aristotle puts it, *katholou* (the universal) and not merely with *kathekaston* (particular). This is a testimony of the substantial nature of the poet's creation as he manifests the immutable traits of human life and thought. Although Sidney and Aristotle relate to each other in their understanding of the poet's way to create his own world, there are comparative points which suggest that while for Aristotle the 'poet is in a sort of competition with nature in order to excel her', the poet for Sidney works towards the idealisation of his material. Thomas Kishler notes that 'Aristotle's universal forms are perfect, but their perfection is realized only in the concrete. In this sense, then, Aristotle's concept of mimesis is basically realistic. Sidney's poet employs the concrete as a springboard to intuitions of the world of perfect ideas'.[48] For Aristotle, art was either directed to the necessities of life or to its 'recreation' where the inventors of the latter were naturally always regarded as wiser than the inventors of the former because their branches of knowledge did not aim at utility. Many aspects of reality lie beyond the premises of poetry proper and when the 'poet does deal with his legitimate object (human action) he is not to be understood as making truth bearing statements or claims, but as offering plausible yet fictional structures of possible (rather than actual) events. The poet is a dramatiser, not an interpreter, of human life. And where interpretation or judgement takes from mimetic representation, Aristotle does not consider the result as 'poetry' but as some other kind of discourse, needing to be assessed by a different set of criteria'.[49] For Sidney and Aristotle, the poet need not have the *enthusiasmos* but surely possesses the unrivalled competence to lend form to thoughts—mimetic representations that are more creative and less interpretive. Motored by trans-habit, we find here an Augustinian notion of imitation at work. Augustine integrates the 'lights of noetic order' and the 'order of making' with an illumination. Monroe Beardsley argues that

> it is possible for the mind, by taking away, as has been said, some things from objects which the senses have brought within its knowledge, and by adding some things, to produce in the exercise of imagination that which, as a whole, was never within the observation of any senses; but the part of it had all been within such observation, though found in a variety of different things: eg., when we were boys, born and brought up in an island district, we could already form some idea of the sea, after we had seen water even in a small cup.[50]

If a small cup of water helps one to imagine a sea, the invention in poetry can be qualified to be a lie, feigning, which does not aim to deceive, but to delight in the way a joke is a lie but intended to evoke laughter. The poet does not choose to be fallacious; the bent oar in the water is illusory but what the artist represents is necessitated by his will, creative transcription of objects. This does not approximate much to the way in which Aquinas looks at the artist's operation with the phenomenal world—*ans imitator naturum in sue operatione phantasia*. The phantasm is an image of a thing, and the imagination is, thus, a receptacle for images; it qualifies to be the sole way by which the intellect can know things in their individuality. The operating intellect of the poet, while preconceiving the form of what is made, has an idea; this idea is the very form of the thing that the poet chooses to imitate. So the idea is not the *form* as an object of perception but the *form* of the substance that the poet selects in his mimetic operation. In Thomistic conception of art, the ontological value of artistic form cannot excel the natural form. Aquinas believes that artistic form (poetry as *infima doctrina*) is ontologically dependent and so composition (*ratio factibulum*), not creation, is the indispensable principle in the medieval theory of art. Sidney's poetics, by contrast, established poetry as both 'doing' and 'making'. What art seeks to reproduce is primarily an inward process which, as psychical energy, works on the outward manifestations in deeds, incidents, events, situations. The poet delights in rhythm and imitation. This rhythm contains a familiar and ordered number of movements in a regular manner.[51] Art takes the form which is in the soul of the artist and the poet's world is both ideal and real.[52] Here visual epistemology[53] connects with poetic imitation to generate a mental picture which can impel the readers to action. This actional thrust of speaking picture makes Sidney's understanding of poetic mimesis interesting. Paula Payne explains it well:

> Aristotle's perception of imitation "mimesis" differs only verbally from participation "methexis". Plato used this term "methexis" to describe the relationship between the appearance or constitutive nature ("eide") and sensible particulars. For Aristotle, imitation remained an active process of joining the inner intelligibility of a form or idea with its sensible effects. Aristotle did not view the "eidos" as a separate substance apart from its sensible particulars, but rather as a complete entity. The mind recognizes the thing it knows when the "eidos" of the object enters the soul. Sidney imitates when his poetry stimulates this joining of "eidos" and sensory details in the reader's mind's eye.[54]

Sidney's notion of imitation then stands opposed to Petrus Ramus's heavy reliance on dialectic with its attendant paradigms of invention, judgement and disposition. Ramism invests in a logical system dealing with the normative problem of language and formation of concepts, emphasis on what is called 'natural' dialectic, its preoccupation with clear statement, and celebration of the common-sense point of view (a point of view, that is, quite opposed to that of logic in the Aristotelian sense of the word, and, one might perhaps add, poetry).[55] A prominent English Ramist of his day, William Temple, could not have accepted poetic imitation as an extension on nature, a 'golden' coming through as a higher form of creation. Decrying poetry as a stimulus to learning and endorsing poetic knowledge as made possible through 'arguments', Temple, unlike Sidney, considers poetic imitation possible only through logical arguments:

> In fact, there is no such thing as poetical imitation, only dialectical. The creative process involved in writing poetry differs in no way from that involved in any kind of writing: "*Quamobrem fictio erit idem quod rei, quae nondum extiterit inventio, id si ita est, ars fictionis non ad poesin sed ad dialecticam inventionem pertinebit: qua non solum res verae sed etiam fictitiae cogitantur.*" In other words, since the only way in which we perceive anything, whether it exists in actual fact or not, is through the arguments and since the only way we can express what we have perceived is likewise "conceptually," then obviously the only "mimesis" is dialectic—in the Ramistical sense.[56]

But Sidney's poet arrives intuitively at glimpses of an ideal world, far removed from the bare transcript of life. His primary motive force in composition is in response to a 'light of nature', making art function as an active discovery by the employment of an interminable skill which is akin to the ability of Pamela in *Arcadia* as she works her stitches into an embroidery.

Does Sidney's poet, then, revolutionise the logos of creativity to secularizse the poet through divine supplantation? It is difficult to accept the argument that sees the creature turning into a creator through a self-articulation achieved by 'reoccupation' of medieval theological categories of divinization of creativity. The poet does not succumb to the habits of creativity that sees dedivinization as part of a strident segregation between nature and art, god and man, faith and reason. The poet's creative effectiveness owes to a divine centre—a transcendent impulsion—and not merely to a secularization of *techne*, mimetic skill, and sparkling wit. The complicated matrices of 'fall', 'brazen', 'deliver' and 'golden' point to a world which is both sacral, secular, theological and theoretical. Deeply entrenched habits to compartmentalise the secular and the sacred betray a prejudice, as Mack rightly notes, 'in favor of reductive theories of secularization'.[57] Sidney's poet challenges such reduction to develop a habit of making which is at once human and divine. Perhaps, straddling both worlds epistemologically exemplarises Sidney's poetics, disconnecting him from the fiercely anchored positional understanding of creativity within anthropological frameworks of artistic production. This, indeed, becomes an inspiration to hermeneuticise Sidney's idea of the poet within the dynamics of trans-habit that looks into the divergent and discretionary parameters ranging across both religious and secular sources. The 'golden' is alchemised to deliver a *sense* that rescues the poet from the monological bind into an opening that makes it an enticing piece of knowledge—solemn, skilled, subtle and sublimatory.

Notes

1. Edmund Spenser, *The Faerie Queene* (ed.) Thomas P. Roche Jr. (New York: Penguin, 1979), 2.1.50, lines 5–8.
2. *The Sermons of John Donne* (ed.) Evelyn M. Simpson and George R. Potter, 10 vols. (Berkeley: University of California Press, 1953–62), 9, 98.
3. *The Origins of Criticism: Literary Culture and Poetic Theory in Classical Greece* (Princeton, N.J.: Princeton University Press, 2002), 133.
4. Joel Spingarn observes: 'The introduction of Aristotelianism into England was the direct result of the influence of the Italian critics; and the agent in bringing this new influence into English letters was Sir Philip Sidney. His Defence of Poesy is a veritable epitome of the literary criticism of the Italian Renaissance'. See his *A History of Literary Criticism in the Renaissance* (New York, 1908, reprinted 1963), 170. Also see Kenneth O. Myrick, *Sir Philip Sidney as a Literary Craftsman* (Cambridge, Mass.: Harvard University Press, 1935) for a restatement of Sidney's alleged lack of originality. However, Sidney's intelligence, temper and unity of thought come in for uniform praise.

5. J. W. H. Atkins, *English Literary Criticism: The Renascence* (London, 1947), 137.
6. Visvanath Chatterjee (ed.) *An Apology for Poetry* (London: Sangam Books, 1975), 12. All quotes from the text are parenthetically provided in the body of the chapter.
7. Michael Raiger, 'Sidney's Defence of Plato' *Religion & Literature*, 30, no. 2 (Summer 1998), 39.
8. Ibid., 39–40.
9. Roger E Moore, 'Sir Philip Sidney's Defence of Prophesizing', *Studies in English Literature 1500–1900*, 50, no. 1 (Winter 2010), 38.
10. Ibid., 53.
11. Michael Mack, *Sidney's Poetics: Imitating Creation* (Washington, D.C.: The Catholic University of America Press, 2005), 91.
12. I waited patiently for the Lord;/ he inclined to me and heard my cry./ He drew me up from the desolate pit/ out of the miry bog,/ and set my feet upon a rock,/ making my steps secure./ He put a new song in my mouth. / a song of praise to our God. Psalm 40. See *Bible*, Standard Version, The Bible Societies, Oxford University Press, 1952 Old Testament, 1946 New Testament.
13. See Hans-Joachim Kraus, *Theology of Psalms* (Minneapolis, Minn.: Fortress Press, 1992), 15.
14. Prabas Jiban Chaudhury, *Tagore on Literature and Aesthetics* (Calcutta: Rabindra Bharati, 1965), 29.
15. David Daiches, *Critical Approaches to Literature* (Calcutta: Orient Longman, 1998), 65.
16. D. M Beach, 'The Poetry of Idea: Sir Philip Sidney and the Theory of Allegory', *Texas Studies in Literature and Language*, 13, no. 3 (Fall 1971), 369.
17. Donald R. Kelley and David Harris Sacks (eds.) *The Historical Imagination in Early Modern Britain: History, Rhetoric, Fiction, 1500–1800* (Cambridge University Press, 1997), 69, 83; William Nelson, *Fact or Fiction: The Dilemma of the Renaissance Storyteller* (Cambridge, Mass.: Harvard University Press, 1973), 23.
18. Blair Worden, 'Historians and Poets', *Huntington Library Quarterly*, 68, no. 1–2 (March 2005), 83. Also see Blair Worden, *The Sound of Virtue: Philip Sidney's "Arcadia" and Elizabethan Politics* (New Haven, Conn.: Yale University Press, 1996). For more on the history and poetry interface, see Paulina Kewes, *The Uses of History in Early Modern England* (Berkeley: University of California Press), 79–86.
19. Ernesto Grassi, 'Humanistic Rhetorical Philosophizing: Giovanni Pontano's Theory of the Unity of Poetry, Rhetoric, and History', *Philosophy & Rhetoric*, 17, no. 3 (1984), 152.
20. See M. H. Doherty, *The Mistress-Knowledge: Sir Philip Sidney's Defence of Poesie and Literary Architectonics in the English Renaissance* (Nashville, Tenn.: Vanderbilt University Press, 1991), 42. Also see https://tspace.library.utoronto.ca/bitstream/1807/4350/1160/displayprose59ec.html for the full text of Puttenham's *The Art of English Poesie*. Accessed 21.03.2016.
21. David Quint, '"Alexander the Pig": Shakespeare on History and Poetry', *boundary 2*, 10, no. 3 (Spring 1982), 60.
22. See Alan D. Isler, 'Heroic Poetry and Sidney's Two "Arcadias"' *PMLA*, 83, no. 2 (May 1968), 374.
23. Bernard Weinberg, *A History of Literary Criticism in the Italian Renaissance* (Chicago: Chicago University Press, 1961), II, 1011–1012. The neo-Latin

jurisconsult Andrea Alciati observes: 'You should understand that both studies embrace each other mutually, as if an alliance had been entered on, and you must consider them the same and not different. For when you say Philosopher, you mean also Poet, and when you say Poet you mean Philosopher'. See Robert J. Clements, *Picta poesis* (Rome: Edizioni di storia e lutteratua, 1960), 98.
24. S. K. Heninger, Jr., Susan C. Staub, John T. Shawcross and Anne Lake Prescott, 'The Interface between Poetry and History: Gascoigne, Spenser, Drayton' *Studies in Philology*, 87, no. 1 (Winter 1990), 117. Also see George E. Rowe, Jr. 'Interpretation, Sixteenth-Century Readers, and George Gascoigne's "The Adventures of Master F. J."', *ELH* 48, no. 2 (Summer 1981), 271–289; Gillian Austen, *George Gascoigne* (Cambridge: D. S. Brewer, 2008).
25. Robert M. Strozier, 'Poetic Conception in Sir Philip Sidney's *An Apology for Poetry*', *The Yearbook of English Studies*, Vol. 2 (1972), 59.
26. Aristotle, *Physics*, 199a; *Politics* IV, VII, 17. See http://classics.mit.edu/Aristotle/physics.html.And http://classics.mit.edu/Aristotle/politics.html. Accessed 22.01.2016.
27. Echo can be found in Giacopo Mazzoni's treatise *On the Defense of Comedy* as well as in Tasso. See M. A. R. Habib, *A History of Literary Criticism and Theory: From Plato to the Present* (Oxford: Blackwell, 2005), 245–249.
28. Mack, *Sidney's Poetics*, 63, 70.
29. Ibid., 71.
30. See John P. Mcntyre, 'Sidney's Golden World', *Comparative Literature*, 14, no. 4 (Autumn 1962), 357.
31. See J. W. H. Aitkin, *English Literary Criticism* Vol. II (Jaipur: Surabhi Publications, 1999), 189–92.
32. John P. McIntyre, 'Sidney's Golden World' *Comparative Literature*, 14, no. 4 (Autumn, 1962), 364.
33. E. Panofsky, *Idea: A Concept in Art Theory* (Leipzig and Berlin, 1924), 108.
34. Mary Ellen Lamb observes that 'Sidney's famous evocation of the poet's golden world is one such text haunted by the ghosts of childhood. As set apart from astronomers, mathematicians, musicians, and other intellectual professionals, poets alone attain true masculinity through the creativity of their minds." The musculature of the creative mind "surpasses nature and bypasses the female role in reproduction" aligning art with the "masculine and the divine". It is an overbalanced dialectic between masculinised intellect with the pleasure and delight of a subjectivity centred on the body'. 'Apologising for Pleasure in Sidney's "Apology for Poetry": The Nurse of Abuse Meets the Tudor Grammar School', *Criticism*, 3, no. 4 (Fall 1994), 508. 'It has been perceptively observed,' notes Doherty, 'that the poet fructifies his creation—also see as a 'male sexual adjunct of a female ruling power'—through a 'coupling of the craftsman and the mistress-knowledge when the "erected wit" of the poet is "lifted up with the vigour of his own invention"'. It is rightly observed that 'the appropriation of power is operative in the male poet's treatment of the royal mistress poesie in Sidney's gendered metaphors of the Defence; consequently, the subject and the structure of the text politically engage the reader in the subject-sovereign relationship of Sidney and the Queen'. Doherty, *The Mistress-Knowledge*, 11.
35. A. C. Hamilton, 'Sidney's Idea of the "Right Poet"', *Comparative Literature*, 9, no. 1 (Winter 1957), 57.
36. Harold Bloom (ed.) *The Art of the Critic*, Vol. II (New York: Chelsea House, 1986), 403.

37. Raiger, 'Sidney's Defence of Plato', 36.
38. 'Now for the poet, he labors not to tell you what is or is not, but what should or should not be. And therefore though he recount things not true, yet because he telleth them not for true he lieth not. There seems an obvious conflict between Sidney's humanism, expressed in the claim that the poet tells us what should be, and the idea that the poetry makes no assertions. Even if the poet makes no empirical claims (about what is), by telling what should be, he or she does affirm something. The poet is therefore capable of mistake or error, even deception. I lack ample space to pursue exegetical issues, except to note that there is sufficient textual evidence to suggest that Sidney was genuinely torn. There are passages where he writes, more circumspectly, of the poet showing, rather than telling, what should be. This is consistent with some forms of humanism, since poetic justice, for instance, requires merely that we be shown virtue always rewarded, not told that crime does not pay. Perhaps Sidney meant the distinction between showing and telling to buttress his denial of literary statements, but this argument implicitly trades on a faulty view of assertion'. See Daniel Jacobson, 'Sir Philip Sidney's Dilemma: On the Ethical Function of Narrative Art', *The Journal of Aesthetics and Art Criticism*, 54, no. 4 (Autumn 1996), 331.
39. Richard Hillyer, *Sir Philip Sidney, Cultural Icon* (Basingtoke: Palgrave Macmillan, 2010), 93.
40. Norman Farmer, 'Fulke Greville and the Poetic of the Plain Style', *Texas Studies in Literature and Language*, 11, no. 1 (Spring 199), 66.
41. Vicente Cantarino, *Arabic Poetics in the Golden Age* (Leiden: E. J. Brill, 1975), 35.
42. Quoted in Cantarino, *Arabic Poetics*, 165. For more on al-Jurjani's distinctions between veracity and poetic truth see Roger Allen, *The Arabic Literary Heritage: the development of its genres and criticism* (Cambridge University Press, 1998), 382–83.
43. See Ibn Rashīq's *Al-'Umdah fī maḥāsin al-shi'r wa adabihi wa naqdihi* for further elucidation on these lines. See G.J.H. Van Gelder, *Classical Arabic Literary Critics on the Coherence and Unity of the Poem* (Leiden: Brill, 1982), 112–126.
44. See Al-Qartajanni, *Minhaj Al-Bulagha*, in Cantarino, *Arabic Poetics*, 214. Also see Mansour Àjami, *The Alchemy of Glory: The Dialectic of Truthfulness and Untruthfulness in Medieval Arabic Literary Criticism* (Washington, D.C.: Three Continents Press, 1988).
45. Nabil Matar, 'Alfārābī on Imagination: With a Translation of His "Treatise on Poetry"', *College Literature*, 23. no. 1 (Feb. 1996), 104.
46. Gábor Katona, 'The Cultural Background of Sir Philip Sidney's "Defence of Poesy"', *Hungarian Studies in English*, 22 (1991), 95.
47. Raiger 'Sidney's Defence of Plato', 25.
48. Thomas C. Kishler, 'Aristotle and Sidney on Imitation' *The Classical Journal*, 59, no. 2 (Nov. 1963), 64. Silvia Carli rightly observes: 'It is the essential connection between mimesis and form that explains why Aristotle discerns a meaningful kinship between poetry on the one hand, and philosophy and universality on the other. Their difference, however, is not blurred: the former exhibits or shows the form of a chain of particular events enacted by individuals and is thus never severed from the experiential. The latter moves from what is most intelligible for us to what is most intelligible in itself and provides rational and general accounts of the nature of the human world'. See Silvia Carli, 'Poetry is more Philosophical than History: Aristotle on Mimesis and Form', *The Review of*

Metaphysics, 64, no. 2 (December 2010), 306. Aristotle does not think that the ergon of the poet is to imitate certain kinds of things, that is to say, the things that could happen. Rather his function is to imitate things as they might happen: the emphasis is on modality or on the way in which things happen (namely, according to probability or necessity).
49. Stephen Halliwell, *The Poetics of Aristotle* (London: Duckworth, 1987), 74.
50. Monroe C. Beardsley, *Aesthetics from Classical Greece to the Present: A Short History* (New York: The Macmillan Company, 1966), 98.
51. *Problemata* 920b; http://www.gutenberg.org/files/12699/12699-h/12699-h.htm. Accessed 22.02.2016. Also see S. C. Sengupta, *An Introduction to Aristotle's Poetics* (Calcutta: N.M. Publishers, 1971), 10–20.
52. See 1032a in Aristotle, *The Metaphysics* (New York: Dover Publications, 2008).
53. See Forest G. Robinson, *The Shape of Things Known: Sidney's Apology in its Philosophical Tradition* (Cambridge, Mass.: Harvard University Press, 1972).
54. Paula H. Payne, 'Tracing Aristotle's "Rhetoric" in Sir Philip Sidney's Poetry and Prose', *Rhetoric Society Quarterly*, 20, no. 3 (Summer 1990), 247.
55. J. P. Thorne, 'A Ramistical Commentary on Sidney's "An Apologie for Poetrie"' *Modern Philology*, 54, no. 3 (Feb. 1957), 162.
56. Ibid., 163.
57. Mack, *Sidney's Poetics*, 182.

3 'To you I submit my selfe, and worke. Farewell'
The Poet and the Reader

'- *neque, me ut miretur turba./ laboro: / Contentus paucis lectoribus*' [I do not work so that I will be admired by the crowd, but am content with a few readers]
—Horace[1]

The Master said, Look closely into his arms observe the means by which he pursues them, discover what brings him content—and can the man's real worth remain hidden from you, can it remain hidden from you?
—Confucius[2]

Can the notion of the poet be configured through the role that the reader plays in the understanding of poetic intention? Can the anxiety and suspicion that the reader breeds in the mind of the poet contribute to the formation of the idea of the poet? Are we to assume that the construction of the poetic self depends on the trueness of the reader—the loyalties to the poetic intention—and also the creativity and license that the reader is expected to enjoy in the appreciation of the poetic content? It, thus, makes for an interesting reading to see how the notion of an*tagonism* can be appropriated in comparative aesthetics to generate a concept of the poet under Jonsonian protocols and propositions of an understanding of poetic meaning.

Antagonism is not about a class of opposites, but a kind of refusal to accept the existence of opposites. It is negotiation and debate over contraries in a space which does not isolate one from the other; rather, it makes room for progress by acknowledging opposition as friendship.[3] Ant*agonism*, in our trans-habitual understanding of literature, speaks of 'world-making' which discounts a 'false universalism' usually set up through the absolute standards of thought and reductive norms of acceptability. By presuming on our abilities to appreciate simultaneously the relational and the disrelational, ant*agonism* in transcultural poetics of meaning-generation places us in continuous prospects of diverse figurative circulations. It becomes a way of overcoming incommensurability in cultural negotiations, most often, the product of inveterate essentialism and monadic nativism. Ant*agonism* is about finding the 'unpeace' amidst contesting territories of power, domination, obscurity, obfuscation and elision. This unpeace renders 'strangeness' to our transgeneric experiences of literature so that we cannot ignore certain things that stay undocumented and quaintly fragmentary, thereby avoiding serious historicist embeddings and 'historical efficacy'. Cultural specificity, then, is not alienation; rather, it is a part of a process where circulation and comparison consort ant*agonistic*ally without ignoring certain 'irreducible' differences. It, thus, intensifies and complicates the 'exchange value'. So, moving beyond bland cosmopolitanisation, this studious curiosity—critical inclusiveness—challenges limitations of thought to admit a chance of connection. In this inclusive engagement time collapses, historical distances are fused and liberties are taken with historical contexts—transcontextualisation emerges. Borders become 'mending walls' and, the acts of returning in certain modes and thoughts to the past and traditions allow us to project texts into the future. Didier Coste points out that

> we should move away from the priority of any single origin and consider the one-and-whole both as origin and goal, and thus itself bi-centered. Comparative thinking, as it moves away from that one-and-wholeness in order to make sense, creates its own bipolarities, around which it is up to our anthropological self-consciousness to move—elliptically also in the sense of an omission, an abbreviation, an encryption and a forgetting.[4]

These 'moves', as Coste suggests, import a 'radical openness', a liminality and simultaneously a new-found familiarity among correspondences of ideas, paradigms and literary meaning-generation which are widely separated in time, context and culture. Not embedded in resolutions of paradigm conflicts, these transcultural negotiations in literary studies contribute to the extension of the world comprehension. There is exchange and play, borrowing and bartering, trade and profit, deficit and loss.

In what follows, I try to place Ben Jonson's relationship with his readers (the complex poet-reader interface) and the consequent modes of reception generated by his works against the concurrent ideas emerging from certain traditions of Chinese, Sanskrit and Arabic literary criticism. Premised within the deep investments that trans-habit makes through complexity theory our arguments can unfold at two levels: one, it shows the ant*agonism* with which Ben Jonson is affected in his negotiations with his readers, both in his performance as a poet-man and a poet-artist; and, second, Jonson's idea of the reader is then transculturised agonistically with the ancient and medieval Chinese notion of the reader and the text, the ideal reader in the Abbāsid period in Arabic literary history and the philosophy of *sahridaya* drawn from Sanskrit aesthetic theories. This, I argue, opens up a fresh pathway to see how we can reach at a concept of the poet in Jonson through the ant*agonism* of the trans-habit.

I

A seeming autodictat, apparent plainspeaker, putatively magisterial and pre-emptory, Ben Jonson was riven by unrest and disquiet: a life where combativeness mapped every corner and every move was prefaced by a niggling dread of oppugnancy. His character was *epigrammatically* judgemental yet he also offered himself to be judged, indulging in the sacrosanct closedness of a reading aesthetic and allowing the needle-pricks of being imperiously doctrinaire. He revelled in the teasing crossroad of masque and play; he was a poet-artist who, caught in the tumult of 'performance' and 'print', grappled with the domains of an aesthetic life which demanded precision and stability. Jonson was a poet-man who acknowledged the 'larger life', not without its flux, incompletion and vastness, existing beyond his aesthetic territorialisation in honest self-assurance. As an 'artistic schizophrenic'[5], he claims order, admits disorder around it, commits to organise without the continual antagonism of being ideologically subverted, solemnly endorses 'honesty' and yet does not lose sight of the excitement that life offers in its diversity, absurdity and complexity.

Jonson was deeply suspicious of his texts being appropriated by readers in ways that might contradict authorial intention. Uncomfortable with anything in transition and turmoil, the protean theatre—which is why he ensured his works appeared in print to avoid theatrical contamination (1616 folio *Works*)—Jonson opted for an antitheatricalism; his 'bibliographic ego'[6] was directed at authorisation and valorisation of the literary artefact. The threat from 'theatrical plunder and counterfeiting' drove him to supervise the printing of his plays, practically making the author alone accountable for the play's performance. Antagonising the Poet-Ape, Jonson cultivated, with self-conscious ardour, the poet-artisan who inflicts the labour of art on his reader or spectator to achieve a 'hard-edged effect'.[7] Specificity, craft and artistic completeness can ensure the readers' staying on rails even if they fail to make a very clear sense of the poet's ideas and intent. Timothy Murray observes that

> an ordered text, thought true to its author's thoughts and unchanging in its transmission, contributes much more to a tuneful community of meaning than the shrieks and groans of the best players. Jonson's priorities centred on the control of his texts. To clean up his "foul sheets", he transferred them from the playhouse to the printshop. He was, so far as we know, the first public dramatist in England to oversee actively the printing of his plays.[8]

Jonson's ant*agonism* with his readers reflects the tension between the playhouse passion and disciplined evaluation, instantaneous emotional gratification and evaluative clarity. In "To the Reader" he asks: 'Pray thee, take care, that tak'st my booke in hand,/ To reade it well: that is, to understand'.[9] For him, art and artisanship went closely together when he insisted on his own right to the text. The 'text's possession of Jonson is at base enabled,' as Richard Newton argues, '*by* their possession by Jonson'.[10] Ant*agonism* here lies in making poetic intention grow in apposition with the reader's reception: the success and worth of a poem depending on the 'correctness' of the reader's reading of the writer. He writes,

> For, as one coming with a laterall viewe,
> Unto a cunning piece wrought perspective,
> Wants facultie to make a censure true:
> So with this Authors, Readers will it thrive:
> Which being eyes directly, I divine,
> His proofe their praise, will meete, as in this line
>
> (*Ungathered Verse*, II, ll. 5–8)

In "To the Earl of Pembroke", Jonson underscores the need to persevere with the trueness of the text and its fidelity to the author. His presentation of the text to his patron, Pembroke, exposes it to censure but nevertheless he hopes it will be judged as a 'legitimate' poem whose 'innocency would appear before a magistrate' (431). He distanced himself from the print marketplace requesting that booksellers avoid advertising his writings. Also, by producing expensive volumes, he tried to ensure that his writings remained out of the common people's reach and that only 'learned' men had access to them ('Thou, that mak'st gaine thy end, and wisely well,/ Call'st a booke good, or bad, as it doth sell,/ use mine so, too: I give thee leave'. "To my Book Seller", *Epigrams*, 3). Marotti notes that 'Sidney did not have to live under the burden of being a (self-promoted) contemporary classic. Jonson, however, did and he responded by returning to the socioliterary environment of manuscript transmission'.[11] He framed himself as an 'instant classic'.

Jonson writes in *The Magnetic Lady*:

> For I must tell you, (not out of mine owne *Dictamen*, but the *Authors*,) a good *Play*, is like a skeene of silke, which, if you take by the right end, you may wind off, at pleasure, on the bottome, or card of your discourse, in a tale, or so; how you will: But if you light on the wrong end, you will pull all into a knot, or elf-lock; which nothing but the sheers, or a candle will undoe, or separate. (135–41)

Evading stigmatisation in being *mysomousoi*, readers are expected to hold the text at the right end to ward off 'invading interpreters', the censures of the Court Witlings and Groom Idiots who 'professe to have a key for deciphering everything … cunningly, and often, utter their owne virulent malice, under other mens simplest meanings' (62–67). As Cordatus responding to Mitis in *Every Man out of his Humour* exclaims, 'O, what else? it's the speciall intent of the author, you should doe so: for thereby others (that are present) may as well be satisfied, who happily would object the same you doe' (II. iii. 305–8). George Rowe shows how the verb 'wrest' encountered in *Sejanus* (I. 143–7; III. 223–9) became the 'code word' for such destructiveness. This pivoted on the ant*agonism* that interpretation evoked in the mutual tension between the poet and the reader to possess and proprietorise the text. Influenced by William Camden, Kenelm Digby, John Selden and Sir Robert Bruce Cotton, Jonson ventures into the paradigms of historical writing, championing the historicist modes of thought, and hence, the method, as opposed to allegorical discourse such as imbibing verisimilitude, decorum, literary convention and imitation.[12] Discommoded by the prospect of destructive malice—'Foul wrestling, and impossible construction' (*Sejanus*, 3.227–29)—and, hence, textual termination, he insisted that addresses to the reader, frontispieces, prologues, epilogues and dedicatory epistles hold strictly to his position which was clearly an antagonism against readerly freedom and licence in interpretation, disallowing, as they say, *de gustibus non disputandum*. Within an ethics of persuasion, the poet prevails upon the reader, invading and breaking upon them, and 'making their minds the thing he writes'[13].

Jonson advocates that the poet's art is no mere license, gleefully misused and abused. Poets cannot borrow indiscriminately what is good or raw or undigested; like the bee he gathers honey from the flower; he chooses the best and the fairest. The poet chooses a theme, simple and uniform, and suited to his power.[14] *Grai*, the ideal poets, achieved a unity of content and form, talent and art. So here *prodesse* (poetic instruction) and *delectare* (poetic fiction) are joined in an ideal unity. Close to Quintilian and Horace, Jonson maintains that even a river flows with its maximum force when its natural and uneven bed is cleared of all impediments. The poet for Jonson is provided with a recipe: read the best authors, observe the best speakers and exercise one's own style with a careful study of the masters. A poet, in his opinion, must have a taste for 'choiceness' of phrase, round and clean composition of sentence, weight of matter, worth of subject, soundness of argument, life of invention and depth of judgement. So Jonson believes that one should not think that

> hee can leape forth suddainely a Poet, by dream hee hath in Parnassus, or having washt his lipps (as they say) in Helicon. There goes more to his making, then so. For to Nature, Exercise, Imitation and Studie, Art must bee added, to make all these perfect And, through these challenge to themselves much, in the making up of our Maker, it is Art only can lead him to perfection, and leave him there in possession as planted by her hand. ... (4–5)

Good writing is preferred over ready writing and Jonson wants his readers to acknowledge the difference. Within the aesthetics of literary appreciation Jonson sees care, vigilance and industry as requirements that are as compelling in the poet as they are in the readers. He warns the artist to judge others rightly and understand what one ought to imitate specially in himself. The reader, thus, must demonstrate an understanding of the ethics of poetic commitment. So his warning to Alphonso Ferrabosco is relevant:

> When we doe give, ALPHONSO, to the light,
> A worke of ours, we part with our owne right;

> For, then, all mouthes will judge, and their owne way:
> The learn'd have no more privilege, then the lay.[15]

This obviates 'miscommunication' but also decimates possibilities of agonism. It separates the 'learned' from the 'lay' readers and also identifies Jonson as a poet distinguished from those who write 'for claps' and to whom 'Pui'nees, porters, players, praise delight'.[16]

In his mind, Jonson evinces an honesty, class, and authenticity in poetic vocation set apart from the petulant and covetous witlings whose writings were destined to cheap fame and lust. As Miles notes, 'poetry set the standard which he hoped all his work would attain, and by which he hoped to be judged. He always described himself as a poet if the not the poet, and his dramas not as plays, but poems'.[17]

> When, in my booke, men read but CECILL's name,
>   And what I write thereof find farre and free
> From servile flatterie (common *Poets* shame)
>   As thou stand'st cleere of the necessitie.

The ideal reader 'legitimises' a poem by ascertaining its truth as covenant with the poet's faculty of judgement and taste and thereby judges the creator on the basis of mutually endorsed and sanctioned truth. Jonson's classicist rigour was inscribed in the ant*agonism* against the 'noise of opinion' (*Catiline*, 5: 431) and also 'clever speaking' (in the words of Confucius)[18]—the collaboration implicit in the poet-reader dialectic based on anticipation and identification. At times, the poet becomes the ultimate reader. No less, Jonson establishes a self-antagonism where becoming famous is only being famous among a select community, where art is antagonised into the possession of a few and literary judgement is agonisingly limited to certain means of 'rapport' which speak less about enfranchisement and more about alienation. Jonson, thus, falls into a time-freeze, a reading of literature that discounts the 'literary' for a certain inflexible interpretive appropriateness. Did Jonson, then, respond to his writings as mere texts and not literature?

II

Jonson's prescriptions within the text-reader dynamics seriously agonise the profound and difficult dialectic between literature and language, word and meaning, intent and inference. Caught in the productive ant*agonism* of the trans-habit—in a, rather, uncanny transcultural negotiation—we can choose to inhabit a Sinocentric hermeneutic space where the entitlements and licence that the reader enjoys in his/her relationship with the text and the poet can be considered meaningfully. Within the categories of *guanshi* (observing poetry) in ancient Chinese literary criticism, intention was clearly inscribed in the rationale of both *fushi* and *yinshi* practises. More than *fushi*, where intention was, most often, instrumentalised and malappropriated self-servingly, the *yinshi* or citation of *Shijing* (Book of Poetry) that flourished in Warring States period (475–221 B.C.E.) prevented harmful decontextualised reading and instead made poetic interpretation an earnest, direct exposition of intent and understanding. However, riding Mencius's insistence on meeting the intent of the author (*zhi*), the *dushi* mode of reading emerged with new modes of conceptualising poetry and poetic intent. The *yi* (poetic conceptualisation, the *kavyasarira* in Sanskrit poetics) and the *zhi* are locked in 'never too simple' formulations which Mencius has stressed as *wenyi*, the meaning of the poem in full, involving authorial intent, poetic integrity and readerly *recreative* interpretations—'Those who speak of the Odes should not let their literary qualities [*wen*] harm the words [*ci*], nor take the words in such a way as to harm the aim [of the poet]'[19]. In a close parallel with the Jonsonian anxiety over intentionalism and textuality, Mencius argues that the reader's mind (the *zhiyin*) interacts with the meaning of the text in the delineation of the authorial and the poetic intent—'the interpreter of a poem should not let the words obscure the text, or the text obscure the intention. To trace back to the original intention with sympathetic understanding: that is the way to do it'.[20] Despite a hermeneutic incontestability that Jonson endorsed in his exasperation over textual predations, he, like Cheng Yi, would unequivocally consider the danger of becoming *ni* (to be enmired)—the debilitation that uncritical and unquestioned clinging to the 'given' and the 'processed' can bring. The complexities surrounding the 'literal meaning' and 'literary significance' in the wake of the breakdown of exegetical authority and the foundationalist critique of the classics since the eleventh century in Chinese literary criticism is peculiarly a Jonsonian problem too. Cheng Yi, in a *Jinsilu* passage, writes:

> In reading books one must not cling to [*ni*] a [single] significance [*yii*] [simply] because [the characters] are the same or similar. Otherwise every word will be a hindrance. One must observe the intention of the context and the direction [of the piece].

Steven van Zoeren has argued that 'becoming enmired in significance meant insisting upon or clinging to a view of language where words were univocal in their meaning and trying to formulate understandings that would embrace all their occurrences. Such readers remained "stuck" at the level of what we might call dictionary meanings, unable to see the animating intentions of the contexts in which individual words get their meanings'.[21] Jonson would surely approve of readers who would make sense of a sedative collapse into *ni* and actively espouse *niwenyii* which is about going beyond literality to excavate contextual intentionalism emerging through language and poetic intent.

Jonson, however, shared a vexed relationship with language and identity which underlined a smoldering struggle to establish and, subsequently preserve, a unified authorial subjecthood and resolve the tension between intent and linguistic eventuality. In the *Epigrammes* he betrays his failure to univocalise language and set up the autonomy of identity and subjectivity by complaining that he cannot fully express what he knows and wants. An uncertainty in language obtrudes on the self-consciousness of the poet's meaning-making, creating a deference to and defiance of the inter-dwelling of the speaker, the subject, the referents and the poetic voice—'scarse one knows, / To which, yet, of the sides himself he owes' (102.7–8). Owning the meaning that language expresses and the continued anxiety over reclaiming what careless readers would make out of poetic expressions obliquely point to the paradox of language and the consequent inevitable trials which no poet can avoid, even Jonson, despite the trenchancy to keep literature within the classical canon and epitomise John Donne and the Countess of Bedford as ideal readers. This resonates, in certain ways, with what we find in *LaoZi*: 'Straight words seem contradictory' (chapter 78). How 'straight' could Jonson train his language to get? Isn't his simmering anxiety to see an interpretive fidelity from his readers a challenge to the success of his vaunted straightness of expression? Zhuang Zi writes resonantly:

> What the world values as speech are books. Books are nothing more than words; words have something that it valued. What is valued in words is meaning; meaning is derived from something. That from which meaning is derived cannot be transmitted in language. Yet the world, because it values language, transmits books.[22]

In contrast, books for Jonson remained as logoi of stability executed in print to antagonise the 'betrayal' and distress that language was capable of producing. Jonson would consciously turn himself against what Zhuang Zi implicates through the parable about the wheelwright and Lao Zi in the paradox which states that 'great eloquence seems inarticulate'. He could not have relied on the 'silence' and non-communication which language produces. Historically, threatened by plagiarists, bawds and usurers and looming on the margins of transgression and misrepresentations, Jonson had to eschew such literary devices which, I would contend, he could not have left unappreciated. Repeated revisions to 'straighten' language—Jonson resorts to 'repetition' and redundancy achieved through words, phrases, rhymes and emphasis on the same subjects and persons—so as to find the centre of meaning reveal an abiding though, largely unacknowledged, consternation over the outbounding ability of the language and the disturbing prospect of the poem eventually overpowering the poet. However, the silence intoned through Zhuang Zi's parable about forgetting the snare after the rabbit is caught and the articulate silence that Sikong Tu in his *Twenty-four Moods of Poetry* mentions implicate the reader's intuitive contemplation and cognition—the zone of *yan wai zhi yi*, the meaning beyond words (the *yizhi*, meeting with the spirit). Jonson rigorously disapproves the invocation of positive silence, *hanxu*, 'the implicit expression', as ways of constructing meaning. Rather, in a serious antagonism to poetic art and ontological slippages of poetic language, he creates a world that exists 'immovable' on the intricate surface of the text, ready for our examination. So Chan precepts to literary writing where 'spirits' are hailed beyond words, 'the tone beyond the rhythm' (*yun wai zhi zhi*), 'the image beyond images' (*xiang wai zhi xiang*), and 'the scene beyond scenes' (*jing wai zhi jing*) would end up with Jonson as 'perverted' means to construe poetic meaning. Jonson is committed to providing a ladder to his readers to reach the meaning and remember the raft after it has reached the shore.

Descanting on 'reading', Jiang Kui (ca. 1155–1221), in his treatise *Baishi Daoren shishuo* (The white-stone Daoist discourse on poetry), recommends how reading the discourse of poetry can make one a poet; yet, he is not oblivious to the 'secrets' that a discourse can never unearth and teach. Jonson's recommendations on reading preclude the 'secret' that his poems could have revealed, something that left his readers imprisoned in a sovereignty of meaning. He could not have joined ranks with Xianqiu Meng's synchronic approach to reading poetry where certain lines culled out of the poem are recontextualised through the radiant proliferation of the meaning-volume. Firmly opposed to such extratextual meaning generation, Jonson preferred clinging on to the 'raft' and exhausting the possibilities of 'experiencing' a boat. This exposes the limitations of the 'tribe of Ben'. Thus, Jonson, in his poems, as Stanley Fish rightly observes, establishes 'an alternate world of patronage and declares it (by an act of poetic fiat) more real than the world in which he is apparently embedded'.[23] This is one of Jonson's negations where he antagonises the 'hybridization of his medium and his audience'[24] and in making demands on the reader to identify with him we encounter both integration and separation. This is a confused conflict where suspicion to sustain identification executed through well intentioned yet somewhat belaboured reiteration in sequences, themes and figures, expires in an isolation and alienation which he could not evade.

Jonson's interpretation of authorial intention, however, is a troubled one for although he was committed to 'directing' the reader he also knew that 'The Writ, once out, never returned yet' (I. 580). In the Prologue to *The Sad Shepherd* we find these loaded lines:

> He that hath feasted you these forty yeares,
> And fitted Fables, for your finer eares,
> Although at first, he scarce could hit the bore;
> Yet you, with patience harkning more and more,
> At length have growne up to him, and made knowne,
> The Working of his Pen is not your owne. (ll. 1–6)

The collaborative note struck here—the mutuality sounded in the working and the appreciation of the 'pen'—renders Jonson's relationship with the readers and spectators an inconclusive and troubled one. These readers resent the insolence of the satirist's self-magnifying authority and his low estimation of their own faculties of judgement. Unlike the contributors to *Jonsonus Virbius*, Chapman, Inigo Jones and others preferred to turn on their accuser, taxing him with his own ethical and artistic failings.[25] Jonson realised, as Rowe shows us, that the 'total dominance of author over reader smacks of fraud, deception, and, more ominously, tyranny'. Consequently, his seething anxiety wanted to secure 'fit readers' who, as Rowe notes, 'are detached, patient, receptive yet critical, willing to unravel the author's threadlike argument from the correct end but unwilling to cede complete authority to that author or anyone else'.[26] Standing apart from the mutability of the world stage, these people are deemed equipped not merely to understand but judge the author's work without turning into his mouthpiece. Fit readers, not someone like the imperious Damplay who declares the reader's dominance over the writer, put a curb on authorly eccentricities and provide intelligent commentaries on the work in question; they do not usurp and yet enjoy a liberty to respond individually and critically, antagonising their perpetual posture of defense.

No doubt, Jonson, through a flurry of injunctions, astutely undermined the self-confidence of the reader who lost his security amidst strong calls to avoid perpetrating 'ill deeds': a serious collapse of the self-judgement and the self-regarding criticality that are required to judge a work of art. However, it is interesting to take note of Jennifer Brady's observations here:

> The poet dispenses decrees, and sentences our vicious follies as though he had an all-seeing eye, yet when we recall that we are likewise "destin'd unto judgement, after all", the rationale behind his authoritarian tactics becomes more clear. Jonson intends to place us between the fools and the heroes. He wants us to wonder which portrait is our own.[27]

In the Prologue to *The New Inn* we find 'welcome all' (l. i), but not without the implicit suggestion that only the able are 'in' and the rest are 'out'. He indeed makes solemn and arduous claims on his readers—becoming 'fit readers' is about making the difficult transition from fools to heroes—to consort with the 'heroes' and prepare themselves for such wise acts of judicious interpretation. This is close to Liu Xie's observations in "Zhiyin" where Xie dissuades critics from allowing temperamental vagaries to have a sway over literary judgement encouraging, in the process, careful insight into poetic growth, structures of sentences, form, arrangement of words and the changes and diversions of meaning.[28] The attribution of the 'wise eye' to Jonson's reader is analogous to Liu Xie's critic, the ideal reader, endowed with clear and insightful eyes and a sharp mind which can take commendable measure of all diverse manifestations—'Good men, and virtuous spirits, that lothe their vices, / Will cherish my free labours, loue my lines'

(Induction, II. 134–5). Was Jonson as 'Father Ben' then making unaccomplished readers aware of their failings and making the rest see how siding with the guilty could contaminate their powers of judgement and criticism? His role as the literary taskmaster, the intimidating poetic voice, was perhaps at once the means to secure the 'solemnity' of his art and to warn erring and lazy readers to train and prepare adequately for enabling poetic judgement. This has a moderate correspondence with how Mencius proposes to attenuate the divide between the author and the reader by suggesting how the readers need to 'prepare' verbally, conceptually and scholastically to understand the author, the text, and the intent. Making 'friends with the ancients' is not an easy task; it requires reconstruction, evaluation and sensibility for accomplishments. Later under the threat of Mao's prefaces, Zheng Xuan (127–200), undergirded by the Mencian principles of interpretation, provided painstaking commentaries on individual poems so as to safeguard the sacrosanct intents of the ancient. It clearly echoes Jonson's ire and insecurity over misinterpretation. Indeed in a combination of Confucian moralism and Mencian intentionalism, we notice how the poetic intent and craft directed readers to know contextually the man behind the art: interpretive activity leading both to the unveiling of the poetic intent and the poet himself in person and in life.

III

This is the juncture at which, in a moment of comparatist ant*agonism*, Jonson's 'fit' reader and Liu Xie's trained reader can aesthetically come together with what we know as *sahridaya* in Sanskrit poetics and literary understanding. Can *sahridaya* take issue with Jonson's anxiety over the performance of the misreader to optimise a 'space' that doesn't encourage extremism on the side of either the reader or the artist? Does *sahridaya* in its conceptual peculiarity and ramification configure a qualitatively better rejoinder to this crisis of authorial anxiety and readerly misappropriation? Could Jonson have philosophically and poetically benefited had he been aware of the notional uniqueness of this aesthetic episteme?

Participatory communion (*sakhya*) goes back to the *Rig Veda* where bonds of friendship are built around degrees of participation and eagerness of the participants—'*atra sakhayah sakhyani janate/ bhadraisam laksmir nihitadhivaci*' (*Rig Veda*, x, 71). *Sakhya,* in its Sanskritic roots, is attachment, a deep interest in the other which results in intense identification with an entity outside the self. It involves a 'sacrifice' where the other and the self give up on a few things in order to seek integration. The ritual of the space generated has a strong participatory aesthetic to it where the consciousness of the experience enjoyed by the two is tuned into the same register, a synergic note where the integrative activity works on anticipation, preparation and permanence. The *sahridaya* is integral to the work of the poet as much as the poet cannot do without the *sahridaya*. Vidya Misra writes:

> Going into the genesis of the word *Sahridaya* we find it is a compound of *sa* and *hrdaya*; *sa* (*saha*), indicating the sense of same *saha*, *samana*—with, together, in a harmonization, co-existent and *hrdaya* indicating an internal organ which is distinct from *manas*, *citta* and *akuti* (thinking). The word *hrdaya* is derived from the root *hr* it means to take away, to carry away. It is not the physical heart though that physical heart may reflect through its vibration some of the function of *hrdaya*, it is a functionary of supramental activity where mental processes such as intellection, recollection, and contemplation are yoked together in a manner that *hrdaya* becomes nothing but a complete merger or a total communion of the sensate, supersensate and the highest level of consciousness.[29]

Misra sees *samana* as an active present participle from the root *as* = to be, which points to being oneself and being in harmony with the other. So *sahridaya* is both being and becoming where the integration is occasioned through *bhava* (emotions) collectively. It turns into a phenomenon where understanding, desires, likes and opposition are brought into a contemplative play of communication and communion. Misra observes, 'A *sahrdaya* thus requires a keen recollection and an intense contemplation as a preparation for the melting process, which takes place when there is an aesthetic engagement'.[30] So, does Jonson's 'fit' reader become the *sahridaya* within the dynamics of a cross-conceptual ant*agonism*? Clearly, his reader is *samana* which is inscribed in *bhava* and where distinctions as to the understanding of sensual enjoyment and aesthetic pleasure are problematised. Jonson's reader is expected to receive, synthesise and synergise in an intense moment of 'returning back' to the text circumscribed through transcendence of subject and an identification with the object. There is a call to create the state of *hridayasamvada*, the remarkable empathy leading to the mood of *tanmayibhava* (total absorption). The *sahridaya* endowed with sound aesthetic instinct, imagination and an astuteness to investigate the hieroglyphics of poetry, connects the poet with humanity at large. Also, empowered with an alive intellect, the cogniser grasps both the literal and symbolic meaning of the poetic content, declaring the essence of poetry as conjointly represented by the *kavi* (poet) and the *sahridaya*. Abninavagupta argues elaborately on the 'sympathy' that poetic appreciation requires. This sympathy does away with spatiotemporal and personal distinctions, and we find the individuality giving way to a profound communicative mutuality— the *hridaya-spanda* (sympathetic vibrations) endotelically moving towards the *rasena* (aesthetic relish). 'Sensitive readers' as *sahridayamnam* are 'persons who are capable of identifying with the subject matter, as the mirror of their hearts has been polished by the constant study and practice of poetry, and who respond to it sympathetically in their own hearts'. As has been said, 'the realisation (*bhava*) of that object (e.g., *vibhava*) which finds sympathy in the heart is the origin of *rasa*. The body is pervaded by it as dry wood by fire"'.³¹ Also, Anandavardhana urges readers and spectators to reproduce in themselves their own 'feeling equipment' (*vibhavas*) which should be similar to the one under the spell of which the poet presented his poem. Indeed it is only in the *sahridaya* that *rasa* can emerge.

Jonson, truculently and in an expressly self-defeatist way, was not creating reader-slaves. His reading of Shakespeare is antinomical in the endorsements that he provides for soaring inspiration, out-of-the-rule ways of creativity, and the value of artful diligence and critical patience. Strategically supportive of both craft and genius, inspiration and method, invention and artifice, Jonson, caught in the delicate contradictions of belief and practise, chose to be inconsistent, at times, by choosing one paradigm over the other when it suited him. He was aware of art and nature having separate rules and how that could meaningfully impact on our understanding of literature. Jonson would surely agree to the combination of *kavyanirmana* (creation of poetry) and *kavya-asvadana* (appreciation) leading to a *rasa* experience for all relishers—*samasta-bhavaka-svasamvedya*. However, contrasted with Jonson's reader who abnegates the claim to equal voice with the poet, *sahridaya* is seen as possessed with a mind that appreciates and clarifies the poet's being and thought—working on both the expressed and the suggested (*dhvani*) content. The longing in the *sahridaya* for the poet is deeper and fairly removed from dread and authorial imperialism—the '*paryatsikibhavana*' (an immersion into an unexplained yearning, in spite of the process of intellection) where the reader undergoes a transference in a separate aesthetic of time and space. The *sahridaya* is not a mere 'enjoyer' but is someone who aestheticises the intent and emotion in a tension, throwing into a broader relief the world of senses and the world at large, the world of aesthetic (here poetic) construct and the world of common knowledge and experiences. It is an experience not in pleasure or pain or idealization; neither in defeat and defense nor aggression and toadyism. Rather, argued as *adhikarin* (aspirant, in the words of Vamana), Abhinavagupta perceives a productive duality in the *kavi* and the *sahridaya* towards working out of the essential aspects of the goddesses of speech and filling the world with their relish. Even Rajashekhara in *Kavyamanjari* accentuates the diadic effectiveness of the faculties—the creative and the appreciative—inscribed in the poetic art, which can only lead to aesthetic relish. Indeed Vamana, to echo Jonson, emphasises the need for the reader to appreciate 'craft', the art that goes into composition, qualifying them as the *rasika*, a *samajika*.

This evokes an identification, the *sambandha*, which is endotelic listening (*bhavanavyapara*) and also a truth of which Jonson's aesthetic domains of appropriate reading would have benefitted but to which, unfortunately, he seemed fairly inimical. The gamut and the arc of the *sahridaya* in relation to the aesthetic meaning-generation are more expansive than Jonson's extraordinary reader. *Sahridaya* has greater powers of coherence and compass, a fact to which Jonson probably would not have comfortably subscribed. So 'this *sahridaya* is neither the *nagar* a civil city dweller as against the barbarian nor the *vicaksana* (erudite), this *sahridaya* is a pundit which fact helps him in the requisite distancing and at the same time he is a *Vidagdha* (wit), the Sanskrit word means literally 'specially burnt', thus this witticism as against the western usage is acquired by passing through a fire'.[32] Jonson probably wanted to see his reader more as a *vidagdha* than a mere 'erudite' person: a reader who would combine powers of judgement with keen sensibilities of evaluation and aesthetic attunement. Difficult to conjure through a definite pattern of education, *sahridaya*, like a rock that subsides into dust and is swept down in a river, is not a quiescent unit in the production of meaning but a part of a continuity.

But does not *sahridaya* come with a literary habit cultivated and sustained through repetition and diligence? Does not the fact about the *sahridaya* growing a resonant sensibility with authorial intent and the product achieved through continued aesthetic relish (*charvana*) come agonistically close to the education of the readers about which Jonson was so articulate? Education is the compelling prelude to *sambandha*. The conceptual lubrication that *sambandha* provides intones a 'delectable' listening which is qualified as *asvada* or *rasana* or *bhoga*. However, Jonson's idea of the *sambandha*, the 'listening', has its own differences with the rasamatrix of the *sahridaya*. Two points of antagonism are clearly evident here. *Sahridaya* as *vidagdha* contributes to the enrichment of the aesthetic space and is not seen merely as a force that effectuates the authorial sanctity and privilege. Close to *Einfuhlung*, *sahridaya* constructs the poem in his own mind alongside apprehension (*pratiti*). And the degree to which Jonson was conscious of the education of the reader meant that his appreciator could only have a denotational fixity to his ability and interference. Jonson looks into training of his readers—a deliberate process of enculturation, a 'cultured audience'.[33] Jonson's learned reader can attune to and, consequently, explicate the truth and merit of the text, whereas *sahridaya* being *vidagdha* can make his own contribution in a unique appointment with the poet achieved in a 'complementary trance'[34] through emotional education. This is not mere scholasticism but an artistic—the reader becomes the poet—commitment to the *kavya sarira* (poetic tissue) and the *aucitya* (poetic propriety). Even the poet is a *sahridaya* in that he holds deep appreciation and empathy for the audience.[35]

Liu Xie in *Wenxin diaolong* sees an emotional connect (*wenqing*, an oriented emotion) between the author and the interpreter—an underlying *sambandha* in aesthetic pleasure and the working of the literary minds (*wenxin*)—which the author manifests in his writing and the reader demonstrates in his creative and deep understanding obtained not by dictating to the author but by becoming his 'fellow worker and accomplice'[36]. There is, thus, an *ananda*, both in the *sahridaya* and in Xie's reader who becomes the *junzi* (cultured) much like the *vidagdha*. This is the true basis of the communication between the poet and the reader, enhancing and engendering poetic merit and meaning—the *hridaya-samvad* (heart-dialogue), the *wanwei* (play

'*To you I submit my selfe, and worke. Farewell*' 57

with and savour). Perhaps, the injunction to be "easy" (*yi*), derived from the teachings of the Chengs and Zhang Zai, applies to both *sahridaya* and Jonson's ideal reader: 'Whenever one [seeks to] understand a text, let him only make his heart easy [*yi qi xin*]; then he will naturally see the principle [there in the text]'.[37] Zhang Zai drives the point home more directly:

> In seeking to understand the Odes, the important thing is a straightforward easiness. One must not be too overcautious. One should seek to match the poet's *emotional* nature—his gentility, his equipoise, and his maturity. Now if one is too overcautious, his heart will be constricted before [he begins] and he will be unable to see the poet's *emotions*.[38]

Indeed both *zhiyin* and *sahridaya* exceed the limitations of Jonson's reader through their breadth, immanence, and continuity in growth and volume—acknowledging the limitations of *vaikhari-vak* (the heard word as opposed to the unheard) and preparing a mind responsive to *pasyanti* (the seen word) and the *madhyama* (the unarticulated word) to unconceal the strengths and sources of *vaikhari* (communicated and manifested meaning).

Here the inevitable momentum of trans-habit leads us to look into the resonant collaboration between the Abbāsid poets and their audience in Arabic literary history. The *majlis* (literary circles) provided the space for a refined interaction where the poets got engaged with an educated audience, 'chancellery scribes (*kuttāb* s. *kātib*), linguists, and other experts for whom poetry was performed'. They combined deep appreciation with criticism, not in hostility but in fine sensibility and mutual ardour. Huda Fakhreddine claims that

> this well-versed audience was fully aware of the poetic tradition and able to recognize its influences and echoes. A poet could rely on the audience's knowledge of images and motifs, and expected them to appreciate his manipulation of these motifs. Both poet and audience were conscious of the pre-Islamic *qasīdah* as a model with which poets of the Abbāsid age were in constant negotiation. In this sense, the point of reference, both for the poet and his audience, was pre-existing poetry. What the audience listened for in fact was the way this pre-existing poetry was echoed or challenged or even rejected by the new poets.[39]

This clearly spoke of an 'education' of the readers considered as both *vidagdha* and erudite. Like Jonson's 'fit' reader, the *sahridaya* and Liu Xie's ideal reader, the *zhiyin*, the well versed audience was competent and engaging, gifted with a 'sharp ear' and poetic acumen to make prudent and profound poetic judgements; they were the deeply sensitive 'magistrates'. Fakhreddine points out that 'when al-Basrī inquired about one of the poet's problematic verses, al-Mutanabbī responded: "Had he [meaning Ibn Jinnī] been present, he would have been able to explain it. Do you think this poetry is intended for these patrons? Very little suffices them. I compose it for you and your likes".[40] This is indicative of the poetic consciousness which had grown depending on and in expectation of readerly appreciation—the *charvana* or *asvada*. The poets in general believed in finding a more adroit and knowledgeable appreciation in the readers—undoubtedly in the finer insights and relish of the *rasikas* and *adhikarin*—than their patrons. Although *jā'izah* (reward) was an important consequence of artistic or poetic work, the poet, most often, looked up to connoisseurs (among whom were poet-patrons) whose deep and subtle understanding of the work left him meritoriously accredited. Poetry could be truthful or untruthful (cf. al-Marzuql) in the context of the early Abbāsid poets who in their New Style employed imagination and intense metaphoricity over factual and direct poetry. But the ideal reader would appreciate the 'artful deception' that the poet brought, deftly sieving out the poetic intent from figurative rendition of thought and, also, surrendering to the aesthetic relish (*bhoga*) that such poetry generated. This also was a challenge for we find Abd al-Qahir al-Jurjani and Hazim al Qartajanni making readers work hard to ferret out the authorial intent, making, in the process, due exactions on the reader's ability and acumen. However, there was a self-conscious urgency and vehemence, close to what Jonson felt, to see one's work finding its life among well-meaning appreciators of poetry, the *samajikas*. In line with Jonson's sensitiveness to the readerly community where, as I have argued, the poet and the critic nearly become the same person, the Abbāsid poets, by 'inventing' an ideal reader became both the creators and the internal critics of their work. This self-conscious move rendered a small coterie of *rasikas* as an extension of the poetic self, privatising an act generally considered as public and allowing the praised to see him in the praiser and the reader becoming the poet.

The notion of the creative self in Jonsonian aesthetics then is built as much around the poet's dependence on the reader as on the reader's submission to the poet. Ant*agonism* is a way of reaching at a point of poise and convergence where the reader and the poet become one: the poet choosing to survive through his reader and the reader keeping the poet alive through his understanding and sanity. The creative self is figured out in mutual attestation where each of them can become the cause for worry, anxiety, delight and security. So the politics of 'farewell' is invested in an ant*agonism* where submission is about negotiation and dependence is about approval.

Notes

1. *Sermones*, 1.10.73–74.
2. *Confucius: The Analects* (translated and annotated) Arthur Waley (Hertfordshire: Wordsworth Classics, 1996), Book 2, no. 10, 10.
3. See William Blake, *The Marriage of Heaven and Hell* in *Collected Poems* (ed.) W. B. Yeats (London: Routledge Classics, 2002).

4. Didier Coste, 'Is a Non-Global Universe Possible? What Universals in the Theory of Comparative Literature (1952–2002) Have to Say about It' *Comparative Literature Studies*, 41, no. 1 (2004), 43.
5. Arthur Marotti, 'All About Jonson's Poetry', *ELH* 39 (1972), 209.
6. See J. Loewenstein, 'The Script in the Marketplace', *Representations* 12 (1985), 101.
7. Jonson writes, 'But before wee handle the kindes of Poems, with their speciall differences: or make court to the Art it selfe, as a Mistresse, I would lead you to the knowledge of our *Poet*, by a perfect Information, what he is or should bee by exercise, by imitation, by Studie; and so bring him downe through the disciplines of *Grammar, Logicke, Rhetoricke*, and the *Ethicks*, adding somewhat, out of all, peculiar to himself, and worthy of your Admittance, or reception (2). Jonson admits that poet chooses his own rules of husbandry and expects his readers to subscribe to similar ways of exercise, study and knowledge. It is significant how the 'fit' reader reads his poems because an *appropriate* reading will vindicate how Jonson conceives the poet.
8. Timothy Murray, 'From Foul Sheets to Legitimate Model: Antitheater, Text, Ben Jonson', *New Literary History*, 14, no. 3, 651.
9. See *Ben Jonson* (ed.) C. H. Herford & Percy and Evelyn Simpson, 11 vols. (Oxford: Clarendon Press, 1925–1952). All quotations from Jonson's work are parenthetically provided from this volume.
10. Richard Newton, 'Jonson and the (Re)Invention of the Book', in *Classic and Cavalier: Essays on Jonson and the Sons of Ben*, (eds.) Claude J. Summers & Ted-Larry Pebworth (Pittsburgh: University of Pittsburgh Press, 1982), 44.
11. See Arthur I Marotti, *Manuscript, Print and the English Renaissance Lyric* (Ithaca, N.Y.: Cornell University Press, 1993), 244. But how much was this also an antagonism against moth and fire (not always the censor's fire)? He escaped the gallows after the fatal scrimmage with Gabriel Spencer by evincing his ability to read a verse from the Bible. Probably, Jonson chose to be 'saved by the book' as Ian Donaldson insightfully notes; it was in the same month that Jonson lost his books in fire and Shakespeare's folio was probably published (November, 1623). Donaldson observes: 'Jonson regarded books as vehicles of fame, couriers to posterity, monuments to art. But he could not quite avoid seeing them also in another light: as mere commodities, easily 'devoured' and dismembered, used to wrap spices, line pie-dishes, and clothe tobacco; as material objects that were as vulnerable as the authors who created them. Despite his hopeful statements to the contrary, Jonson knew very well that books, like their makers, were susceptible to Jove's anger, to fire, sword, and the gnawing tooth of time'. See Ian Donaldson, *Jonson's Magic Houses* (Oxford: Clarendon Press, 1997), 211. Amusingly, he swore by the book, lived by it, was hugely possessive of it, clung onto it for survival, sustenance and security. Ant*agonism* clearly worked in both life and art.
12. George E. Rowe, 'Ben Jonson's Quarrel with Audience and its Renaissance Context' *Studies in Philology* 81 (1984), 457.
13. An other Age, or juster men, will acknowledge the vertues of his studies: his wisdom, in dividing: his subtility, in arguing: with what strength hee doth inspire his Readers; with what sweetnesse hee strokes them: in inveighing, what sharpnesse; in Jest, what urbanity hee uses'. Ben Jonson, *Timber: or, Discoveries*, in *Ben Jonson*, ed. C. H. Herford & Percy and Evelyn Simpson, 11 vols. (Oxford: Clarendon Press, 1925–1952), 8, 587–88.

60 'To you I submit my selfe, and worke. Farewell'

14. By simple theme, Horace means one from familiar material, or from 'life and customs' to which grace can be imparted by the power of 'order' and 'connection'. It has to be uniform or one whole, with nothing extraneous or irrelevant to the 'matter' at hand. Although appreciative of Shakespeare's native excellences and unschooled genius, Jonson points out—'wherein he flow'd with that facility, that sometime it was necessary he should be stop'd; *Sufflaminandus erat*; as Augustus said of Haterius. His wit was in his owne power; would the rule of it has beene so too'.
15. *Epigrammes* 131, "To the Same", 1–4. Richard Helgerson notes that Jonson wants 'his audience to judge as well as to enjoy, to regard sense above spectacle, to use its ears before its eyes, to remain detached and observant, not allowing itself to be caught up, carried away, or taken in. Where Shakespeare and the other professional dramatists agree in seeking "a loving audience," Jonson prefers "an understanding one". *Self Crowned Laureates: Spenser, Jonson, Milton and the Literary System* (Berkeley: University of California Press, 1983), 154–55.
16. *Epigrammes* 52, "To John Donne", 9–10.
17. Rosalind Miles, *Ben Jonson His Craft and Art* (Savage, Md.: Barnes and Nobles, 1990), 169.
18. See Adele Austin Rickett (ed.) *Chinese Approaches to Literature from Confucius to Liang Ch'i-ch'ao* (Princeton, N.J.: Princeton University Press, 1978), 26.
19. See Steven Van Zoeren, *Poetry and Personality, Reading, Exegesis, and Hermeneutics in Traditional China* (Stanford, Calif.: Stanford University Press, 1991), 198.
20. See Zhang Longxi, *Allegoresis: Reading Canonical Literature East and West* (Ithaca, N.Y.: Cornell University Press, 2005), 93.
21. Steven Van Zoeren, *Poetry and Personality, Reading, Exegesis, and Hermeneutics in Traditional China*, 204.
22. See James J. Y. Liu, *Language-Paradox-Poetics: A Chinese Perspective* (Princeton, N.J.: Princeton University Press, 1988), 9.
23. Stanley Fish, 'Author-Readers: Jonson's Community of the Same', *Representations* 7 (Summer 1984), 38.
24. Peter Stallybrass and Allon White, *The Politics and Poetics of Transgression* (London: Methuen, 1986), 76.
25. Jennifer Brady, '"Beware the Poet": Authority and Judgment in Jonson's *Epigrammes*', *Studies in English Literature, 1500–1900* 23, no. 1 (Winter 1983), 98.
26. Rowe, 'Ben Jonson's Quarrel with Audience and its Renaissance Context', 458.
27. Brady, 'Beware the Poet', 107.
28. See Zhu Yingping, (ed.) *Wenxin diaolong suoyin* (Shanghai: Shanghai guji, 1987). The legend about Bo Ya, the musician, and his friend Zhong Ziqi is relevant to this context.
29. Vidya Niwas Misra, 'The Concept of *Sahrdaya*', in C. D. Narasimhaiah (ed.) *East West Poetics at Work* (New Delhi: Sahitya Academi, 1994), 49.
30. Ibid., 51.
31. See *The Dhvanyaloka of Anandavardhana with the Locana of Abhinavagupta* (trans.) Daniel H. H. Ingalls, Jeffrey Moussaieef Masson, & M. V. Patwardhan (Cambridge, Mass.: Harvard University Press, 1990), 70.
32. Misra, 'The Concept of *Sahrdaya*', 54–55.

33. See A. R. Hardikar, 'The Aesthetic Appreciator or *Sahridaya*', *Annals of the Bhandarkar Oriental Research Institute*, 75, no. 1/4 (1994), 266.
34. Robert Graves, *The Common Asphodel* (Hamish Hamilton, 1949), 1.
35. For some interesting thoughts on this subject see P. N. Virkar, 'Was Sahrdaya the name of the author of the Dhvanikarikas?' *Annals of the Bhandarkar Oriental Research Institute* 57, no. 1/4 (1976), 192–98 . Virkar writes: 'The word *Sahrdaya* is, in point of fact, used to mean a *rasika*. It is abundantly used in the *Dhvanyāloka*. It need not be argued on that strength that it has been used liberally in the *Dhvanyāloka* deliberately, because it happens to be the name of the *Kārikākāra* also and hence the author of the *Kārikās* derived an indirect pleasure in using that word in his own *Dhvanikārikās* and *Snandavardhana*, too, used it throughout the *Dhvanyāloka* as it afforded him so many opportunities to mention the *Kārikākāra*, his Guru. For, the *Kārikā- kāra* was not the first to use this word. It was used before the *Dhvanyāloka* or even before the *Dhvanikārikās*...' 193–94.
36. Virginia Woolf, *The Common Reader* (London, 1932), 259.
37. Steven van Zoeren, *Poetry and Personality,* 209.
38. Ibid. Italics are mine.
39. Huda J. Fakhreddine, 'Defining Metapoesis in the ʿAbbāsid Age', *Journal of Arabic Literature* 42 (2011), 221.
40. Ibid., 222.

4 'Launch not beyond your depth but be discreet'
The Tulip Poet

> The best criticism of any work of art is another work of art.
> —Pablo Picasso[1]

> There is but one way for the moderns to become great, and perhaps unequalled; I mean by imitating the ancients.
> —Johann Joachim Winckelmann[2]

'The most common effect of habit', writes Maine de Biran, 'is to take away all resistance, to destroy all friction'.[3] Habits of thinking and intellectual movements fear friction and prefer settlement in a generality that is undergirded by common agreement and well-meaning approbation. This engenders belief which, in turn, leads to habit that Charles Pierce qualified as the appeasement of the irritation of doubt.[4] But habit, as Plato points out, is no 'small matter' and, indeed, habit cannot be 'ease' always. Habits come with appetite, imagination and reflection. In the conceiving of what I call the tulip poet, the habits of neoclassical understanding—the general emphasis on a common perimeter of comprehension—show tendencies to escape its formations, provoking an intimate reflection on settled and sedimented thought-crust (like, a near heliocentric trust in generality and the distrust of imagination). Within the double-bind of habit, the conceptualisation of the poet and creativity refuse to exist as merely repetitive and imitative in their neoclassical rigour and discipline—habits existing both as movement and process, a doubt on the determinacy of belief. This is the zone of 'active habit'[5] where repetition unconceals gainful possibilities: repeated commitment to perform habits of creativity and art bring out discriminative judgement about the dialectics of obsession and necessity, passion and perception. It grows a tendency to challenge habit, a kind of distress that habit undergoes before 'something' comes into being. The transitivity in habit comes from a variety of thinking on how one looks at the notion of the poet—some being strictly neoclassical, some wedged in protoromanticism, and some impregnated with an anticipation for a change. Neoclassical habits of creativity have always oscillated a bit between habits repeated, revisionary habits and a dash of flight beyond settled habitual premises.

I

A habitual habitation in Lord Shaftesbury can be our starting point. He is said to have founded 'the first really comprehensive and independent philosophy of the beautiful'[6], being as he was, a dominant figure in British aesthetics of that period. Shaftesbury through his conception of the 'inner senses'—forms that determine the taste and natural affection—established certain predispositions that refused to get corrupted by stale social norms and customs. He aimed for the 'just standard of nature'. But *following* nature requires an intuitionism which, again, is processed out of a labouring mind that has an inevitable 'commerce with the world'. So the inner senses cannot be claimed to solely govern the taste of the poet. Standards of nature appeal to memory and the experiences derived out of the world at large generate the conflict that grounds creativity:

> Whatever philosopher, critic, or author is convinced of this prerogative of nature, will easily be persuaded to apply himself to the great work of reforming his taste, which he will have reason to suspect, if he is not such a one as has deliberately endeavoured to frame it by the just standard of nature. Whether this be his case, he will easily discover by appealing to his memory; for custom and fashion are powerful seducers; and he must of necessity have fought hard against these to have attained that justness of taste which is required in one who pretends to follow nature. But if no such conflict can be called to mind, 'tis a certain token that the party has his taste very little different from the vulgar. And on this account he should instantly betake himself to the wholesome practice recommended in this treatise. … All other speculations should be suspended, all other mysteries resigned, till this necessary campaign was made and these inward conflicts learnt; by which he would be able to gain at least some tolerable insight into himself and knowledge of his own natural principles.[7]

The insight is dialectically ruled by an antagonism between the holistic order and the limited fragmentary power of things. So the habits of creativity have their ultimate roots in a pre-established harmony which is organic and fundamental. Morality and poetic creativity are closely connected. This is where poetry gets a moral organicity to stay dialectically attuned to the *partium-totum* tension. However, creativity and imitation share a different order in that producing mimetic fidelity through copying of human manners, passions and actions seeks a replacement through the desire to reveal true beauty. This beauty inheres in universal attributes of order and proportion and through inventive measures stand assuredly removed from all forms of servile imitation. Robert Marsh keys onto the right note when he argues that the 'method of inward colloquy has its special significance in this connection chiefly as the preliminary corrective means by which the objective of accurate, natural description, upon which all writing depends, can be achieved. It must, beyond any other science, teach us the turns of humour and passion, the variety of manners, the justness of characters, and truth of things, which when we rightly understand we may naturally describe. And on this depends chiefly the skill and art of a good writer'.[8] Creativity has this dialogic marrow to it where the ordered and the unruly, the limits and the ultimate, invention and symmetry, reside in a resonant cheer. Poetics then has a strong inscription in divine creative acts which hold superiority in power ('sovereign mind') and are of great value (an 'impowered creatress' and 'substitute of Providence' that Shaftesbury calls 'Nature'). Shaftesbury finds divine presence in poetic inspiration of a high order but is sceptical of considering inspiration as wholly inspired by divinity. The divinity factor surrounding the poet-head owes to the significance of order and balance that he ascribes to all forms of creation. Judging and making one's spirit work is validated by a composure, and all creativity that dialecticises the divine head with the poet head must consider its existence. A good poet is a 'second maker', generally 'copy from another life, studying the graces and perfections of minds'.[9] As master or architect he is capable of describing both men and manners and giving 'to an action its just body and proportions'. Sure about the 'boundaries of passions' and 'exact tones and measures', the poet 'marks the sublime of sentiments and action, and distinguishes the beautiful from the deformed, the amiable from the odious'.[10] Marsh points out that 'although Shaftesbury does not (and, given his conception of the perfectly self-sufficient creator, cannot) adopt the Platonic doctrine of the "persuasive" act of the demiurge in bringing recalcitrant materials into harmony and order, the concept of persuasion appears, as an attribute or power of deity, in another sense. Through created things, a contact between the mind of God and the mind of man is made; in Shaftesbury's view, it is characterised, in the recipient, both by intellectual apprehension and by feeling, by movements of the affections. A true poet, therefore, imitates the sovereign genius also in the act of causing fellow human beings to think and to feel according to the ultimate principles of beauty, virtue, and truth; he is especially God-like when he causes them to recognize themselves in the mirror of human nature which he presents for their benefit'.[11]

Nothing in life is without harmony; things and events await an inspection on them for a chord of harmony ('interior numbers') without prejudgements that ascribe their evil nature. Poetic virtuosity selects the harmony and is the 'beautifying' power because Shaftesbury knows that 'beautified' is not really the beautiful. This is the vital principle—'the great and general ONE of the world'[12]—which animates all good work. We can infer that poetic interest is conative as against axiological—*interestedness* as revealed or executed through an active agential performance. Shaftesbury who can rightly enjoy the 'distinction of being the first thinker to bring the phenomenon of disinterestedness to light and analyzing it', understands disinterestedness as privative 'not motivated by self-seeking'—non-selfish as the antonym for selfish and not unselfish as is commonly known. Disinterestedness cannot spring from self-concern and any private interest of the perceiver—'advantage of the private system'. It is the key to creativity in that more than self-passion it is the 'love of truth, proportion, order and symmetry in the things' which come home to matter.[13] Shaftesbury considers the terrible and the frightening as aesthetically valuable. In an aesthetic attitude underwritten by neoclassical virtues of harmony, proportion and symmetry, the poet's vision accepts nature as having features that lack these attributes—the emphasis being on the distinction between the beautiful and the sublime. Such features were regarded as a revelation of God's majesty and not merely parts, but necessary parts, of the whole. In the poet's aesthetic vision the grand and the terrible aspects of nature are appreciated. It is the encompassing vision that perceives the ghastly and the hideous for their peculiar beauties—'the wildness pleases'.

The poet expected to engage with the world—its figures and forms, morals and manners—knows the tension of conjugation and opposition. He tries to find forms within the world, not weaning away from the world but allowing such engagements to 'correct' one's taste. Shaftesbury's neoplatonism hinges on the significance of expression:

> One would think there was nothing easier for us than to know our own minds, and understand what our main scope was; what we plainly drove at, and what we propose to ourselves, as our end, in every occurrence of our lives. But our thoughts have generally such an obscure implicit language, that 'tis the hardest thing in the world to make them speak out distinctly. For this reason, the right method is to give them voice and accent.[14]

But this dependence on the world may not be interpreted as a blunt submission to materialism and empirical veracity. There is a truth beyond the mere epidermal status of things:

> Something therefore there is in every design, or designatory work of imitation, and copy after nature (be it even in animals, fruit, or flower-pieces), which answers to the history in a truly epic or poetic work. This is in truth and strictness historical, moral, characteristic. The note or character of nature, the form, natural habit, constitution, reason of the thing, its energy, operation, place, use or effect in nature: if ill and mischievous to us, that we may record and avoid; if salutary, record and improve. This is the moral, the intelligence of the fable.[15]

Within a neo-Platonic speculative aesthetics, the creative mind holds a ground which cannot be strictly fenced out with classicism and metaphysics. His inward colloquy and internal sense are not metaphysical effusions alone; they demand being tested, judged and evaluated for their immediacy, efficacy and worth.

Perception and judgement are held in a co-habitative tension where a keenness for form and order precludes any passive engagement with the object perceived or intended to be experienced. Objects pass the threat of phantasm of mind through tests founded on inner sense. This is not naive empiricism though. The poetic art within Shaftesburian aesthetics is inscribed in taste and interest. Fancy needs taste as 'controller or manager' for without taste madness or loss of reason sets in.[16] So poets should

> add the wisdom of the heart to the task and exercise of the brain, in order to bring proportion and beauty into their works. That their composition and vein of writing may be natural and free, they should settle matters in the first place with themselves. And having gained a mastery there, they may easily, with the help of their genius and a right use of art, command their audience and establish a good taste.[17]

Taste does not speak of character, but forms and norms poetic creativity. Habits of creativity—taste, interest and form—do not allow poetry to be a mere act of copying or generalised representation. The business of the poet is not just to hold a mirror to reality: rather, in imitating, he transforms. This activates the Shaftesburian aesthetic which does not acknowledge the status in natural order as having any alliance with associationist psychology; it celebrates the living organic growth of natural order. So Hobbes and Locke come under fire—'These philosophers together with the antivirtuosi may be called one common name, viz. Barbarians'—as beauty, virtue, and music assume their individuality to the point where beauty and order of affections are celebrated and a mechanist and an associative functioning of the mind are debunked in favour of a creative imagination considered analogous to the operations of the divine mind.[18] However much Cartesian rationalism shows its disrespect for imagination—positing it at best between passive faculty that forms images and recombines images and Malebranche's skepticism in *Recherche de la Verite*—there is no denying of its proactivism:

> But for the man who truly and in a just sense deserves the name of poet and who as a real master, or architect in the kind, can describe both men and manners, and give to an action its just body and proportion, he will be found, if I mistake not, a very different creature. Such a poet is indeed a second *Maker*; a just Prometheus under Jove. Like that sovereign artist or universal plastic nature, he forms a whole, coherent and proportioned in itself, with due subjection and subordinacy of constituent parts.[19]

The poet's imitative ways demand originality and not mere subservience to the general nature of things—Aristotlean probable impossibility is better than a possible improbability. Imitation of the ideal world is possible by using, as R. L. Brett argues, 'the temporal and spatial forms in which the ideal manifests itself'—an ideal world that is not 'caught and fixed in dead and immutable symbols. It is a living force working in the changing forms of this world; the natural order is not fixed and dead, but a living organic growth'.[20] Shaftesbury's Platonism leads him to believe that beyond the natural order there is a transcendent and ideal world to which this present world only approximates. But the ideal reveals itself not in the fixed and dead entities of a mechanical construction; it is embodied in the changing forms of a world which is a living and organic growth. Art, which is an imitation or representation of nature, must also be creation in a real sense, and poetic invention must be a creative process. Suspicious of associationist psychology, the poet works on the principle of plastic power that *shapes* up the raw materials into new forms—a modifying and propulsive power that gleans out a 'form' from the 'unformed' and lends a 'shape' to the 'unshaped'. The imagination that compounds under associative laws the various units of mental experience underlines mechanical causation to which Shaftesbury is never seen to subscribe. The 'indifferent' artist may produce a work by bringing together from memory the bits and pieces of his material that Shaftesbury ascribes as the injudicious and random use of wit and fancy. There is a patent emphasis on perception that does not include the compounding of the sense-data (cf. John Stuart Mill's *System of Logic*), but points to an active power of the mind with an amalgamatory or assimilatory strength. It is what Thomas Parnell would attest as the 'passive mind' in his "The Gift of Poetry" and the power of imagination as 'celestial fire'.

Shaftesbury's poet knows the difference between enthusiasm and fanaticism for he is the admirer of the kind of enchantment or magic which we call *enthusiasm*.

> ... all sound love and admiration is enthusiasm: the transports of poets, the sublime of orators, the rapture of musicians, the high strains of the virtuosi—all mere enthusiasm! Even learning itself, the love of arts and curiosities, the spirit of travelers and adventurers, gallantry, war, heroism—all mere enthusiasm!... T' is enough; I am content to be this new enthusiast in a way unknown to me before.[21]

So the poet can be an enthusiast as well. Mark Akenside in his *The Pleasures of the Imagination* points out that Shakespeare pursued the vast, alone, the wonderful and the wild, and, Edmund Waller sighs for harmony, grace and sublime beauty, enabling a true poetic vision that encompasses both. The enthusiasm of the true artist is diverted towards both ends. The poet need not be cramped mercilessly and unflinchingly by rules or set precepts for poetical reason is not the same as mathematical reason. He has an aesthetic truth in mind, a truth that is qualitatively measurable, manifesting a capacity to carry his enquiries closely into men, manners and human nature. John Dennis's *Advancement and Reformation of Modern Poetry* traces a creative self which believes in art as the expression of passion and highest art as the communication of the most intense passion. The 'trueness' of the poet is in the expression of such strong enthusiasm which he believes are six in number: admiration, terror, horror, joy, sadness and desire. Dennis's state of enchantment while crossing the Alps is analogous to Thomas Burnet's appreciation of 'sublimity' ('sacred theory') in the ruins of the mountain, the old temples, fractured earth or great gurgling ocean which, in their inherent magnificence, raise great thoughts and passions invoking God and his greatness. They overbear the mind with their *excess* and cast it into a pleasing kind of stupor and admiration. Dennis reflects:

> If these Hills were first made with the world, as has been a long time thought, and Nature design'd them only as a Mound to inclose her garden Italy's Then we may well say of her what some affirm of great wits, that her careless, irregular and boldest strokes are most admirable. For the Alps are works which she seems to have design'd and executed too in a Fury.[22]

The poetic universe 'follows nature' in that the great and the worthy in nature owe to proportion, situation and interdependence of parts—a kind of regularity that brings order, a submission to reason. Dennis points out that a 'poet is capacitated by that which is commonly call'd Regularity, to excite the ordinary Passions more powerfully by the Constitution of the Fable, and the Influence which that must necessarily have, both upon the Words and Thoughts'.[23] The evocation of passion—enthusiasm—provides delight to the mind, moves us with pleasure and urges us to action and contemplation. Sublimity is a way of getting 'moved' when heightened thoughts overwhelm our formal regular structure of contemplation without being oblivious of the inward harmony of faculties—a transcendence of ordinary passions without losing its connection with regularity because it is not a mere display of stunning effects' but a communication of sense of causality. The poet has his role to enact in the use of language, utilising the peculiar energies of his medium. Also, Edmund Burke's distinction between a clear expression and a strong one is crucial to a proper understanding of poetic language. The Burkean aesthetics suggest a natural affinity between language and the sublime. So, the poet's status becomes somewhat subservient to an 'affective sublimity'. The poet is not there to make an ideal class but to make it *affecting* to the imagination.

Brett rightly observes that Shaftesbury 'adopts the "judgement-fancy" distinction by which Hobbes explains the process of poetic invention, and yet he upholds the Platonic doctrine of reminiscence. He is a well-meaning advocate of reason and at times seems to suggest that it is the faculty which makes aesthetic judgements, and yet he is the English critic most responsible for the introduction into criticism of "taste" and the use of the term *je ne sais quoi*'.[24] The tension in his understanding of aesthetic taste emerges out of the predominance of universalities and the insistent and unignorable prevalence of peculiarities and particularities. With the faith in Aristotlean understanding of imitation Shaftesbury notes that 'they are mean spirits who love to copy merely, nothing is agreeable or natural but what is original'[25]. The poet's mind is not mere associationist, not just a mechanism that subordinates wit to judgement; it builds on innate ideas. To govern and subjugate everything to reason meant understanding how one defined reason in the context of poetic creativity. As science promulgated order and propeudetically recognised coherence, poetic creation failed to configure itself beyond such frames of thinking. John Dennis sees a meaningful collaboration between nature and reason and believes that 'poetry cannot swerve from the Laws which Reason severely prescribes' and the 'more Irregular any Poetical composition is, the nearer it comes to Extravagance and Confusion, and to Nonsense, which is nothing'.[26] However, Shaftesbury's taste declares a new direction, not particularly pronounced—a refigurative stress on habits—which spoke of charm, particularity, flexibility of mind and attitude, and enchantment. It is a perception that homes in on the sense data to *create* an object, imposing an order on the disorder. This is 'a repetition in the finite mind of the eternal act of creation in the infinite I am'.[27] Shaftesbury attributes it to the power of reason (with a respectable analogy with Kantian reason) that apprehends the truth by an immediate act of awareness. It is a power that need not be confused with mere discursive ability but is the product of the poet's imagination that has its epistemological propinquity with Kant's aesthetic imagination. Shaftesbury believes that an inward eye distinguishes and sees the fair and shapely, the amiable and the admirable apart from the deformed, the foul, the odious or the despicable, reneging on the principle of harmony. In fact the concept of taste for Shaftesbury is never relative as he fought shy of the schism between relativistic and absolutistic tendencies and believed that aesthetic sense makes way for universal standards of judgements. The active principle in the poet's mind which is analogous to the 'plastic nature' is the shaping spirit of imagination that embodies the poet's thought in sensible forms, just as the creation is the embodiment of God's thought. Indeed in likening the mind of the poet to the mind of God, Shaftesbury is not making a psychological analysis of the art of writing poetry, nor is his description of the poet something which can be directly and empirically verified as scientific statements can be.[28]

II

The refigurative habits of creation involving imagination and reason find a somewhat restive stretch in John Dryden. Invested in an artistic dualism of thoughts and words, in a 'conception of art as a thing with interior and exterior aspects, imaginative and expressional', Dryden's art accentuates an indivisible imagination.[29] The first happiness of the poet's imagination, as Dryden notes, is 'invention' which includes the sudden eruption of the germ of a new poem, perhaps merely as a state of feeling. The second happiness is fancy or variation which calls for the capacity of moulding thought with due emphasis on judgement, making it, hence, proper to the subject. The third happiness of the poetic process is elocution which is the art of clothing and adorning the thought in apt and sound words. Based on the preface to *Annus Mirabilis*, imagination, working through its fraught inscription in memory, can be considered as a reproductive faculty with some inexpungeable conservatism and reservation that springs from judgement and mimetic performance. Dryden observes:

> I am of opinion, that they cannot be good poets, who are not accustomed to argue well. False reasonings and colours of speech are the certain marks of one who does not understand the stage; for moral truth is the mistress of the poet as much as of the philosopher. Poesy must resemble natural truth, but it must be ethical. … Therefore that is not the best poesy which resembles notions of things that are not, to things that are: though the fancy may be great and the words flowing, yet the soul is but half satisfied when there is not truth in the foundation.[30]

In *Dramatic Poesy*, fancy carries the 'connotation of licentiousness, lack of selectivity'—the 'wild imaginations' of 'hypercritics' produce 'things out of nature' ('Examen poeticum', ii. 159)—and imagination connects with the creative process (with greater emphasis on this line in the preface to *An Evening's Love*). In fact, the quickness of the responsive imagination is demonstrated in the invention, the fertility is exhibited in the fancy and accuracy is manifested in the expression.

Alexander Pope, in the preface to his translation of the *Iliad,* emphasises Homer's power of 'invention', his ability to supply a great variety of incident and events, thronging the narrative with speeches, battles and episodes of all kinds. Homer's 'invention' is the imaginative force. To Homer's strength of invention, one can attribute 'Fire' and 'Rapture' and *Iliad* is kindled all throughout by a true poetical spirit. The poet achieves a 'Grace beyond the Reach of Art' ("An Essay on Criticism" I. 155) or Boileau's *je ne sais quoi*. This closely resembles Addison's secondary pleasures of imagination that meaningfully connect with the conjurement of art (*Spectator* no. 411). Shakespeare could not have afforded 'weak sight' (natural genius as contrasted with genius developed by study in *Spectator* no. 419) gifted, as he was, by invention and noble extravagance of fancy. Imagination, for Addison, comes with aesthetic enjoyment and discrimination which is identified with taste:

> Let every one here consider, how different we must suppose the Perception to be, with which a Poet is transported upon the Prospect of any of those Objects of natural Beauty, which ravish us even in his Description; from that cold, lifeless Conception which we imagine in a dull Critick, or one of the Virtuosi, without what we call a fine Taste.[31]

Addison, as Clarence Thorpe argues, was 'essentially a sensationalist who began with sense perception not pre-sensation, as did Shaftesbury'.[32] So the poet with good imagination should have a mind 'stocked with sense impressions, gathered, first from the Works of Nature,' then from the 'Pomp and Magnificence of Courts,' and from all the noble works of art, including statuary, painting, and architecture.[33] The poet's pleasure of imagination builds on associationism and if, as Thorpe rightly argues, 'Shaftesbury thought of a mental process through which the imagination refers the immediate perception to preconceived or innate ideas of harmonious form', Addison 'conceived of primary aesthetic response as something quite independent of any idea of absolute form; as being, indeed, only a natural response of a nervous organization so constituted by the creator as to experience pleasure upon the perception of certain objects'.[34]

The poetic art is built around the affective difference between the copy and the original—the mending nature excelling reality (*Spectator* no. 418, 421) and constructions beyond the realm of sight (*Spectator* no. 419) which, again, Dryden ascribes as a 'fairy kind of writing'.

> The fancy must be warm to retain the print of those images it hath received from outward objects: and the judgement discerning, to know what expressions are most proper to clothe and adorn them to the best advantage. A man who is deficient in either of these respects, though he may receive the general notion of a description, can never see distinctly all its particular beauties; as a person, with a weak sight, may have the confused prospect of a place that lies before him, without entering into its several parts, or discerning the variety of its colours in their full glory and perfection.[35]

On the principal habit where perception determines expression, imitation holds a preponderant sway on creative aesthesis. At the beginning of his career as a literary critic, Dryden struggled a bit with his Aristotelian habits of poetic imitation by considering imitation to be a spiritual process—the vital force needed for excellence in art and generating the 'illumination'. Imitation then is both reflective and reflexive—a sort of following or adherence which is never without a plan and, certainly with a recreative consciousness. Here the stress on the *lively* imitation of nature goes back to the Renaissance aesthetics where *enargia*, 'vivid illustration' or 'representation,' 'living truth,' and 'eyes of the mind' premise the concept of liveliness.[36] The *enargia* inspires representations of human nature—certain fundamental and psychological truths—inscribed more in delight and transport than insipid instructions. This is in line with the power of poetry to *move* something that we encountered in Sidney without a lapse into the alluring enchantments of *furor poeticus*—something that his poetics could simply ill-afford given his reservations about fancy's ways as found in 'Discourse on Satire' (ii.i), 'The Character of Polybius' (ii. 68) and 'To My Dear Friend Mr Congreve' (1694). The poet is 'like that of a curious gunsmith or watchmaker: the iron or silver is not his own; but they are the least part of that which gives the value: the price lies wholly in the workmanship'.[37] Poetry's ability to move comes with a measured adjustment between the part and the whole—a complicated role-sharing among the creator, imitator and the instructor. In this context and, also on a kind of a theoretical obligation to the ancients, Dryden is close to Tasso where both agree on keeping the beauty of the whole, precluding variety from becoming a 'confused and perplexed mass of accidents'.[38] John Sherwood working on this comparative axis points out that Tasso 'demanded that the poet defer to the ancients on the "foundation of the design" ("l'unita della favola") but granted him freedom with reference to the "customs of countries" and "idioms of language"—"la maniera del- l'armeggiare, i modi dell'aventure, il rito de' sacrifici e dei conviti, le cerimonie" as well as the "idioma"'. For Dryden, though, the poet works more on providing 'novel materials than in forming and embellishing material which may well have come from others'.[39] Committed habits, confidence in closely repeated habits, and habits denied, then, have a disturbing constellative presence in Dryden's conceptual figurations.

The *enargia* must accompany good sense as much as judgement—John Dennis ascribes it as the fine discernment of truth—and discretion which contribute to the enlargement and extension of the poet's fancy, keeping the harp in tune. This comes with the consciousness to adorn the expression—the art of clothing a thought with appropriateness and measure. Robert Hume observes that in 'Dryden's more usual use of "wit" to mean propriety of thoughts and words or the ability to produce it, judgement serves to correct the labours of fancy. Here, though, wit itself becomes the creative faculty which must be checked by judgement. This usage is a development of the position taken in the Apology for Heroic Poetry and it reflects the increasingly verbal sense in which Dryden had come to think of creation'.[40] The poet is largely defined by expression, the charming impact of the art of words, the tropes and figures, 'the versification, and all the other elegancies of sound, as cadences, turns of words upon the thought'.[41] Accenting suggestiveness in poetry, Dryden finds the primary secret of harmony in his choice of words and, by this, he means the elegance of expression where the 'propriety of sound' is varied in response to the 'nature of the subject'—the 'rhythmus by the ancients'.[42] So diction or elocution is identified by Dryden as a significant component of poetic creativity, having 'aptness (decorum with regard to genre, subject, purpose), significance (expressiveness, meaningfulness), and harmonious sound (sweetness, sonority)' which certainly contradicts any uncritical claim that Dryden's diction is literal and denotative'.[43] The poet writing in English, says Dryden, 'must have a magazine of words, and have the art to manage his few vowels to the best advantage that they may go the farther. He must also know the nature of the vowels, which are more sonorous and which more soft and sweet, and so dispose them as his present occasions require'.[44] The entropy of trans-habit continues to makes us 'veer' into Liu Hsieh's *Wen-hsin tiao-lung* where we encounter again the agreeable negotiation between eloquence and emotion—'emotion is the warp of literary pattern and the linguistic form the woof of ideas.

'Launch not beyond your depth but be discreet' 73

Only when the warp is straight can the woof be rightly formed, and only when ideas are definite can linguistic form be meaningful'.[45] This precipitates into a diffractive correspondence between Liu and Dryden on musical expression where the gift of nature and learning become a sort of creative combo, enabling the 'wind' and the 'bone' into a synthesis which T'sao P'ei has called the breath. This 'breath' repremises our idea of the genius where *studium* cannot avoid being a respectable part of the narrative of creativity. Liu's conception of organic unity, for me, makes for a close correspondence with neoclassical poetic structuring. In chapters like 'Organization' (*Fu-hui*) and 'Discussion on the Art of Writing' (*Tsung-shu*), he underlines a comprehensive view of a literary piece, an underlying unity that is empowered with a critical and discrete exclusionist-inclusionist rationale. This makes 'structure' articulate, making for the organicity of the literary production. Perhaps the trans-habitual journey does not continue further when Liu sees a 'mystic subtlety of imagination' with a corresponding emphasis on vital force (*chih-ch'i*)—the creative dialectic involving spirit, rhetoric, tranquillity and reason is far more intricate than what we find in Dryden.

So, based on his complex understanding of poetic art, Dryden could not have allowed literary evaluation to be left in the hands of the hoi polloi—'If by the people you understand the multitude, the hoi polloi, 'tis no matter what they think; they are sometimes in the right, sometimes in the wrong: their judgement is a mere lottery'[46]; it means, indirectly, he considers the poet of superior merit whose art is not a simple business to attend and judge. Judgement helps the poet to manage his powers skilfully and artfully. Hoyt Trowbridge points out that to 'succeed by chance is no credit to an artist, for discrimination in the choice of means is inherent in the very definition of an art. For Dryden, if not for some critics of later times, a poet without art is a contradiction in terms'.[47] However, such habits of creativity, come under revisionary stress when Dryden, speaking of Shakespeare as the 'largest and most comprehensive soul,' looks into a few aspects of creativity differently: 'All the images of nature were still present to him, and he drew them, not laboriously, but luckily; when he describes anything, you may see it, and feel it too. Those who accuse him to have wanted learning, give him the greater commendation; he was naturally learned; he needed not the spectacles of books to read nature; he looked inwards, and found her there'.[48] Somewhere his poetic insight was inflicted by a paradox where dogmatic limitations are threatened to be superceded by the challenging ways of an isolated genius[49]—'the flights of fancy in *The Tempest* and *Midsummer Night's Dream* may be excused, because poets should have the liberty of describing things which do not exist if the descriptions are founded on popular belief'.[50]

III

Johnsonian poetics is another good instance of a struggle of a literary mind caught in the dialectic between *feng* and *ku*, *pratibha* and *prayojana*—the organicity of art that combines felicity and skill, emotion and imagination as evident in the well-known wheelbarrow metaphor in ancient Chinese literary criticism. Johnson's low estimate of imagination can be traced to his disinclination to privilege imagination over fancy like many of his contemporaries. Imagination for Johnson is 'a licentious and vagrant faculty, unsusceptible of limitations, and impatient of restraint, has always endeavoured to baffle the logician, to perplex the confines of distinction, and burst the inclosures of regularity'.[51] He attributes the strangeness and irregularity of imagination to the weakness of human nature. The combinatory and evocative power of imagination does guarantee 'new formations' but not absolutely new planes of transcendence and transformative realities. Creation, rather, is a distillate formed out of the combination of imagination and reason, vouchsafing a formidable connection with life experiences—an incessant preying upon life. However, imagination, passion and reason share a combinatory poise that does not have a whole scale anti-imagination bias of Cartesian mathematicism or an exaggerated neoclassical rationalism. The novelty in the poet's art is something that Johnson never denies; the aesthetic pleasure is also never disclaimed. But the poet needs to distinguish between 'to please' and 'to direct'. Truth, to be poetic, has to be pleasure-giving. The Johnsonian aesthetic, thus, cannot leave out the restrained but decisive function of imagination ('the power of forming ideal pictures' as defined in his *Dictionary*) and imitation where representation is not mnemonic but, to a large extent, aesthetically mimetic with a cardinal commitment to life and nature. Since nature should not be 'promiscuously' described and proper imitation calls for distinguishing appropriate parts of nature, imagination, as Johnson notes, is 'useless without knowledge', demanding agreeable observation and experience. This engagement with reality has its own limitations and, imagination is solicited to generate possibilities—an unavoidable aesthetic-political contradiction. Reality as the poet encounters is not free from particular forms of unsightliness and defacement. So what Reynolds did in painting, Johnson proposed for poetry by claiming that the general order of nature is what the imagination must endeavour to seize with an eye to generate possibilities. In his sixth *Discourse*, Joshua Reynolds, in a somewhat trans-habitual stress, points out that imitation meant incorporation and distillation without losing sight of originality. He writes:

> The mind is but a barren soil; a soil which is soon exhausted, and will produce no crop, or only one, unless it be continually fertilized and enriched with foreign matter.
> When we have had continually before us, the great works of Art to impregnate our minds with kindred ideas, we are then, and not till then, fit to produce something of the same species. ...
> It is vain for painters or poets to endeavour to invent without materials on which the mind may work, and from which invention must originate. Nothing can come from nothing.[52]

He observes further:

> He who borrows an idea from an ancient or even from a modern artist not his contemporary, and so accommodates it to his own work, that it makes a part of it, with no seam or joining appearing, can hardly be changed with plagiarism; poets practice this kind of borrowing without reserve. But an artist should not be contented with this only; he should enter into a competition with his original, and endeavour to improve what he is appropriating to his own work. Such imitation is so far from having anything in it of the servility of plagiarism, that it is a perpetual exercise of the mind, a continual invention. Borrowing and stealing with such art and caution will have a right to the same lenity as was used by the Lacedemonians; who did not punish theft, but the want of artifice to conceal it.[53]

Referring to the Second *Discourse* Floyd Martin explains that invention

> is little more than a new combination of those images which have been previously gathered and deposited in the memory: nothing can come of nothing: he who has laid up no materials, can produce no combinations. Invention, then, was the placing of the painter's mental picture of actions, expressions, and characters on the canvas. The mental picture was made up of the artist's previously gathered images from nature and art. In the eighteenth century, it was assumed such a picture would be generalized and moral, addressing the minds of the spectators.[54]

Within the 'nothing can come from nothing' principle, the poet must connive at the romantically 'marvellous' and subscribe to the 'probable'; this precludes a disorganised discharge of 'inventive' energies, bulwarking his mind against scatty 'incredibilities'—laws of nature are superior to the 'accidental prescriptions of authority'. Imbibing the values of the toil of study and the knowledge of nature or the acquaintance with life, the poet must avoid the dominance of subjective impulse over objective insight, doing things *de justesse*; he 'does not number the streak of the tulip'[55] and so never loses sight of the grandeur of generality. Despite being acknowledged for their originality and learning, the metaphysical poets come under the prescriptive politics of 'generality'—their novelty is often clogged by labored particularities denying them the access to the sublimity of 'general life'.[56] They stand disqualified—failure to make just measure of astonishment and rational admiration—before the Johnsonian dictum that sees great thoughts as always general; their descriptions are always analytic and fragmentary, ridden by particularities and unsuited to the true nature of poetic creation ('Poetry cannot dwell upon the minuter distinctions, by which one species differs from another, without departing from that simplicity of grandeur which fills the imagination; nor dissect the latent qualities of things, without losing its general power of gratifying every mind, by recalling its conceptions').[57] Johnson's apprehensions about the potentiality and limitations of human life contribute to his penchant for generality. The seeming polarity between reason and imagination owes to the limitations of the human mind ('human mind is so limited that it cannot take in all the parts of a subject, so that there may be objections raised against anything'[58]) and its inability to look beyond a certain point in understanding things. Particularity baffles because, as Johnson notes, humans are finite beings 'furnished with different *degrees of attention*, and discovering consequences which escape another, none taking in the whole concatenation of causes and effects, and most comprehending but *a very small part*'.[59] Steering clear of individual caprice, the poet must see through the endeavour of self-authorised legislators who try to clamp fixity to rules that are born for their self-serving reflexion. To highlight his antipathy towards a misplaced accent on rules, Johnson told Fanny Burney that the people who judge her work are those who know no rules, but pronounce entirely from their natural taste or feelings or those who know or judge by rules or those who know and are above the rules. In *Discourse* XIII, Reynolds describes 'sound reason'—distinguished from 'partial reasoning' or 'cold consideration'—which 'does not wait for the slow process of deduction, but goes at once, by what appears a kind of intuition, to the conclusion'. Both Reynolds and Johnson appreciate the artist's ability to isolate 'ideal beauty' from the accidents of time and place, emphasising a 'skill in selecting' and 'care in digesting'. For Reynolds, the imagination—going a bit out of the Johnsonian habitual prescriptions—appears to be the faculty which is captivated or 'delighted' by the embodiment of ideal beauty and, which, immediately recognises its truth, 'whereas the faculty which enables the artist to distinguish and embody the ideal is 'sound reason' (the adjective being necessary to distinguish this kind of reason from the analytical variety)'.[60] The 'friction' on strict habits of neoclassical creativity can be found in Reynolds's attention to particulars without which creation in its wholeness cannot be approached—'a minute attention to particulars with neither selection nor modification is incompatible with the grand style of painting which represent the invariable, the great and general ideas fixed and inherent in universal nature'.[61]

The neoclassical simplicity in ideating a poet can be deceptive—the inevitable problematic of the 'friction' of habit comes into play. Through Shaftesbury and Francis Hutcheson, as much as through Johnson, we encounter a contradictory and complexified understanding of what constitutes and enables a poet and his functioning.[62] René Wellek does not see Johnson as an unflinching neoclassicist but, also, not a precursor to romanticism. He finds in Johnson an understanding of reality with a strong undertow of morality and sincerity of feeling—a combination that puts Johnson's notion of creativity under a refigurative mode. Prolonged and panoramic contemplation of nature evoke possibilities to redeem nature of its imperfection, throwing the poet in the midst of general and transcendental truths. This mooring in the grandeur of generality owes itself to the advancement of particularly mathematical science, for it is with the general truth, as James Sutherland argues, that 'the man of science deals'. Sutherland observes that progress in science 'quickened men's interest in natural laws, and, more generally, in that sort of truth which was universal and above all particular instances'.[63] However, the configuration of the poet based on generality finds some opposition in Joseph Warton who falls out on Johnson because of his heavy reliance on generalities and an alleged sunderance from the 'true and lively, and minute, representations of Nature'. Warton saw the sublime and the pathetic as fundamental to poesy and Johnson failed him. Generality prevails in both Johnson and Joshua Reynolds as a neo-Platonic aesthetic trait which, however, is not a transcendent reality but a general experience of mankind, a collective experience of humanity on 'the passions of men, which are uniform' rather than on 'their customs, which are changeable'.[64] The poet's knowledge cannot be merely qualified by propensities that are fundamentally general in nature. Poetic creativity owes to all ways and modes of life. In *Rasselas* we find Johnson arguing for the necessity of a combination of a variety of emotions emerging from various institutions and 'accidental influences of climate or custom'—an active ambivalence as to the merit of particularity and generality in poetic creativity.

In fact the 'friction in habit' is intensified further through Johnson's appreciation of the 'rough' genius of Shakespeare, whose composition 'is a forest, in which oaks extend their branches, and pines tower in the air, interspersed sometimes with weeds and brambles, and sometimes giving shelter to myrtles and to roses; filling the eye with an awful pomp, and gratifying the mind with endless diversity. Other poets display cabinets of precious rarities, minutely finished, wrought into shape, and polished into brightness. Shakespeare opens a mine which contains gold and diamonds in inexhaustible plenty, though clouded by incrustations, debased by impurities, and mingled with a mass of meaner minerals'.[65] Working on the grandeur of generality Johnson sees Shakespeare as holding up 'to his readers a faithful mirror of manners and of life. His characters are not modified by the customs of particular places, unpractised by the rest of the world;… they are the genuine progeny of common humanity, such as the world will always supply, and observations will always find' (10–11). For the reader recognises in it his own thoughts, words and deeds 'those general passions and principles by which all minds are agitated and the whole system of life is continued in motion' (11) and language that seems 'to have been gleaned by diligent selection out of common conversation and common occurrences' (12). It is from this 'wide extension of design' (11) that he believes so much instruction can be derived. Johnson's defence of Shakespeare is somewhat a reworking on his neoclassical habits where virtue, vocation, verisimilitude and values are caught in a reaccented orientation. To consider Shakespeare as having the ability to probe into the 'happiness and misery of every condition', observe the 'power of all passions in all their combinations, and trace the changes of the human mind as they are modified by various institutions and accidental influences of climate or custom' speak about the importance of particulars in the understanding of the general. Such weighing in of the particulars contradicts the consideration of the right and wrong 'in their abstracted and invariable state'. Johnson's treatment of Shakespeare, much like Dryden's, then is an intelligent defence of habit where defending one's habit is also a way of falling a victim to its transcendence.

IV

The category of genius[66]—a subject that provokes another dimension of transcendence of the habitus of strict neoclassical creativity—individualises the poet as distinguished from common men and men of talent. In the entangled politics of invention, imagination and genius, the poetic mind inheres in an oppositional space caught, as usual, between volition and verve and decorum and deliberation—a lively friction of habits. It is primarily in Albert Gerard (*Essay on Genius*), Edward Young (*Conjectures on Original Composition*), William Duff (*Essay on Original Genius*), William Sharpe (*Dissertation on Genius*) and James Beattie (*The Minstrel; or, The Progress of Genius*) that we encounter a separate line of creative epistemology where genius and originality exist as refigurative paradigms and art and nature are caught in a fecund antagonism. Trans-habitually, working through Denis Diderot, Abbe Du Bos, D'Alembert, Condillac and Batteux, we find that the genius in eighteenth-century French aesthetics is artistic having inventiveness and a separate order of perception: *Nous prenons l'imagination dans un sens plus noble & plus precis, pour le talent de creer en imitant.*[67] Discounting divine inspiration and unrestrained feeling, artistic genius is more adept at organising feelings and perceptions. This builds an inspiring analogy with the British neoclassicists' suspicion about 'enthusiasm' considered as an aesthetic category. Johnson, Shaftesbury, Diderot and M. de Cahusac perceive enthusiasm and reason as superarched by the powers of imagination and, great art, as all resoundingly concur, can scarcely overlook the mutual pull of the competing paradigms. The habits of creative enthusiasm meet with a different treatment as much with Shaftesbury as with Diderot. The notion of the poet as artistic genius inheres in two concepts: *avoir du genie* and *etre un genie* or *un homme de genie*. The former deals with special ability and the latter betrays a supernal power close to *furore poeticus*. Herbert Dieckmann notes that with the advent of an opposition between feeling and 'sensibilite' in eighteenth century, a 'work of art is no longer judged by the degree of conformity with traditional patterns and rules, but by the degree of delight it gives, and this delight is caused, not by rational structure and intellectual simplicity, but by the free play of imagination and emotion. At the same time a keen interest in the creative powers of the artist and in the psychological process of creation awakens'.[68] However, the free play of imagination did not meet with much endorsement from Diderot who weighed in the importance of reason in all imaginative works of art. The friction in habit was conspicuously in play. The poet for Diderot, as much for Gerard or Young or Shaftesbury, is inspired by a genius that is not 'some ephemeral spirit that hovers near its owner'. Helvetius looks into the formation of genius as both innate and externally engineered through education, appropriate cultivation of circumstances conducive to such a development and general concurrence. But Diderot saw genius as different from Helvetius's understanding of it as a product of chance. Genius, as Jaffe deftly explains, is that 'fundamental attribute of a great artist that makes him what he is. The only way one can understand these incredible men is by looking inside them; all the theories that have relied on external factors have ultimately been disproved. There are no promptings by voices or Muses, no daemons that possess the unsuspecting human, no well-ordered nature that sustains the artist and guides his pen or brush. But there still is inspiration, there still is madness, and there still is a world that affects the genius' artistic vision. To integrate these three troublesome ideas, Diderot utilized a word that would dominate the vocabulary of his Romantic successors: imagination'.[69] Poesis inheres in imagination which is also about self-control, development of an ability that bulwarks against emotional vacillation towards the creation of a higher reality. The success of genius (*homes sublimes*) is not in volatility—in Diderot's *Neveu de Rameu*, Moi points out genius as 'un dans la multitude'. And Lui's idea of the inhospitability of genius has a contradictory note which, however, spells out the character of genius—but surely in working out on a settlement in composure which only reason or imagination in their isolated capacity cannot generate. At the end of *Neveu de Rameau* Lui describes the statue of Memnon whose powers are harmonic, distinct from the perception of ordinary men. This power rises above mediocrity and enables one to see the truth and serve the moral guide. Borrowing from the Memnon image, James Mall shows us that the 'solar' laws are extraordinary and terrestrial laws are relegated to mediocrity. But a genius is not divine; he is both human and not ordinary and, hence, obligated to function on 'two mutually exclusive levels at once'. This projects a dual character which qualifies the genius as a monster—not familiar and yet not wholly bizarre and beatific.[70]

The genius of the poet is the energy, as Johnson observes, that 'collects, combines, amplifies, and animates'. Poetic genius subverts existing rules (*Rambler* Nos. 125 and 156) and sometimes inspiration—'sudden elevations of the mind'—can intervene beyond the poet's usual *techne* and talent. This again throws up Johnson's ambivalence within neoclassical premises of regulative functioning. Johnson looks into the complex contact between aesthetic (the combination of the good, true and the beautiful) and moral sensibility. Unlike Shaftesbury's 'moral sense' where beauty becomes an attribute of the perceiver's mind, Johnson associates beauty with empiricism and not impressionism. The poet performs through an attention to experience and human activity. Johnson appreciates the breadth of life with things that are both familiar and unfamiliar, disclosing a world that knows the ways to *refresh* tradition. In a critical parallelism with Reynolds's aesthetics which is inscribed in a moderate enthusiasm for the abilities of 'genius' ('we are sure that in the hands of a man of genius it is capable of inspiring sentiment, and of filling the mind with great and sublime ideas'[71]), we find the poet failing to exist on his own potential alone. Creativity is not all chance and genius can produce excellence but not without the presence of rules—selection, digestion, recreation and methodization come in a fraught operational cluster. The artist of genius will permit the lower painter like the florist or the collector of shells to exhibit the minute discriminations which distinguish one object of the same species from another while he, like the philosopher, will consider nature in the abstract and represent in every one of his figures the character of its species.[72]

Like Abbe Du Bos with his penchant for method, Gerard sees genius as reducible to two ends: the discovery of truth and the production of beauty. Genius is considered as the *power of invention,* either in science or in arts, either of truth or of beauty. Gerard argues that our intellectual powers may be reduced to four paradigms: sense, memory, imagination and judgement. But the redoubtable significance of imagination needs the close association of judgement. Fancy cannot be left entirely to itself for that renders it unworthy of any invention. The poetic mind thrives on a connection built between imagination and judgement: imagination produces genius and the other intellectual faculties lend their assistance to 'rear the offspring of imagination to maturity'.[73] So imagination *sans* judgement would be extravagant—I ascribe this as neoclassical unease—and Gerard notes that 'without imagination, judgement could do nothing. A bright and vigorous imagination joined with a very moderate judgement, will produce genius, incorrect, it may be, but fertile and extensive;' but a very nice judgement unattended with a good imagination, cannot bestow a single spark of genius.[74] James Engells argues that 'judgment is not, as it is in Dryden, Dennis, and Addison, a power to control and subordinate imagination. Instead it is a complementary aid to perfect and assure the justness of the "design" already sketched out by the imagination. When a genius judges his own work, he is simply developing a "regularity of imagination," which is by no means the same thing as subjecting a completed imaginative work to some higher power. When a genius changes his work, he exercises "the posterior essays of imagination, affected by new associations in repeated views of the subject"'.[75]

The poetic genius (*Genielehre*) need not wilt into a psychopathological problem as a consequence of an overbalance of imagination and enthusiasm in the way in which Diderot described it. Even the adult genius (following the categorical distinction that Edward Young makes with 'infantine' genius) cannot infuse his poetic art with fine frenzy[76]: as a dialectical product of nature and art, poetry owes its origin to the genius who is a 'grand architect'. Bernard Fabian makes us see that, although Gerard 'substitutes the image of the plant for that of a magnet, we cannot interpret this conceptual substitution as a transition from mechanism to organicism'. He points out that 'undoubtedly the vegetative analogy was felt to be more suggestive in an age that had turned from the contemplation of the majesty of the cosmos to the observation of the minuter objects in physical nature. While Shaftesbury's revival of the demiurgic analogy interpreting the artist, in almost Sidneyean terms, as an *alterdeus* seems appropriate for the age of Newtonian physics, Gerard's likening of genius to the plant reflects, with corresponding fidelity, the dawning of the era of Linnean botany'.[77] In fact, Gerard notes that 'when a vegetable draws in moisture from the earth, nature, by the same action by which it draws it in, and at the same time, converts it into the nourishment of the plant ... In like manner, genius arranges its ideas by the same operation, and almost at the same time, that it collects them'. This speaks of an inbuilt associative power but clearly more intense and profound in character—not a Coleridgean esemplasticism but particularly organic and passionate. The poetic genius, therefore, through an inner tension and congruence finds its own connect with virtue and cannot disregard learning altogether: creativity without learning is cankered with a 'lack', overvaluing learning shows the effects of an inevitable harm. If learning gives us pleasure, genius gives us rapture, if one informs, the other inspires, if one qualifies as borrowed knowledge, the other has its own power of innateness.[78] However, going beyond the imitation-imagination-reality problematic of Charles Batteux[79], William Duff in his *Essay on Original Genius* sees genius as inseparable from imagination and somewhat, within a politics of antagonistic thinking, approximates its plastic abilities: imagination as defining the inner life of the mind, a unifying faculty that is combinatory, assimilative and, to an extent, transformative. But there exists a common agreement over the counterbalancing act that harmonises the volatility and radicality of imagination with reason and judgement. Genius, thus, builds taste, the aesthetic judgement, the 'internal sense' which form five principles: 'the elevation and pleasurable exertion of the mind in conceiving the new phenomenon; surprise; compositions with other passions and emotions; reflection on success in surmounting difficulty, or self-gratulation on acquisition of the new perception; sympathy with the original genius displayed in inventive works of science and art'.[80] The taste of novelty then does not produce certainty of affective knowledge always. Aesthetic categories produced by the poetic mind inhere in a delight that becomes a consequence of comparison, ingenuity, powerful principle of association, discernment and intense acts of imitation. Imitation, somewhat paradoxically, comes with its own strictness and liberty—a conception that does not aim to copy existing things with utmost resemblance and rigour:

> In a word, poetry is called an imitation, not because it produces a lively idea of its immediate subject, but because this subject itself is an imitation of some part of real nature. It is not called an imitation, to express the exactness with which it copies real things; for then history

would be a more perfect imitation than poetry. It is called an imitation for the very contrary reason, to intimate that it is not confined to the description only of realities, but may take the liberty to describe all such things as resemble realities, and on account of that resemblance, come within the limits of probability.[81]

Such acts of imitation points to the inner coherence of a poetic work and, enabled by an Aristotlean notion of probability, finds a connect with Dominique Bouhours's *je ne sais quoi*[82]; this points to an indefinability of experience and aesthetic formation, contributing to the delight. So imagination for the poet is no 'unskilful architect' which means that the mind cannot leave an undigested chaos unattended because it is through repeated attempts and transpositions, through collection and choice, it reaches at a design, a 'regular and well-proportioned edifice'.[83]

The production of art, thus, owes both to mechanical felicity and the inventiveness of the genius. There cannot be a genius without training and learning because 'by being conversant with the inventions of others that we learn to invent; as by reading the thoughts of others we learn to think'.[84] It is interesting to observe that the painter who takes nature as he finds it is no better than the prose historian. Rembrandt's penchant for exact representation of individual objects does not support the argument that his imitation of nature is more faithful than what the idealising Raphael does. The painter of the ideal landscape has the cherished independence and the remarkable power to 'select' his material. Reynolds's painter or the *poetical painter* varies and combines his material to correspond with the general idea of his work and the elevation of the theme: 'a landskip thus conducted, under the influence of a poetical mind, will have the same superiority over the more ordinary and common views, as Milton's *Allegro* and *Penseroso* have over a cold prosaik narration or description; and such a picture would make a more forcible impression on the mind than the real scenes, were they presented before us'.[85] So Reynolds equates the power of the poet and the painter in his study of Michelangelo. With more poetical 'inspiration' Michelangelo's ideas grows vast and 'sublime' which is the highest excellence a human composition can attain. In the fifteenth and the last *Discourse,* Michelangelo is singled out for praise as he is said to possess a 'poetical part' with the virtue of an elevated imagination; he is ranked with Homer and Shakespeare, highlighting the power that explores the unknown regions of imagination—'so far therefore is servile imitation from being necessary, that whatever is familiar, or in any way reminds us of what we see and hear every day, perhaps does not belong to the higher provinces of art, either in poetry or painting. The mind is to be transported, as Shakespeare expresses it, *beyond the ignorant present* to ages past'.[86] However, the artist's sublimity should not transgress the limits of classical decorum—a celebration or vindication of rational firmness which is the true testament of a sound and true genius. It is a Longinian state of transport that accentuates

'Launch not beyond your depth but be discreet' 83

the *vigour* in a firm realisation of the ideal or the *beau ideal*. So in the context of imitation, Reynolds does not subscribe to a work that is a mere copy of Nature. Imagination, for him, is the 'residence of truth'.[87] The art of the painter or the poet is addressed as the highest province for, by evading any correspondence with the gross senses, he can summon the sparks of divinity that reside within all of us. Reynolds points out that genius 'begins not where rules, abstractedly taken, end; but where known vulgar and trite rules have no longer any place. It must of necessity be, that even works of Genius, like every other effect, as they must have their cause, must likewise have their rules'.[88] Originality, therefore, holds an opposition within it—the demos of exuberance continuously tamed by artistic reliance on refinity, stylistic adroitness and thematic modulation and décor.

> In almost all countries, the most ancient poets are considered as the best: whether it be that every other kind of knowledge is an acquisition gradually attained, and poetry is a gift conferred at once; or that the first poetry of every nation surprised them as a novelty, and retained the credit by consent which it received by accident at first: or whether, as the province of poetry is to describe Nature and Passion, which are always the same, the first writers took possession of the most striking objects for description, and the most probable occurrences for fiction, and left nothing to those that followed them, but transcription of the same events, and new combinations of the same images. Whatever be the reason, it is commonly observed that the early writers are in possession of nature, and their followers of art; that the first excel in strength and invention, and the latter in elegance and refinement.[89]

So the habit of notionising the poet brings the problematic of 'rules' to it. The inherent unease coming from a complicated investment involving making rules, following rules, standardising rules and opposing rules make the poet a far more colourful creature than what inane understanding of neo-classicism would allow—a simmering antagonism between the idealising and generalising strain of reflective configuration. Caught in the complex dynamics of inward sense, imagination, reason, study and genius, the concept of a poet then becomes mostly about a poetics of 'launch'—an intensity and caution to launch beyond depths. Habit-formation is a complex game that hides constitutive forces more than we get to understand. The 'launch' in creative aesthetics is the *enargia* that builds around discretion, deference and daring. Launching not beyond depths then is riddled in an opposition where staying within depths is caution against the urge and the latency of surging beyond. Counting the petals of the tulip, watching the tulip, relishing the wholesome beauty, imaging and imagining a tulip, go into the making of the creativogenic society that holds on to its habits of creativity knowing well that the trans-factor is disturbingly present to push the frontiers of possibility and potency—the tulip poet always in retrospective and anticipative negotiations with the vatic, the seer, the platinum, the quantum and the transcendental poet.

Notes

1. Quoted from Martin C. Battestin, ed., Preface to Henry Fielding's *Joseph Andrews and Shamela* (Boston: Houghton Mifflin, 1961), xix.
2. See Stephen C. Behrendt, 'The Best Criticism: Imitation as Criticism in the Eighteenth Century', *The Eighteenth Century*, 24, no. 1 (Winter 1983), 4.
3. Maine de Biran, *The Influence of Habit on the Faculty of Thinking*, (trans.) Margaret Donaldson Boehm (Westport, Conn.: Greenwood Press, 1970), 47.
4. C. S. Pierce, 'How to Make Our Ideas Clear', in *The Essential Pierce: Selected Philosophical Writings*, (eds.) Nathan Houser and Christian J. W. Kloesel (Bloomington: Indiana University Press, 1992), 129.
5. Joseph Butler, *The Analogy of Religion, Natural and Revealed, to the Constitution and Course of Nature* (Oxford: Oxford University Press, 1907), 102.
6. Ernst Cassirer, *The Philosophy of the Enlightenment* (Boston: Beacon Press, 1955), 312.
7. 'Soliloquy; Or Advice to an Author', III. 3, *Characteristics of Men, Manners, Opinions, Times*, etc., (ed.) John M. Robertson (London, 1900), 228–29.
8. Robert Marsh, 'Shaftesbury's Theory of Poetry: The Importance of the "Inward Colloquy"' *ELH*, 28, no. 1 (Mar. 1961), 58.
9. 'Soliloquy', I. 3, 135.
10. Ibid., 136.
11. Marsh, 'Shaftesbury's Theory of Poetry', 65.
12. 'Soliloquy', II, 102.
13. Jerome Stolnitz, 'On the Significance of Lord Shaftesbury in Modern Aesthetic Theory' *The Philosophical Quarterly* 11, no. 43, (April 1961), 108.
14. *Characteristics*, 'Soliloquy or Advice to an Author,' Vol. I, 113. Quoted in Dabney Townsend, 'Shaftesbury's Aesthetic Theory' *The Journal of Aesthetics and Art Criticism*, 41, no. 2 (Winter 1982), 207.
15. Second Characters, 'Plastics,' 124; quoted in Townsend, 'Shaftesbury's Aesthetic Theory', 208.
16. *Characteristics*, 'Advice to an Author,' Vol. I, 207–08.
17. Ibid., 180–81.
18. Benjamin Rand (ed.) *Second Characters of the Language of Forms* (Cambridge: Cambridge University Press, 1914), 178.
19. *Characteristics*, I, 135–6. The comparison of the poet, or the artist, to God as Creator can be found, for instance, in George Puttenham's *The Art of English Poesy* (1589) or in Tasso's *Discorsi del poema eroico* (1594) or in Julius Caesar Scaligeri's *Poetics* (1561). In Scaligeri's big work, one reads this praise of poetry: 'But the poet makes another nature and other outcomes for men's acts, and finally in the same way makes himself another God, as it were. The other sciences are as it were users of what the Maker of them all produced; but poetry, when it so splendidly gives the appearance of the things that are and of those that are not, seems not to narrate the events as other sciences … do, but as another God to produce them; therefore the poets have got their name, which is common to them and Him, not through the agreement of men but through the providence

of nature'. See E. N. Tigerstedt, 'The Poet as Creator: Origins of a Metaphor' *Comparative Literature Studies*, 5, no. 4 (1968), 457.
20. R. L. Brett, *The Third Earl of Shaftesbury: A Study in Eighteenth-Century Literary Theory* (London: Hutchinson's University Library, 1951), 103–104.
21. See Andrew Ashfield, Peter de Bolla (ed.) *The Sublime: A Reader in British Eighteenth-Century Aesthetic Theory* (Cambridge: Cambridge University Press, 1996), 77. For more on this subject, see Marjorie Hope Nicolson, *Mountain Gloom and Mountain Glory: The Development of the Aesthetics of the Infinite* (Seattle: University of Washington Press, 1997), especially chapter 7, 'The Aesthetics of the Infinite', 271–323.
22. E. H. Hooker, *Critical Works of John Dennis* (Baltimore: Johns Hopkins University Press, 1943), 381.
23. Jeffrey Barnouw, 'The Morality of the Sublime: To John Dennis', *Comparative Literature*, 35, no. 1, (1983), 30.
24. R. L. Brett, 'The Third Earl of Shaftesbury as a Literary Critic', *The Modern Language Review*, 37, no. 2 (Apr. 1942), 133.
25. Ibid., 135.
26. See John Dennis, *Advancement and Reformation of Modern Poetry*, 1701, in *Critical Works of John Dennis* (ed.) E. H. Hooker (Baltimore: Johns Hopkins University Press, 1943), I, 202.
27. Shawcross, *Biographia Literaria*, I, 202.
28. R. L. Brett, *The Third Earl of Shaftesbury: A Study in Eighteenth-Century Literary Theory* (London: Hutchinson's University Library, 1951), 116.
29. John M. Aden, 'Dryden and the Imagination: The first Phase' *PMLA*, 74, no. 1 (Mar. 1959), 28.
30. W. P. Ker (ed.) *The Essays of John Dryden* (Oxford: Clarendon Press, 1900), 121.
31. See Clarence Dewitt Thorpe, 'Addison and Hutcheson on the Imagination', 2, no. 3 (Nov. 1935), 219.
32. Ibid., 224.
33. *Spectator*, No. 417.
34. Thorpe, 'Addison and Hutcheson on the Imagination', 227.
35. See B. B. Das & J. M. Mohanty (eds.) *Literary Criticism: A Reading* (New Delhi: Oxford University Press, 1985), 24.
36. See Mary E. Hazard, 'The Anatomy of Liveliness as a Concept in Renaissance Aesthetics', *The Journal of Aesthetics and Art Criticism*, 33, no. 4 (Summer 1975), 408.
37. Preface to *An Evening's Love*, in *Of Dramatic Poesy and Other Critical Essays*, (ed.) George Watson, 2 vols. (London, 1962), I, 155.
38. See John C. Sherwood, 'Dryden and the Critical Theories of Tasso' *Comparative Literature*, 1, no. 4 (Autumn 1966), 353.
39. Sherwood, 'Dryden and the Critical Theories of Tasso', 354.
40. Robert Hume, 'Dryden on Creation: Imagination in the Later Criticism', *The Review of English Studies,* 21, no. 83 (Aug. 1970), 308.
41. 'A Parallel Betwixt Painting and Poetry,' in *Of Dramatic Poesy and Other Critical Essays* (ed.) Watson, II, 203.
42. *Preface to Albion and Albanius*, in Watson, *Of Dramatic Poesy and Other Critical Essays*, II, 40.

43. Thomas H. Fujimura, 'Dryden's Poetics: The Expressive Values in Poetry', *The Journal of English and Germanic Philology*, 74, no. 2 (Apr. 1975), 203–04.
44. See Watson, *Of Dramatic Poesy and Other Critical Essays*, II, 235. Through the inevitable trans-(in)fusionist apercus, Dryden's conative tension in his habits of studium and grace—what I call the poetics of launching—gets operatively close to some classical and medieval Arabic aesthetic criticism that problematises poetic excellence through a dialectical understanding of naturalness and embellishment in poetry and the conceptual attrition within the truthful-untruthful paradigm of poetry. In fact, views differed over the politics of transmission, selectability, compliance with classical norms or methods of the early poets, verifiability of poetic indulgences, figurative exaggeration and poetic resonance. Habits of poetic doing throws the group that supports untruthfulness and excess in creativity against the group that accentuates poetic embellishment and order. See Mansour Ajami, *The Neckveins of Winter: The Controversy over Natural and Artificial Poetry in Medieval Arabic Literary Criticism*, (Leiden: E.J. Brill, 1984), chapter 1 'Polarization of the Issue', 1–50.
45. *The Literary Mind and the Carving of Dragons* (trans. & annotated) Vincent Yu-chung Shih (Hong Kong: The Chinese University Press, 1983), xxxv.
46. See Keith Walker (ed.) *John Dryden the Major Works* (Oxford: Oxford University Press, 1987), 124.
47. Hoyt Trowbridge, 'The Place of Rules in Dryden's Criticism', *Modern Philology*, 44, no. 2 (Nov. 1946), 90.
48. Ker (ed.) *The Essays of John Dryden*, I, 79.
49. See Irving Ribner, 'Dryden's Shakespearean Criticism and the Neo-Classical Paradox', *The Shakespeare Association Bulletin*, 21, no. 4 (Oct. 1946), 170.
50. Preface to *The State of Innocence and Fall of Man* (1674), V, 121. See John Olin Eidson, 'Dryden's Criticism of Shakespeare', *Studies in Philology*, 33, no. 2 (Apr. 1936), 278.
51. Raymond D. Havens, 'Johnson's Distrust of the Imagination' *ELH*, 10, no. 3 (Sep. 1943), 253.
52. Quoted in William L Pressly, *The Artist as Original Genius: Shakespeare's "Fine Frenzy" in Late Eighteenth-century British Art* (Newark: University of Delaware Press, 2007), 28.
53. Ibid., 29.
54. Floyd W. Martin, 'Sir Joshua Reynolds's "Invention": Intellectual Activity as a Foundation of Art' *Art Education*, 40, no. 6 (Nov. 1987), 7.
55. See Geoffrey Tillotson & Brian Jenkins (ed.) *Samuel Johnson: The History of Rasselas* (Oxford: Oxford University Press, 1977), 28. Tulip gets the longest definition—a 263-word account—in Johnson's *Dictionary*.
56. Robert Folkenflik provides further contexts for Johnson's tulip. In the botanical semiotics of the day, the tulip was assumed to be a highly individualised flower (no two tulips were alike), and it connoted gaudiness, extravagance and needless luxury, even sinfulness. The tulip is an epitome of individuality and particularity. Poems by Richard Leigh and Cowley, which Johnson must surely have read, are devoted to tulips and their numerous streaks—one thinks again of Johnson's complaint that the metaphysicals dwelt too much on particulars and thus perverted the function of poetry. Pronouncements similar to *Rasselas* X can be found in the "Preface to Shakespeare" and in the *Lives of the Poets*. In the "Life of Cowley" Johnson explains why the metaphysical poets failed to

reach sublime conceptions: "Sublimity is produced by aggregation, and littleness by dispersion. Great thoughts are always general, and consist in positions not limited by exceptions, and in descriptions not descending to minuteness."' See Jose Angel Garcia Landa, '"The Enthusiastick Fit": The Function and Fate of the Poet in Johnson's *Rasselas*', 1991, https://dialnet.unirioja.es/descarga/articulo/69021.pdf Accessed 25.11.2015.
57. *Rambler* No. 36.
58. Boswell, *Life of Johnson* (ed.) G. B. Hill, rev. L. F. Powell (Oxford: Oxford University Press, 1934); see Arieh Sachs, 'Generality and Particularity in Johnson's Thought', *Studies in English Literature*, 1500–1900, 5, no. 3 (Summer 1965), 494–95.
59. See Sachs, 'Generality and Particularity in Johnson's Thought', 495. In *Idler* No. 5, Johnson writes: 'Of all extensive and complicated objects, different parts are selected by different eyes; and minds are variously affected as they vary their attention'.
60. W.P. Albrecht, *Hazlitt and the Creative Imagination* (Lawrence: University of Kansas Press, 1965), 68–69.
61. Ibid., 79.
62. See '"The Enthusiastick Fit": The Function and Fate of the Poet in Johnson's *Rasselas*' https://www.unizar.es/departamentos/filologia_inglesa/garciala/publicaciones/enthusiastick.html.
63. William Youngren, 'Dr. Johnson, Joseph Warton, and the "Theory of Particularity"', *Dispositio*, 4, no. 11/12, Change and Stability (Verano-Otoño 1979), 165; also see Youngren's 'Generality, Science and Poetic Language in the Restoration,' *ELH*, XXXV (1968), 158–87. See W. R. Keast, 'Johnson's Criticism of the Metaphysical Poets,' *ELH*, XVII (1950), 59–70; David Perkins, 'Johnson on Wit and Metaphysical poetry', *ELH*, XX, 1953, 200–17.
64. *Rambler* No. 36.
65. 'Preface to Shakespeare', 18. See D. J. Enright, and E.D. Chickera (ed.) *English Critical Texts: 16th to 20th Century* (Oxford: Oxford University Press, 1962).
66. 'The use of the word "genio" started about 1550 with painter-writers like Leonardo, Vasari, and Telesio. By 1700, according to Lange-Eichbaum, the word "genius" acquired the meaning of an "incomprehensible and mysterious force animating certain human beings." It was generally applied, however, to the individuals manifesting this force'. See Silvano Arieti, *Creativity: The Magic Synthesis* (New York: Basic Books, 1976), 293.
67. Jean le Rond d'Alembert, 'Discours preliminaire des editeurs,' *Encyclopedie, ou Dictionnaire Raisonne des Sciences, des Arts et des Metiers, Par une Societe de Gens de Lettres*, 17 vols. (Paris, 1751–65), Vol. 1, xvi. Quoted in Kineret S. Jaffe, 'The Concept of Genius: Its Changing Role in Eighteenth-Century French Aesthetics', *Journal of the History of Ideas*, 41, no. 4 (Oct.–Dec. 1980), 590.
68. See Herbert Dicckmann, 'Diderot's Conception of Genius', *Journal of the History of Ideas*, 2, no. 2 (Apr., 1941), 155; also see Otis E. Fellows, 'The Theme of Genius in Diderot's Neveu de Rameau' *Diderot Studies*, 2 (1952), 168–199.
69. Jaffe, 'The Concept of Genius: Its Changing Role in Eighteenth-Century French Aesthetics', 594; see Margaret Gilman, 'Imagination and Creation in Diderot,' *Diderot Studies*, 2 (1952), 200–20. Also see chapter 2 'Genius Obscured: Diderot', in Ann Jefferson, *Genius in France: An Idea and its Uses* (Princeton, N.J.: Princeton University Press, 2015), 35–44.

70. James Mall, 'Le Neveu de Rameau and the Idea of Genius' *Eighteenth-Century Studies*, 11, no. 1 (Autumn 1977), 28–29.
71. Morris Weitz, *Problems in Aesthetics* (New York: Macmillan, 1959) 46–7.
72. R. R. Wark, *Discourses on Art* (New Haven, Conn.: Yale University Press, 1975), 50.
73. Alexander Gerard, *An Essay on Genius* (ed.) Bernhard Fabian (Munchen: Wilhelm Fink Verlag, 1966), 27, 37.
74. Ibid., 38.
75. James Engell, *The Creative Imagination: Enlightenment to Romanticism* (Cambridge, Mass.: Harvard University Press, 1981), 82.
76. For description of genius as glorious enthusiasm see John Gilbert Cooper, *Letters Concerning Taste* (London, 1755).
77. Bernhard Fabian (ed.) *An Essay on Genius*, xxvi.
78. George J. Buelow, 'Originality, Genius, Plagiarism in English Criticism of the Eighteenth Century' *International Review of the Aesthetics and Sociology of Music*, 21, no. 2 (Dec. 1990), 125.
79. See *Charles Batteux: The Fine Arts Reduced to a Single Principle* (translation with an introduction) James O Young (Oxford: Oxford University Press, 2015).
80. Walter John Hipple, Jr. *The Beautiful, The Sublime, & the Picturesque in Eighteenth-Century British Aesthetic Theory* (Carbondale: The Southern Illinois University Press, 1957), 70.
81. Hipple, *The Beautiful, The Sublime, & the Picturesque in Eighteenth-Century British Aesthetic Theory*, 77.
82. Dominique Bouhours, 1705, *The Art of Criticism*, (ed.) Philip Smallwood (Delmar, NY: Scholar's Facsimiles & Reprints, 1981) 227. Jean-Baptiste Du Bos, *Critical Reflections on Poetry, Painting and Music*, (trans.) T. Nugent (London: John Nourse, 1748). He speaks of the ability of the genius through a plant metaphor which is more organic and assimilative and deterministic. http://plato.stanford.edu/entries/aesthetics-18th-french/. Accessed 17.12.2015.
83. Gerard, *An Essay on Genius*, 63–5.
84. *Discourse* IV, 167–171; quoted in Martin, 'Sir Joshua Reynolds's "Invention": Intellectual Activity as a Foundation of Art', 8.
85. Weitz, *Problems in Aesthetics*, 44.
86. Ibid.
87. Ibid., 38.
88. Quoted in Walter John Hipple, *The Beautiful, The Sublime, & the Picturesque in Eighteenth-Century British Aesthetic Theory*, 145.
89. *Rasselas*, X, 60. See *Samuel Johnson: Rasselas, Poems, and Selected Prose* (ed.) Bertrand H. Bronson (New York, 1952). Imlac makes the following points in Chapter 10: 1. Poetry is considered the highest learning, and is accorded 'a veneration approaching to that which man would pay to the Angelick Nature'. 2. Ancient poets are regarded as the best, and possess nature while later poets possess art. 3. No man is great by imitation of art alone, and so one must regard nature and life as well. 4. No kind of knowledge is to be overlooked; all appearances of nature are to be utilized for … 5. 'the inforcement or decoration of moral or religious truth' and 6. the purpose of gratifying his 'reader with remote allusions and unexpected instruction'. 7. The poet examines the species, not the individual; general properties, large appearances, the 'prominent and striking features as recall the original to every mind'. He accordingly neglects 'the

minuter discriminations'. 8. He must also know 'all the modes of life, ... all the passions in all their combinations, and trace the changes of the human mind as they are modified by various institutions and accidental influences of climate or custom'. 9. 'He must divest himself of the prejudices of his age or country' and work towards the 'general and transcendental truths which will always be the same'. 10. He will thus 'contemn the applause of his own time, and commit his claims [to fame] to the justice of posterity'. 11. He is 'the interpreter of nature, and the legislator of mankind,' and presides 'over the thoughts and manners of future generations'. 12. He must know many languages and sciences, and must practice his craft in order to acquire 'every delicacy of speech and grace of harmony'. See Howard D. Weinbrot, 'The Reader, the General, and the Particular: Johnson and Imlac in Chapter Ten of Rasselas', *Eighteenth-Century Studies*, 5, no. 1 (Autumn 1971), 84.

5 'Fearful Symmetry'
Quantum Creativity

To know is in its very essence a verb active.

—Samuel Taylor Coleridge[1]

Coleridge often spoiled a book; but in the course of doing this, he enriched that book with so many and so valuable notes, tossing about him, with such lavish profusion, from such a cornucopia of discursive reading, and such a fusing intellect, commentaries so many-angled and so many-coloured that I have envied many a man whose luck has placed him in the way of such injuries …

—Thomas de Quincey[2]

'The poet stands in the ruins', writes Michael Joyce, 'it is the modernist moment. But no, this is not, what we see. The poet makes his way into the ruins, and in so moving the movement in itself reads barrier as gate. What he reads he writes. Against the unassigned space of the dark building—let us call this space the screen—crossed boards read as sign and juncture, axis and nullification, light on light. A gutted foyer no longer opens to another space but is the space of its own opening. Yet in movement the outward dark gives way to memory and metonymy, to multiplicity, the one continually replacing the other. In this crossing "here" and "there" are interwoven as is ivy. Or wire'.[3] Samuel Taylor Coleridge is *here* and *there* with a mind steeped in trans-habit, a quantum mind caught in contrariety, serpentinity and a meandering corridor of interests, desires and provocations. This is a universe of a mind where apparent nonentitites inhere in an interrelatedness, where 'one cannot uproot a flower without disturbing the stars'.[4] Afflicted by opium, inflicted by abstruse research interests[5] and, smitten by the enticing paradox of life and imagination, Coleridge works out a quantum notion of a poet that stays submitted to a complexity phenomenon—interstitial, interstellar and intermediary.[6] Contestation between states of mind signaturises Coleridge's thinking and, hence, 'unconflicted thought' can never be a reality.[7] When a mind shares its thinking and philosophic space with 'chemists and physicists, medical men, politicians of every stripe, farmers, tanners, lawyers, painters and musicians, publishers, newspaper editors and journalists, civil, servants, clerks, housewives, innkeepers, teachers and children, parsons and professors, as well as poets and novelists and an assortment of the *literati*',[8] we can easily understand the accumulated potency of contrariety that creativity inheres and quantumises to deliver. The poet then shows his interest in all kinds of disciplines of life and life forms—a 'myriad-mindedness', a phrase that he used in reference to Shakespeare. The energy of such a mind oscillates between the commonplace and the supernatural, the wonderful and mundane, the strange and strenuous, grammar and imagination, logic and hypothesis—'I am a Starling self-incaged, & always in the Moult,' he laments to Godwin on 22 January 1802, '& my whole Note is, Tomorrow, & tomorrow, & tomorrow'.[9] A psychologist for whom every fact and idea has a relational potency to a greater happening, relishing the disparate, the irrational and the unbounded remained a life-long commitment. A poet, thus, by staying a participant in all flights and foundations of life produces gestaltist ways of understanding—a morphogenetic growth that lives both a manifest and implicate order in the deep whirl of trans-habit.

I

Whenever Coleridge attempts to define poetry, he almost always turns his attention not to the finished product, but to its etiology in the poet and looks into the nature and play of the mental faculties in its composition. Espousing the inherent discordance in things, the poet's mind catches the generative tension and tries to dissolve the individual identities to create a composite new whole.

The imagination, in creating poetry, therefore, echoes the creative principle underlying the universe. Conversely, the whole universe, both in its continuous generation in the 'Infinite I am' and in the repetition of that act in the process of perception by individual human mind, may be said to consist, just as a good poem does, in the productive resolution of contraries and disparates.[10]

With a significant allegiance to the Pythagorean asunder-unity thesis, Coleridge finds opposition and composition in the poet's mind. In his *Lectures on the History of Philosophy*, he observes:

> One cannot help thinking, provided the mind is beforehand impressed with a belief of a providence guiding this great drama of the world to its conclusion, that, as opposites are in constant tendency to union, and as it is the opposites poles of a magnet and not the similar ones which attract each other, that a certain unity is to be expected from the very circumstance of opposition and that these are as it were imperfect halves which after a series of ages each maturing and perfecting are at length to meet in some one point comprising the excellences of both.[11]

This is not the Augustinian ideal where art looks for a 'higher unity'. To the Augustinian mind, the aesthetic object is an illumination of *congruentia partium* in number, form, unity and order which are also expressional, shining out in beauty. For Augustine, the emphasis on *number* does not 'fall into the error of reducing all the aesthetic constituents to formal numerical relations, the kind of reduction which has tempted those who have tried to find in art geometrical laws, the golden section etc'.[12] Number, then, as a principle marks the arrangement of parts, be it equal and unequal, with the teleology of concordance and integration. In the nature of judgement, Augustine brings the *a priori* standard, the presupposition of an ideal order, which the artist aspires to reach and the critic normatively uses as a touchstone. For Coleridge, the artist begins from disunity—an inherent opposition of laws and objects—and, desires for a maturity, a development coming through a productive conjugation whose laws are not inscribed in any presuppositiveness. With an undertow of trans-habit, the poet for Coleridge is caught between the monist and diversitarian—the 'love of variety' contraposed with the 'love of uniformity'. However, forming the composite whole— the unremitting strife to effect a resolution of disparates—is a difficult art needing spontaneity and deliberation, spontaneous impulse and voluntary purpose.[13] What Seamus Perry attributes as an unhappy love with plurality, I call it Coleridge's innate settlement in trans-habit. Perry argues that Coleridge's thinking 'habitually seeks to correct into oneness the apparently incorrigible plurality continually rediscovered in the sharpness of his senses; while (to look at the predicament from the other end), in the teeth of his commitment to universality and oneness, diversity and particularity continue to exert their interest so that, in practice, the unity which he proclaims so vociferously is typically submerged by the protracted exhibition of the contradictory elements he is meant to be to bringing together. This is not just an oblique way of embracing heterogeneity after all; it is trying to have things both ways'.[14] Coleridge's poet revels in the heterogeneity without the sense of something 'one and indivisible', a faith in the abilities of all things to 'counterfeit infinity'. The poet must have the ear of a wild Arab listening in the silent Desert; he has to have the eye of a North American Indian trying to trace the footsteps of an enemy upon the leaves that lie strewn upon the forest floor; he needs to have the touch of a blind man who feels the face of a darling child.[15] So a true poet writes 'from a principle *within*, independent of everything without. The work of a true poet, in its form, its shapings, and modifications is distinguished from all other works that assume to belong to the class of poetry, as a *natural* from an *artificial* flower; or as the mimic garden of a child from an enameled meadow'.[16] He is the man who 'carries the simplicity of childhood into the powers of manhood; who, with a soul unsubdued by habit, unshackled by custom, contemplates all things with the *freshness and wonder* of a child; and, connecting with it the inquisitive powers of riper years, adds, as far as he can find knowledge, admiration; and where knowledge no longer permits admiration, gladly sinks back again into the childlike feeling of devout *wonder*'.[17] It is in poetry that extremes meet—'opposition is a tendency to re-union'[18]—where truths are the most 'awful and mysterious' and yet of universal interest, but are 'too often considered as so true that they lose all the powers of truth, and lie bed ridden in the dormitory of the soul, side by side with the most despised and exploded errors'.[19] So the inbuilt power of contrariety in poetic truths would project the dynamic depths of the unconscious ('sunless sea' in "Kubla Khan"), deep and quiet sensibility, higher intellectual power and the corresponding energy of the lower, all coming together 'as in a war embrace', to effect the *grace* of creation—the 'damsel with the dulcimer'.

> ... He must out of his own create forms according to the severe laws of the intellect, in order to generate in himself that coordination of freedom and law, that involution of obedience in the prescript, and of the prescript in the impulse to obey, which assimilates him to nature, and enables him to understand her, that his own spirit which has the same ground with nature, may learn her unspoken language in its main radicals, before to approaches to her endless compositions of them.[20]

The balancing act of the poet's mind—the 'mental alembic'[21]—as symptomatised through Kubla Khan whose dream is a 'miracle of rare device' ("Kubla Khan", ll. 31–6), becomes a commandeering power that negotiates with the chaos of the world without having to return with a view or understanding that shall have a 'satisfying degree of clearness, distinctness, and individuality'. The poem as a quasi-natural organism constellates in an 'instant'—a deeply troubled investigation into the ordering principle enjoying a latent habitation in a muddle.

For Coleridge, 'deep thinking' is 'attainable only by a man of deep Feeling'—the true inward creatrix works on the relational principle existing between the dignity of passiveness and worthy activity 'when men shall be as proud within themselves of having remained an hour in a state of deep tranquil Emotion, whether in reading or in hearing or in looking'. Deep thinking as generative of poetic creativity knows how the activity of the mind is not a mere bluster but about staying broadly awake even when there is a stir of the tempest and having understanding, retentiveness and receptivity as its glorious byproducts.[22] The poet's mind—tensional situatedness in dialectic and organism—does not revel in chaos but is accepting of chaos and yet not shy of exploring a coherence. Coleridge writes: 'I seem to myself to behold in the quiet objects, on which I am gazing, more than an arbitrary illustration, more than a mere simile, the work of my own fancy. I feel an awe, as if there were before my eyes the same power as that of the reason—the same power in a lower dignity, and therefore a symbol established in the truth of things'.[23] In *Aids to Reflection*, Coleridge sees the power of poetic origination in a discontinuity where 'every appearance of origination in Nature is but a shadow of our own casting'.[24] That Coleridge, cast into the continuity/unity-discontinuity-muddle dialectic, could not produce a systematic philosophy of creativity is what for me distinguishes him and, in fact, contributes to his unique conception of the poet. Coleridge thought over—persistent and protracted—the goings-on of Coleridge the thinker, a kind of Coleridge on Coleridge himself awaiting a 'looking abroad'. The poet mind works both on external observations, experiences and inner associations which achieves points of entangled manifestation. There is a speculative bias to creativity and the associational churches ring a bell of meaning despite their apparent discordance. On a trans-habit axis, a short musing on Paul Valery's engagement with 'intimation' (what Graham Wallas calls 'fringe consciousness') can be interesting. W. N. Ince argues that the 'poet senses that there is potential poetic material (a solution to a problem, an idea, a rhythm, a rhyme, a new development in the poem) just 'round the corner', psychologically speaking, which he will probably be able to seize if he waits a while until this fringe-consciousness becomes focal'. The poet muse brings to bear for this capture a certain will and effort. The fringe-consciousness has to be coaxed into fuller and clearer existence. He must avoid letting it disappear, as it might easily if it is not coaxed and if he does not immediately jot down all suggestions which come into his full focal consciousness. Valery's manuscripts reveal this jotting down of suggestions and provisionally accepted findings more abundantly than is the case with many poets. Rudolf Arnheim notes: 'the indefiniteness of words...suggest that the literary recording of an experience resembles, in its first stages, the trapping of an insect with a large net. The little animal is being confined to a limited area but not yet pinned to a specific spot. The work sheets show how the poet closes in gradually on the adequate formulation'.[25] The poet's art cannot thrive without a 'waking reality', the murmur and might of the unconscious. In his 'Treatise on Logic' Coleridge sees unconscious as a consequence of a 'primary mental act' and endowed with the property of 'synthetic unity'.[26] This makes Coleridge rely on intuitionism to see how by looking into one's own nature the connection between art and life can be produced and understood—'intuition or immediate Beholding' mingles with 'art of reasoning' and 'acts of abstraction'. This is not a representative Image or an intellectual notion or a perception of a thing but clearly 'an intuitive process—It and Time, the *Intuitus puri et omnis perceptionis formae universales*'.[27] In *The Friend*, Coleridge observes:

> The groundwork, therefore, of all pure speculation is the full apprehension of the difference between the contemplation of reason, namely, that intuition of things which arises when we possess ourselves, as one with the whole, which is substantial knowledge, and that which presents itself when, transferring reality to the negations of reality, to the ever varying framework of the uniform life, we think of ourselves as separated beings, and place nature in antithesis to mind, as object to subject, thing to thought, death to life. This is abstract knowledge, or the science of the mere understanding. By the former, we know that existence is its own predicate, self-affirmation, the one attribute in which all others are contained, not as parts, but as manifestations. It is an eternal and infinite self-rejoicing, self-loving, with a joy fathomable, with a love all comprehensive. It is absolute; the absolute

> is neither singly that which affirms, nor that which is affirmed; but the identity and living *copula* of both.[28]

It is in the living copula that contrariety resides and the poet's quantum habit owes to the experience and exploration of what Perry calls the 'muddle'.[29] Perry calls this the 'good muddle' with an informal and determining structure amidst 'conflicting callings or visions of reality', rising above 'the indignity of a sheerly incoherent mess: it comes from entertaining incompatible ideas about the one subject'.[30] The poet knows that there would be occasions where the 'contrary would be true' and aesthetic rhythm is operatively serpentine having its own climaxes and lows—'the reader should be carried forward ... by the pleasureable activity of mind excited by the attractions of the journey itself. Like the motion of a serpent, which the Egyptians made the emblem of intellectual power; or like the path of sound through the air; at every step he pauses and half recedes, and from the retrogressive movement collects the force which again carries him onward'.[31] Serpentinity and sinuousness are deeply inscribed in Coleridge's aesthetic thinking analogising the motion of the serpent as the working of the poet's mind, his inventive faculty, the genius. George Gilpin explains that

> Coleridge may have understood creativity to take a spiraling form because of the Cartesian view that in the beginning God set going the primary matter of the cosmos which by inevitable mechanical laws of fluid motion took the form of whirlpools or vortices from which the earth and other heavenly bodies were born. Coleridge's concept may have been reinforced by his reading of the Divine Comedy in which Dante ascends the mountain of Purgatory to Paradise as if on a spiral staircase. Certainly William Blake in illustrating Dante's poem conceived of the path in this way, and in the water color "Jacob's Ladder" he pictured the intellectual progress of man to heaven as a spiral staircase with five turns. Perhaps because of similar sources in Descartes and Dante, Coleridge applied the metaphor of the spiral staircase to human thought in a manner remarkably like Blake.[32]

This tendrillar and wound pattern of thinking and, hence feeling, exude high energy which calls for the reconciling and mediatory power of imagination, the 'self-circling energies of the reason', giving birth to a system of symbols, harmonious in themselves, and consubstantial with the truths of which they are the conductors'.[33] In an intertwined state with the Apollonian dream and the Dionysiac depth, we encounter a pain in the poetic consciousness—a state of the *daemonic*. A romantic vision becomes a well-endowed response to such a condition of mind, raising hopes of substantiating imagination by anchoring it in the divine ground of being.[34] Working on the concept of 'demonic', Mark Kipperman sees the word as strangely ambivalent. The poetic mind inflicted by the demonic demonstrates 'infinite assertion of self-will' and going by Schelling's reading of the self the mind cannot evade the intrusion of the 'dark *un*conscious remainder'.[35] Coleridge finds the freedom of the creative self-turning against itself through an overpowering higher self whose identity is never revealed in full. The deep contrariety is a 'dialectic of love'[36]—the outward and inward movement occurring in strange simultaneity. This is a smorgasbord of imagination, quest, the demonic, love, tension and opposition that is both therapeutic and instable, hence, ontologically disturbing.

Trans-habit gets us to situate the poetic mind as 'daimonic thinking' within Lui Xie's idea of imagination (*xiangxiang*) as found in *Wenxindiaolong*. Shuen-Fu Lin points out that the word *shen* in *shensi* carries a double meaning: 'on the one hand, it qualifies *si* or thinking as an activity of a person's *jingshen* (spirit) that resides in his mind-heart. On the other hand, it also connotes that this *si* has a marvellous, unfathomable, or daimonic quality'.[37] Quite appropriately, Coleridge would appreciate the unruly power of imagination—the Platonic daimon—but not without the contrary awareness of being ruined by its restlessness. This translates into an urgency about 'literary thinking' (*the wen zhi si*) and the resultant contrariety successfully foregrounds Coleridge's insistence to grow the unifying habit of secondary imagination under hauntings and shadows. Coleridge allowed the 'daimon to roam with things' working on thing-images and idea-images: 'things coast along the ear and eye, language governs the pivot and sill of the door [to their perception by the daimon]. When the pivot and sill allow passage, things do not conceal any aspect of their appearance. When the bolt to the gate is obstructed, the daimon vanishes from the mind-heart'.[38] The daimon is the organising power of the poet's mind—the shaping spirit of imagination. It is not a tranquillity that puts a statis on figurative process; tranquillity (*jing*) inspires 'roaming' but not in uncontrollable chaos.

II

The energy of Imagination distinguishes the poet's mind with the Blakean claim that 'Every Eye sees differently. As the Eye, Such the object'.[39] Writing to Revd Dr. Trusler (23 August 1799), Blake notes:

> I see Every thing I paint In this World, but Every body does not see alike. The tree which moves some to tears of joy is in the Eyes of others only a Green thing that stands in the way. But to the Eyes of the Man of Imagination, Nature is Imagination itself. As a man is, so he Sees. As the Eye is formed, such are its Powers.[40]

For Coleridge the seeing—it is a 'Window concerning Sight'[41]—is infused with energy, a spiraling consciousness to explore the heterogeneity, the goings-on of the environing muddle: Isaiah answered: I saw no God, nor heard any, in a finite organical perception; but my senses discover'd the infinite in every thing …'.⁴² When Coleridge said that the reader of poetry is carried forward by the pleasurable activity of the mind which is excited by the attractions of the journey itself, he is merely pointing at the electricity in the poet's mind that seizes the reader in an intensified pleasure. Mind and nature have a gap to overcome and nature almost always exceeds the abilities of the mind. The poet's art is a unity in multeity: this penchant for organicity makes Coleridge's reason read romantic. This is not practical reason but a process where the whole soul of man is brought into activity 'with the subordination of its faculties to each other, according to their relative worth and dignity'.⁴³ A contrariety is constructed around a sea of flux and the poet's mind seeking organic unity and intelligibility produces a vitality that informs creation.

Here, in a trans-poetical moment, the formative powers of imagination in Coleridge's poetics find a connect with Gaston Bachelard's philosophy of dynamic imagination as a becoming power that de-forms and trans-forms images; it has the demon of excess in it, the aspiring power, the transcending ability similar to Coleridge's secondary imagination which, however, comes with its unease and exemplarity: 'the poetic function is to give a new form to the world which poetically exists only if it is unceasingly reimagined'.⁴⁴ Edward Kaplan argues that 'contemplation is a creative inwardness which takes the world as a companion. Finally—not primarily—the contemplator sees the world somewhat objectively in representation, according to the surface imagination of forms. Only after experiencing the rich depth of the spectacle—and at the same time his own depth—does the poetic spectator truly place himself in the world'.⁴⁵ The oneiric dimension of the poet's mind makes its own distinctions between objective knowledge and the unconscious, producing an affective commitment that transforms the object which Bachelard calls 'valorization'. I see a passionate love for valorization in Coleridge's *homoaleator* too—'all forms are furnished with movement'⁴⁶— resulting in a freedom which is intrinsic and transformatory of ways by which we intersubjectivise the world. In a Bachelardian spirit, he swoops on the intermediary zone that mines the dialectic of being and nonbeing: the dynamicity of oneiric imaginative ability makes him live not in the nonbeing and unfailingly everywhere—here and there—in a vibrant and vital inside. For both Coleridge and Bachelard, the imagination strives towards a 'syncopation of contrary elements' which Bachelard 'demonstrates in his graphic analysis of the fascination shown by artists for images of "roundness" (the synthesis of horizontal and vertical impulses), "androgeny" (the synthesis of the animus and the anima), and "cosmic harmony" (the synthesis of the *natura naturans* and the *natura naturata*)'.⁴⁷ In *La Terre et les reveries du Repos*, Bachelard sees in imagination the integrating powers of the tree: 'it is root and branch. It lives between earth and sky. Imagination lives in the earth and in the wind. The imaginative tree is imperceptively the cosmological tree, the tree which summarises a universe, which makes a universe'.⁴⁸ Coleridge sought the summarising powers of imagination to effect a roundness of understanding, a desire for integration which he was convinced imagination was capable of without forgetting the reality of a counter-force. He observes:

> They and they only can acquire the philosophic imagination, the sacred power of self-intuition, who within themselves can interpret and understand the symbol, that the wings of the air-sylph are forming within the skin of the caterpillar; those only, who feel in their own spirits the same instinct, which impels the chrysalis of the horned fly to leave room in its involucrum for antennae yet to come. They know and feel, that the *potential* works *in* them, even as the *actual* works on them![49]

The creative muddle is also a sort of reverie with a *potential* and *actual* in it where the 'not' does not function because heterogeneity is welcome.

If Coleridge employs the figure of camera obscura to illustrate a passive way of thinking—a critique of Hartley's associationist theory[50]—he also 'invokes the optical mechanism to suggest a mode of writing that exceeds representation' which he connects with poetic imagination.[51] The poet's mind cannot be a 'caput mortuum' that Coleridge was apprehensive photography might reduce it to, disabling its active processual powers. His anxiety with photography much before it became a reality in 1839—its modes of operation, representation and the subject-object divide—betrays a phobic consciousness that is disinclined to feel diminutive and disingenuous. Representation is feared to collapse into an organised set of things without the stir of an active mental principle, a reconfigurative power of the mind, reducing the poet to a 'poor worthless I'.[52] The prospect of rigidified representation akin to the despotism of the eye appals Coleridge for it is the mind of the poet which is ontologically enticing. Poetic imagination unfixes the principles of representation—melting inflexible units into a 'living meaning' ('Eisenoplasy') with passion. Analogous to Kant's cognitive and aesthetic imagination, Coleridge sees primary and secondary imagination as one that is ruled and the other is not. If reason is romantic this dimension of not being ruled cannot be unruly. Robert Hume explains that Coleridge never denies the

> solidity or importance of the conceptual world; secondary Imagination does not supersede Reason, but provides an alternative to it. Conceptual and imaginative constructs of reality are not mutually exclusive; neither destroys the other. Thus when in "This Lime-Tree Bower My Prison" Coleridge sees trees and yet much more than just that, the knowledge that he is looking at trees in no way spoils his intuition or diminishes its significance for him.[53]

It is the productive faculty of cognition that creates another nature out of the material that actual nature gives it—a remoulding experience that does not merely function in correspondence with analogical laws but is inscribed in principles in reason. Kant points out that

> the poet ventures to realize to sense, rational ideas of invisible beings, the kingdom of the blessed, hell, eternity, creation, etc.; or even if he deals with things of which there are examples in experience—e.g. death, envy and all vices, also love, fame, and the like—he tries, by means of imagination, which emulates the play of reason in its quest after a maximum, to go beyond the limits of experience and to present them to sense with a completeness of which there is no example in nature. This is properly speaking the art of the poet, in which the faculty of aesthetical ideas can manifest itself in its entire strength.[54]

Reflective judgement, for Kant, is grounded in imagination, and based on the judgement of taste, imagination opens up the possibility of an intersubjective dialogue. So the functioning of imagination brings about an association with others. The poetic mind embedded in the muddle cannot stay disinterested from intersubjectivity. It is *geist* that endows its own forms of expression providing an enlivening principle of the mind.[55] In fact, Kant finds the spirit of an art as a systematic method which contains a comprehensive idea (*zusammenhangende*). Cassirer prefers to render it as 'soul'.

> *Geist* is simply that which brings about this harmony of the faculties of the mind (subjective or formal purposiveness). It gives life to the work of art, and a work of art which is *ohne Geist* is lifeless since, although in accordance with the rules of taste, its representation does not make us feel the harmonious relation of our mental powers. As long as the artist does no more than not disobey the rules of taste he cannot produce a genuine work of art. He himself is soulless (*ohne Geist*). What he lacks is *Geist,* the animating principle of the mind.[56]

It thus produces the harmonious motions of the powers of the mind (*was die Gemiits Krafte zweckmassig in Schwung versetzt*) and, it is through genius that a coordinating relationship between imagination and understanding can be wrought. This shows itself in the enunciation or expression of aesthetical ideas and in contradistinction to reproductive or the productive imagination thus, represents the imagination as 'free'. The poet as the genius revels in the free employment of his cognitive faculties and for Kant the cognitive importance of aesthetic ideas can be located in their unparaphrasability and transphenomenal application. The poet's aesthetic ideas are both definite thought and not completely intelligible too—the sensibility and supersensible in a difficult, not strictly ruled bound, relationship. Somewhere, the dissipative and recreative power of the imagination connects as much with communicative intelligence as with the unconscious, enabling an obscure impulse to become 'a bright, and clear, and living Idea'.[57]

Coleridge's aesthetic idea relates to Kant's indeterminate judgement opening a course of thinking where imagination furthers man's thinking and representations, presences and experiences do not have much to offer or suggest. Habits of creativity owe to aesthetic intuition, a reconstruction of the past, a heterogeneity in understanding and taste and certain forms of prejudices. Understanding—critical and creative—is preset in contradictions because universal forms of argument and logos of reason are forever short of providing claims of assurance and certitude. This quandary puts added stress on the reformulative habits of imagination as it struggles to represent ideas through repeated abjurement and revision. The poet's mind is then faced with an inadequacy, the unremitting threat of the diminishment of sublimic desire—the imbalance in encounters involving feeling, experience and representation. It is ill-adaptive in the sense of being underwhelmed or overwhelmed by the affective power of an experience or reflective experience: the contrariety emerging out of an ill-preparedness for aesthetic encounters. Coleridge's trans-habit founds itself in such a muddle which, essentially, is not a chaos but a state whose order is always under suspension, susceptible to imaginative involvement and projective of possibilities.

Coleridge's glowing faith in the vitalistic and coadunative powers of imagination are again riddled with contrariety when one discovers his misgivings about the other side of imagination which might hazard the poet into fits of unbridled mental acts.[58] The muddle vitalises itself on the poet's anxiety over the ability of imagination to counterfeit memory; a wavering consciousness insinuates the vexed character of imagination which, on one hand, is gloriously esemplastic and, on the other, an aesthetic stress to import a 'gentle and unnoticed control'—a disturbing balancing game that plagued his aesthetic and critical consciousness all through his life. Quantum creativity then owes to this 'shadowy state of imagination' too—an active-passive state which is romantic with the worm of a neoclassicist turning inside it. Poetic imagination must contrarise an engagement with the great and the ideal and concrete experiences. What the eye sees, the eye conceives, and the things that escape the eye 'coagulate on commixture' to produce the muddle of identities leaving behind a struggling imagination:

> Many a star, which we behold as single, the astronomer resolves into two, each, perhaps, the centre of a separate system. Oft are the flowers of the bind-weed mistaken for the growth of the plant, which it chokes with its intertwine. And many are the unsuspected double stars, and frequent are parasite weeds, which the philosopher detects in the received opinions of men:—so strong is the tendency of the imagination to identify what it has long consociated.[59]

So the symmetricisation of imagination is indeed fearful: 'Reason and Reality can stop and stand still, new Influxes from without counteracting the Impulses from within, and poising the Thought. But Fancy and Sleep stream on. ...'[60] The vestibule of poetic consciousness is quantumised in an imaginary aggravation and the 'force of a diseasedly retentive Imagination'[61]—the golden chariot and nightmare consciousness. So the poetic creativity was reinforced by an anguished imagination—'distempered' and dissipative, fearful and fusive.

Despite an agonised poetic mind, art demanded a reconciliation of form and matter, an integration of the parts and the whole. Coleridge writes:

> Imagine the polished golden wheel of the chariot of the sun, as the poets have described it; then the figure, and the real thing so figured, exactly coincide. There is nothing heterogeneous, nothing to abstract from: by its perfect smoothness and circularity in width, each part is ... as perfect a melody, as the whole is a complete harmony. This, we should say, is beautiful throughout. Of all 'the many' which I actually see, each and all are really reconciled into unity: while the effulgence from the whole coincides with, and seems to represent, the effulgence of delight from my own mind in the intuition of it.[62]

The poet infuses a logic even into the loftiest of poetry where pleasure and emotion become the unifying agents and, conscious will and understanding have their own share of contribution to make in the disciplinising of form without which beauty would be a casualty. This brings us to 'method' which is a 'unity with progression' and an unpremeditated and evidently habitual arrangement of the poet's words. Coleridge argues that poetic method is grounded in the habit of foreseeing in *each* integral, or in every sentence, the *whole* that the poet intends to communicate—a sort of 'progressive transition'. There are two methods: one is the method based on the relations of the Law, the other is the method based on the relation of theory.[63] Despite his own difficulty with organization and easier aptitude for the canvas, Coleridge submitted to a search for methodised thinking in Shakespeare. Shakespeare faced a crowd of thoughts – a difficult traffic to negotiate—but executed his genius to effect a 'harmonized chaos'. He saw 'method in fragments', 'link of association' and the poetic mind could resolve 'many circumstances into one moment of thought to produce that ultimate end of human Thought, and human Feeling, Unity'.[64] There is a reconciliation of the two methods in the mind of God and, to a lesser degree, in the activity of the poet. The poet ought to understand that the sum total of all his intellectual excellence is good sense and method; through good sense the genius distinguishes the various parts of the whole in terms of means and, he derives his position and characteristic from the antecedent method, or self-organising purpose. Trans-(in)fusionally, we find in *Wenxindiaolong* a 'proper and dignified construction' (*yazhi*) of the 'literary mind' and 'dragon carvings'. Poetic mind lives through 'spirit thought' without being inattentive to the existence of 'nature and form' (*tixing*) in that wandering and mapping are considered as close allies—'when concepts soar across empty sky, they easily become wondrous; but it is hard to be artful by giving them substantial expression in words'.[65] Liu Xie looks into a 'literary mind' through a convergence of 'expressive and affective immediacy and spontaneity with moral-cosmological order'. He recounts two dreams—the 'dream of aesthetic longing followed by dream of moral purpose', wanton abandonment with form-giving force.[66] The creative imagination presents the mental antecedents of the poetic method and this antecedent can be an image or an idea obtained through the senses. It originates from without. The inspiring passion which is the immediate and proper offspring of the mind develops into a specific medium and gives birth to a form. The principle of method, therefore, leads to the principle of organic form in the aesthetics of creation.[67]

III

It is in the Psalmist that Coleridge sees the ideal poet:

> It has struck [me] with great force lately, that the Psalms afford a most complete answer to those who state the Jehovah of the Jews, as a personal and national God and the Jews, as differing from the Greeks, only in calling the minor Gods, Cherubim & Seraphim & confining the word God to their Jupiter. It must occur to every Reader that the Greeks in their religious poems address always the Numina Loci, the Genii, the Dryads, the Naiads, Sec Sec? All natural Objects were dead? mere hollow Statues? but there was a Godkin or Goddlessling included in each? In the Hebrew Poetry you find nothing of this poor Stuff? as poor in genuine Imagination, as it is mean in Intellect? / At best, it is but Fancy, or the aggregating Faculty of the mind? not Imagination, or the modifying, and co adunating Faculty. This the Hebrew Poets appear to me to have possessed beyond all others? & next to them the English. In the Hebrew Poets each Thing has a Life of it's own, & yet they are all one Life. In God they move Sc live, Sc have their Being? not had, as the cold System of Newtonian Theology represents / but have.[68]

Imperfect understandings are as much a reality as the labyrinth of ideas that drive a mind to be a wanderer. Impervious to desynonymy, the poetic way betrays a figurative desire to claim a harmonic point, the stability of the beautiful as a diminished form of sublimic eros. Despite the contradiction that Coleridge's theory of poetry has in its Kantian and Schellingian allegiances, it is in the Hebrew notion of creativity and theology that he tries to effect an extraordinary synthesis: 'Doubtless, to *his* eye, which alone comprehends all Past and all Future in one eternal Present, what to our short sight *appears* strait is but a part of the great Cycle—just as the calm Sea to us appears level, tho' it be indeed only a part of a *globe*. Now what the Globe is in Geography, *miniaturing* in order to *manifest* the Truth, such is a Poem to that Image of God, which we were created into ...[69] The poetic mind is the non-Newtonian mind—a compelling complex of excess that is both damaging and fecund. Desire as addiction is the inherent component of a poetic mind that transcends boundaries for harmony that stays elusive.[70] The poetic mind becomes a habit to desire order, a reconciliatory power and an effective conjugation in imaginative reason. However, the excess that the mind produces, produces the deficit that the mind longs to overcome. This is a strange loneliness in creation. Coleridge points out that 'in order to obtain adequate notions of any truth, we must intellectually separate its distinguishable parts; and this is the technical process of philosophy. But having so done, we must then restore them in our conceptions to the unity, in which they actually co-exist'.[71] When 'distinction is not division', the quantum mind functions in thought-packets that are separate and together at the same time—cutting-together-apart, as Karen Barad would put it. This is impassioned discontinuous continuity. So when T. S. Eliot observes that Coleridge was one of those unhappy persons who might have made something of his life, 'might even have had a career', might have been a greater poet, had he not been 'interested in so many things' and 'crossed by such diverse passions',[72] I find something seriously amiss in the understanding of what I have argued as the 'quantum creativity'. Coleridge's career could not have been anything other than having such a quantum mind which could simply have thrived on diverse passions and interests, in contrariety and opposition. A great mind does not always translate into a great poet. What Eliot, like many others, misses is an encounter with a quantum romantic mind, restive in its symmetry, for symmetry is sublime. One must know that staying fearful is staying creative.

Notes

1. Samuel Taylor Coleridge, *Biographia Literaria* (ed.) James Engell and W. Jackson Bate (Princeton, N.J.: Princeton University Press, 1983), 1: 264.
2. *The Collected Writings of Thomas De Quincey* (ed.) D. Masson. 14 vols. (1896), 314.
3. *Othermindedness: The Emergence of Network Culture* (Ann Arbor: The University of Michigan Press, 2000), 13.
4. See John W Murphy (ed.) *The World of Quantum Culture* (Westport, Conn.: Praeger, 2002), 5.
5. See Neil Vickers, 'Coleridge's Abstruse Researches' in *Samuel Taylor Coleridge and the Sciences of Life* (ed.) Nicholas Roe (New York: Oxford University Press, 2001). Coleridge's 'Idea-pot' bubbled over with literary plans and diverse interests ranging across poetry, philosophy, science, politics, criticism and theology. He confessed to Poole that this is kind of disease of the mind which inspires him to launch into massive contemplations whose accomplishment lay beyond him: 'I should not think of devoting less than 20 years to an Epic Poem', he wrote to Cottle; 'ten to collect materials and warm my mind with universal science. I would be tolerable Mathematician, I would thoroughly know Mechanics,

Hydrostatics, Optics, and Astronomy, Botany, Metallurgy, Fossilism, Chemistry, Geology, Anatomy, Medicine—then the mind of man—then the minds of men—in all Travels, Voyages and Histories. So I would spend ten years—the next five to the composition of the poem—the last five to the correction of it'. See Earl Leslie Griggs (ed.) *Collected Letters of Samuel Taylor Coleridge* (Oxford: Clarendon Press, 2000), xxxiii-iv.
6. 'Certainly Coleridge read a great many books, some of them curious, some strange, some of them commonplace enough. But we must not allow the seductive enthusiasm of John Livingston Lowes (for this was not Lowes' intention) to persuade us that Coleridge had in fact read everything. The truth is more plausible and more interesting. He several times called himself a "library cormorant"; as a lover of White's Natural History of Selborne and a fastidious observer of birds, he probably meant what he said. The cormorant is indeed a voracious bird; but he is not nitwitted like the booby, nor - as sailors says of his half-brother the gannet - an indiscriminate glutton. The cormorant Coleridge had a keen appetite and almost flawless digestion'. See George Whalley, 'The Harvest on the Ground: Coleridge's Marginalia', *University of Toronto Quarterly*, 38, no. 3 (April 1969), 253–54.
7. Neil Vickers, 'Before Depression: Coleridge's Melancholia', *Studies in the Literary Imagination*, 44, no. 1 (Spring 2011), 94.
8. Kathleen Coburn, *Inquiring Spirit: A New Presentation of Coleridge from His Published and Unpublished Prose Writings* (New York: Pantheon Books, 1951), 11.
9. *Collected Letters*, 11, 782. Quoted in Max F. Schulz, 'Coleridge Agonistes', *The Journal of English and Germanic Philology*, 61, no. 2 (1962), 277.
10. M. H. Abrams, *The Mirror and the Lamp* (New York: Oxford University Press, 1953), 119.
11. *Lectures 1818-19* (ed.) J. R. de J. Jackson, *The Collected Works of Samuel Taylor Coleridge* Vol 1, (Princeton, N.J.: Princeton University Press, 1975), 50.
12. Emmanuel Chapman, 'Some Aspects of St. Augustine's Philosophy of Beauty', *Journal of Aesthetics and Art Criticism* (Spring 1941), 49–50.
13. J. Shawcross (ed.) *Biographia Literaria* (London: Oxford University Press, 1907), 50.
14. Seamus Perry, *Coleridge and the Uses of Division* (Oxford: Clarendon Press, 1999), 22.
15. See Letter of July 13, 1802. Quoted in L. S. Sharma, *Coleridge: His Contribution to English Criticism* (New Delhi: Arnold Publishers, 1993), 125.
16. Thomas Middleton Raysor, (ed.) *Samuel Taylor Coleridge: Shakespearean Criticism*, Vol. II (London: Dent, 1960), 212. Italics are mine.
17. Ibid., 112. Emphases are mine.
18. *Friend*, Vol 1, 94.
19. Coburn (ed.) *Inquiring Spirit*, 43.
20. Shawcross, *Biographia Literaria* 258.
21. Herbert Read, *The True Voice of Feeling* (London: Faber and Faber, 1947), 36.
22. Cobourn, *Inquiring Spirit*, 13.
23. Richard Haven, *Patterns of Consciousness: An Essay on Coleridge* (Amherst: University of Massachusetts Press, 1969), 2.
24. *Aids to Reflection* (Grant, Edinburgh, 1905), 232.
25. W. N. Ince, *The Poetic Theory of Paul Valery* (Leicester: Leicester University Press, 1970), 139–140.

26. See J. R. de J. Jackson, *Method and Imagination in Coleridge's Criticism* (London: Routledge & Kegan Paul, 1969), 116.
27. *Coleridge Notebooks* III 973, Autumn 1810. Looking into the 'biosociation of matrices', one can see with Arthur Koestler how the 'moment of truth, the sudden emergence of a new insight, is an act of intuition. Such intuitions give the appearance of miraculous flashes, or short-circuits of reasoning. In fact they may be likened to an immersed chain, of which only the beginning and the end are visible above the surface of consciousness. The driver vanishes at one end of the chain and comes up at the other end, guided by invisible links'. See *The Act of Creation* (London, 1975), 211.
28. Cobourn, *Inquiring Spirit*, 15.
29. Perry, *Coleridge and the Uses of Division*, 7.
30. Ibid., 11.
31. Shawcross, *Biographia Literaria*, II, 11.
32. George H. Gilpin, 'Coleridge and the Spiral of Poetic Thought' *Studies in English Literature*, 12, no. 4, Nineteenth Century (Autumn 1972), 642.
33. Ibid., 644.
34. See Douglas B. Wilson, 'The Dreaming Imagination: Coleridge, Keats and Wordsworth' in *Coleridge, Keats, and the Imagination* (ed.) J. Robert Barth & John L. Mahoney (Columbia: University of Missouri Press, 1990), 59–62.
35. Mark Kipperman, *Beyond Enchantment: German Idealism and English Romantic Poetry* (Philadelphia: University of Pennsylvania Press, 1986), 115.
36. See Harold Bloom, 'The Internalization of Quest Romance', *Yale Review* 58 (Summer 1969), 17. Quoted in Kipperman, *Beyond Enchantment*, 116.
37. 'Liu Xie on Imagination', in *A Chinese Literary Mind* (ed.) Zong-qi Cai (Stanford, Calif.: Stanford University Press, 2001), 135.
38. Ibid, 140. Coleridge writes: 'An IDEA therefore contemplates the Alpha and Omega (one-all; Finite-Infinite; Subject-Object; Mind-Matter; Substance-Form; Time-Space; Motion-Rest; Futuration-Presence; & c & c – and it is indifferent which of the Pairs you take, for they are all Symbols of the same Truth produced by different Positions'. *Letters*, IV, no. 1033.
39. Geoffrey Keynes, *The Complete Writings of William Blake* (Oxford: Oxford University Press, 1966), 456.
40. Ibid., 793.
41. Ibid., 617.
42. Geoffrey Keynes (introduction and commentary) *The Marriage of Heaven and Hell* (New York: Oxford University Press, 1975), xx. So poets like prophets 'have each for his peculiar dower, a sense/ By which he is enabled to perceive/ Something unseen before (*The Prelude*, 1805, 303–5). The poet is dowered with the transforming imagination which.

    … in truth,
    Is but another name for absolute strength
    And clearest insight, amplitude of mind,
    And Reason in her most exalted mood. (267–70)

43. Frederic Will 'Cousin and Coleridge: The Aesthetic Ideal' *Comparative Literature*, 8, no. 1 (1956), 74–5. In *Biographia Literaria* Coleridge adhered to the specific link made by Kant in the *Critique of Judgment* between genius and poetry: '[Poetry] is a distinction resulting from the poetic genius itself, which sustains

106   *'Fearful Symmetry'*

and modifies the images, thoughts, and emotions of the poet's own mind. The poet, described in ideal perfection, brings the whole soul of man into activity, with the subordination of its faculties to each other, according to their relative worth and dignity. He diffuses a tone, and spirit of unity, that blends, and (as it were) fuses, each into each, by that synthetic and magical power, to which we have exclusively appropriated the name imagination' (*Biographia* II, 16). The 'perfection' that brings the 'soul of man into activity' seems to be the spring inside of the genius at the beginning of section 49: 'Geist'. Coleridge realised the full potential of Kant's concept of poetic genius: aesthetic ideas bring imagination and the Understanding into harmony, they 'blend' and 'fuse' and render 'the spirit of unity' (otherwise inaccessible within the realm of space and time) as if it were empirically manifest. As mentioned before, the concept of aesthetic ideas is the only hypothesis in the third critique that provides a hint of integration of the supersensible ideas through art. See Monika Class, *Coleridge and Kantian Ideas in England 1796–1817* (London: Bloomsbury, 2012).
44. *L'Eau et les Re'ves, Essai sur V'imagination de la matiere* (Paris: Corti, 1942), 81.
45. Edward K. Kaplan, 'Gaston Bachelard's Philosophy of Imagination: An Introduction' *Philosophy and Phenomenological Research*, 33, no. 1 (Sep. 1972), 23.
46. *L'Air et les Songes, Essai sur V'imagination du mouvement* (Corti, 1943), 58. Quoted in Kaplan, 14.
47. See Richard Kearney, *Poetics of Imagining* (Edinburgh: Edinburgh University Press, 1998), 102.
48. Ibid.
49. *Biographia Literaria*, I, 167.
50. In 1801, he wrote to Thomas Poole: 'If I do not greatly delude myself, I have not only completely extricated the notions of Time and Space; but have overthrown the doctrine of Association, as taught by Hartley, and with it all the irreligious metaphysics of modern Infidels—especially, the doctrine of Necessity' (*Collected Letters*, II, 706).
51. Alexandra Neel, 'A Something-Nothing Out of its Very Contrary': The Photography of Coleridge', *Victorian Studies*, 49, no. 2 (Winter 2007), 208.
52. See 'Memoria Technica', *Biographia*, 429.
53. Robert D. Hume, 'Kant and Coleridge on Imagination', *The Journal of Aesthetics and Art Criticism*, 28, no. 4 (Summer 1970), 493.
54. J. H. Bernard (trans.) *Immanuel Kant, Critique of Judgment* (New York: Hafner Publishing Company, 1951), 157–58.
55. Rudolf A. Makkreel, *Imagination and Interpretation in Kant, The Hermeneutical Import of the Critique of Judgment* (Chicago: The University of Chicago Press, 1990), 97.
56. H. W. Cassirer, *A Commentary on Kant's Critique of Judgment* (New York: Barnes & Noble Inc., 1938), 278–79.
57. Jackson, *Method and Imagination in Coleridge's Criticism*, 117.
58. See Paul Magnuson, for example, in *Coleridge's Nightmare Poetry* (Charlottesville: University of Virginia Press, 1974).
59. Patricia Mavis Jenkins, 'Coleridge and the Perils of the Unbridled Imagination', *Philosophy and Literature*, 1, no. 2 (Spring 1977), 198.
60. Ibid., 195.
61. *Collected Letters*, 2: 974. Hess points out that in May 1808, Coleridge constructed the following plan for a table of the mind's faculties: 'Frame a numeration table of the primary faculties of Man, as Reason, unified per Ideas,

Mater Legum Judgement, the discriminative, Fancy, the aggregative, Imagination, the modifying & fusive, the Senses & Sensations—and from these the different Derivatives of the Agreeable from the Senses, the Beautiful, the Sublime / the Like and the Different—the spontaneous and the receptive—the Free and the Necessary—And whatever calls into consciousness the greatest number of these in due proportion & perfect harmony with each other, is the noblest Poem'. In fact these commonplace books stay cited as mediators between perception and imagination—the action of imagination being synonymous with moulding. See Jillian M. Hess, 'Coleridge's Fly-Catchers: Adapting Commonplace-Book Form', *Journal of the History of Ideas*, 73, no. 3 (July 2012), 479.
62. Shawcross, *Biographia Literaria*, 223.
63. The former is a 'progression of necessary consequents unified by an initiative drawn from the observation of nature'. See Jackson, *Method and Imagination in Coleridge's Criticism*, 102.
64. Theodore Leinwand, 'Shakespeare, Coleridge, Intellecturition', *Studies in Romanticism*, 46, no. 1 (Spring 2007), 87.
65. Owen, *Readings*, 206.
66. Wai-Yee Li, 'Between "Literary Mind" and "Carving Dragons": Order and Excess in *Wenxin diaolong*' in *A Chinese Literary Mind* (ed.) Zong-qi Cai (Stanford, Calif.: Stanford University Press, 2001), 224–25.
67. See P.S. Sastri, *Coleridge's Theory of Poetry*. The Aristotlean theory would take one to over-emphasise the understanding, the conceptual element. But the Platonic Coleridge liked to contemplate understanding distinctly, to look down upon it "from the throne of actual ideas, or living, inborn, essential truths". This throne of actual ideas in the creative act is the realm of imagination. These ideas are visioned as concrete universals by the artist. This transformation has evidently nothing to do with the unconscious or the state below consciousness. If at all we explain it, it proceeds from the superconscious or supra-conscious state which may be viewed as higher immediacy'. 105.
68. Ina Lipkowitz, 'Inspiration and the Poetic Imagination': Samuel Taylor Coleridge' *Studies in Romanticism*, 30, no. 4 (Winter 1991), 617.
69. Paul Hamilton, *Coleridge's Poetics* (Oxford: Blackwell, 1983), 190.
70. Caught between opium, habit, excess, loss, infirmity and desire, Coleridge writes: 'If I could secure you full Independence, if I could give too all my original Self healed & renovated from all infirm Habits; & if by all the forms in my power I could bind myself more effectively even in relation to Law, than the Form out of my power would effect-then, *then*, would you be the remover of my Loneliness, my perpetual Companion?' See Paul Youngquist, 'Rehabilitating Coleridge: Poetry, Philosophy, Excess', *ELH*, 66, no. 4 (1999), 905.
71. *Biographia Literaria*, II chapter xiv, 8.
72. 'Wordsworth and Coleridge', *The Use of Poetry and the Use of Criticism* (London: Faber and Faber, 1933), 68.

6 'Hero as Poet'
Thomas Carlyle and 'Future Poetry'

> At once I came to the world wherein I recovered my full meaning. My mind touched the creative realm of expression....The rhythmic picture of the tremulous leaves beaten by the rain opened before my mind the world which does not merely carry information, but a harmony with my being. ...I felt sure that some Being who comprehended me and my world was seeking his best expression in all my experiences, uniting them into an ever-widening individuality which is a spiritual work of art.
> —Rabindranath Tagore[1]

> Who knows but that, on the lower frequencies, I speak for you?
> —Ralph Ellison[2]

In *Sartor Resartus*, Thomas Carlyle points out how interpretation can be made productive through the impact of language, culture and ideas. He argues how untried and unfamiliar ways of 'seeing' make the nature of interpretation interesting—'To know; to get into the truth of anything, is ever a mystic act—of which the best Logics can but babble on the surface' (5: 57). Emphasising the relativity of the human perspective, he observes that 'nine tenths of our reasonings are artificial processes, depending not on the real nature of things but on our peculiar mode of viewing things, and thereby varying with all the variations both in the kind and in extent of our perceptions'.[3] Although Carlyle claims that meaning exceeds intention, relies heavily on intuition and wonder and submits to the tension between conceptual representation and the stable absolute—a variant of Victorian compromise and consent—he purposes to a locus of meaning which would be stable, permanent and universal, engendering a desire to overcome ossified beliefs and an indeterminacy of signs that make understanding transgressive. His apprehension of truth is hermeneutical—reclothe or freshly clothe[4]; hence, his notion of the poet-hero is exegetical and judgemental, reflecting on his use of language, the structure of thought and fibres of perception. The understanding of the poet hero is materialist, intuitive, imaginative and passionate but not incommensurable with forms of understanding and some exegetical paradigms that clothe ideas and thoughts. His 1840 lecture, 'Hero as Poet', is conceptually grand, founded on a brilliant and deft attempt to understand what the poet as hero should quintessentially be. However, Carlyle, despite being an originalist of a high order[5]—capable of casting sedulously a spell through his singular eloquence and with a mind whose grasp was large and potent—did not have a systematic philosophy to formulate his views. And this text, in my estimate, if read in isolation—appreciated merely within strict Carlylean aesthetic paradigms—fails to configure the poet in his more profound resonances. Since Carlyle acknowledges the terrible difficulty of pinpointing an apposite understanding of things, achieving a comprehensive and complete assessment of the nature of the poet-hero does not come to him easily. He tried to execute several 'peaks' and 'deep edges' in his exposition of the poet as hero, but could not quite muster the philosophical and aesthetic insight needed to render a fulsome treatment to the concepts that his essay sets out to unfurl. Here trans-habit initiates the construction of 'unexpected affinities' between Carlyle's ideas on poetry and the poetic theory of Aurobindo Ghosh (1872–1950), one of India's foremost spiritual visionaries and philosophers. The kinematics of Carlyle's text and the philosophical intricacies underpinning Aurobindo's poetic theory produce an apparent opposition bordering cultural incommensurability. But trans-habit is the way and mechanism to overcome the blinkered, absolutist, nonpluralist relativism that incommensurability legitimizes.[6] In creating an unexpected web of affiliations, trans-habit re-writes our habits of cultural epistemology to incorporate the reality and necessity of 'surprise' and 'shock' into our cross-border thinking.

I

Carlyle's dialectical aesthetics, as much as Aurobindo's, collapse the distinction between religion and poetry—poetry as a moral and an inmost experience, and never an imitative experience, one that emphasises the intuitive faculties over its external, empirical powers. Writing to Froude, Carlyle notes: 'That the Supernatural differs from the Natural is a great Truth, which the last century (especially in France) has been engaged in demonstrating. The Philosophers went far wrong, however, in this, that instead of raising the natural to the supernatural, they strove to sink the supernatural to the natural. The gist of my whole way of thought is to do not the latter but the former'.[7] In 'The State of German Literature' he points out,

> poetic beauty, in its pure essence, is not drawn from anything 'external, or of merely intellectual origin; not from association, or any reflex or reminiscence of mere sensations; nor from natural love, either of imitation, of similarity in dissimilarity, of excitement by contrast, or of seeing difficulties overcome. On the contrary, it is assumed as underived; not borrowing its existence from such sources, but as lending to most of these their significance and principal charm for the mind. It dwells and is born in the inmost Spirit of Man, united to all love of Virtue, to all true belief in God; or rather, it is one with this love and this belief, another phase of the same highest principle in the mysterious infinitude of the human Soul. (xxvi, 55–56)[8]

Carlyle's 'supernatural' and 'inmost spirit' point to the aesthetic of poetic inspiration. Here, Aurobindo, by arguing for a communication between poetic beauty and inspiration and drawing on the myth of Pegasus and Dadhikravan, extends the argument. Acknowledging what Carlyle called the 'mysterious infinitude' (an appointment with the Divine Idea), Aurobindo considers it as a 'thing breathed into the thinking organ from above; it is recorded in the mind, but is born in the higher principle of direct knowledge or ideal vision which surpasses mind'.[9] Poet-heroes, Carlyle notes, are the appointed interpreters of this Divine Idea and they alter the poise of their consciousness to achieve greater poetry.[10] This is what Aurobindo argues as the 'overmind' influence. He writes:

> A fundamental and universal aesthesis is needed, something also more intense that listens, sees and feels from deep within and answers to what is behind the surface. A greater, wider, and deeper aesthesis then which can answer even to the transcendent and feel too whatever of the transcendent or spiritual enters into the things of life, mind and sense.[11]

Carlyle's ideas on the 'inmost spirit of man' and 'highest principle' find a meaningful correspondence with Aurobindo's 'fourth dimension of aesthetic sense'[12] which makes creativity deeply intimate—*vacam artho anudhavati*.[13] Inscribed in a 'divine idea', the universe cannot be an inert automatism. To ordinary men, this 'Divine Idea' of the world is never revealed. The poet-hero in possession of 'genuine virtue, knowledge and freedom' can, amidst the world's multitudinousness, 'discern, seize and live wholly in this idea'(xxvi, 58). Emery Neff rightly notes that 'prowess in war having ceased to be a title to honor and reward, a world of brothers would thereafter cooperate harmoniously in exploiting the resources of the planet. And to inspire mankind with higher than material aims would arise a new, unorganized priesthood of men of letters, whose works would keep men alive to the spiritual significance of the universe, and reveal God's ever-unfolding plan of history'.[14] So, in 'lucid moments', it is to the poet-priests alone that the glimpses of 'our upper Azure Home' (in the words of Teufelsdrockh) are revealed.[15] The 'man of logic' and the 'man of insight' are separable (xxviii, 5–6) and Carlyle believes that the enthusiast for the idea and reason values both in and for themselves irrespective of the 'poetical convenience which their triumph may obtain for him'. Joseph Barrett observes:

> A divine relation, he calls it, in all times unites a great man to other men; and Heroism is the term which he uses to express *the* greatness, the grand elements of which are sincerity, practical earnestness, and unceasing efforts to carry mankind to a higher sphere of light and action than any one man ever before contemplated. Such a one "is the living light-fountain"; his is the light which enlightens, which has enlightened the darkness of the world; and this not as a kindled lamp

only, but rather as a natural luminary, shining by the gift of Heaven; a glowing light-fountain, as I say, of native original insight, of manhood and heroic nobleness.[16]

So, for both Carlyle and Aurobindo, the poet-hero finds in every finite thing a window 'through which solemn vistas are opened into Infinitude itself' (xxvi, 199), becoming a point, as Schegel argues, 'where the vital external forces of mankind converge, and where the inner forces are in most immediate effect'.[17] In *Savitri*, Aurobindo writes:

> A purer perception lent its lucent joy …
> A door parted …
> Releasing things unseized by earthly sense:
> A world unseen, unknown by outward mind
> Appeared in the silent spaces of the soul.[18]

Like Aurobindo, a poem for Carlyle then is a musical thought and the mind behind it penetrates into the heart of the thing, disclosing its inmost mystery, 'the fire that slumbers in it', the melody that lies hidden in it—Goethe's 'open secret'.[19] Discrediting rigid argument and the 'Logical, Mensurative faculty' as against the Imaginative, this secret, which is a power of knowledge, is conscience, a parting door to 'the silent spaces of the soul'. But insight, both thinkers agree, does not come through a mere denunciation of logic chopping dogmatic approaches. The secret, though open to all, was seen only by a rare few, pointing to the difficulty of having 'insight'—the open secret being the vesture, the embodiment that renders it visible. This insight is preceded by a leap that emerges out of a 'loyal heart', an understanding of the silence that consorts with 'secret', and a glimpse of the puzzle occupying the truth of a phenomenon. Carlyle and Aurobindo located this 'leap' in the poet. The leap provides the revelation of the harmony of coherence—'in one way or other, we all feel that the words he utters are as no other man's words. Direct from the inner Fact of things;—he lives, and has to live, in daily communion with that'.[20] Through insight, the poet 'lives in the inward sphere of things, in the True, Divine, and Eternal, which exists always'.[21] David Delaura points out that 'the effect is incalculably strengthened by a seemingly innocent device, Carlyle's constant repetition of "at bottom", a simple adverbial expression which becomes part both of the prophetic message and of Carlyle's credentials as a prophet in his own right'.[22] In the hero-archy, the poet's mind shows reverence for veracity and a natural spontaneity of forms (236),[23] looking through 'the shows of things into things' (63), into the always reverable reality (14). In overmind aesthesis, Carlyle's poet-hero with the 'creative vital' undergoes an intensification of capacity that, as Aurobindo argues, 'looks into the soul of each thing'.[24] It results in *ananda* which is akin to the 'wonder' that Carlyle's poet-hero experiences through the relentless unveiling of vestures of thought.

Although the prophet seizes the moral side of things and the poet the aesthetic side, these two provinces run into one another and cannot be disjoined. The Carlylean aesthetic integrates intellect and morality and considers a 'great' poet as a 'great' man with a clearly developed character, insight, courage and 'real applicable force of head and heart'. It is interesting to note that the poet as hero, the Able Man[25], is described as earnest, fervent and rugged, representative of an 'unconscious' pointing to intuitive apprehension of the divine—a figure who is titanic, melancholic, wild and temperamental. The poet-prophet is *able* to perceive a magic in the interrelatedness of things in the world; this magic is a revelation born not merely out of logic but intuition and sympathy—'The healthy Understanding,' Carlyle insists, 'is not Logical, argumentative, but the Intuitive; for the end of Understanding is not to prove and find reasons, but to know and believe' (xxviii, 5). This is not a mystical attitude towards life but a struggle to bring together several forces involving a moral vision, the divine image in the circumambient reality and a manifestation of spirit. Man (the Able Man) is both the epitome and symbol—'Analogienquelle' for the world, the 'Werkzeug' and organ of divine meaning, the 'Mittler' or mediator between the spiritual and material worlds, the 'Amen of the Universe'. Charles Harrold points out that for Fichte humanity is a high revelation of the Divine Idea and reason (*Vernunft*), 'signified the active principle of the ego' and may be regarded as a manifestation of the Idea in man; for Novalis, reason is 'susceptible to religious interpretation and development', somewhat synonymous to imagination, exalting poetry as the end of human effort; for Carlyle it is spiritual insight, the imaginative reason close to fantasy when he considers fantasy as the 'organ of the Godlike'. Fantasy resembles intuition and imagination and Harrold notes further that 'for Carlyle all three words, Reason, Imagination, and Fantasy, perform a double service: they act as moral criteria, and they serve as organs of knowledge'.[26] The poet-hero possesses the intuitive vision of reason which 'moulds the world like soft wax' and by which he 'lovingly sees into the world' (xxvii, 377). Aurobindo qualifies such a thought as 'a slender river of brightness leaping from a vast and eternal knowledge … which exceeds reason more perfectly than reason exceeds the knowledge of senses'.[27]

The poet, then, is the man of intuitive intellect with the touch of the 'universal' (having the infinitude in him), communicating an *Unedlichkeit*. He creates the world of his choice which is *nirmiti* (new creation).[28] The poetic mind discovers sweetness, intensity, delight and beauty, be it in repose or creation, power or love, silence or the titanic whirl of knowledge. He is a man possessed with 'great heart' (255) and 'clear deep-seeing eye' (ibid.)—'A larger seeing man with nobler heart'.[29] He is a person who combines the politician, the thinker, the legislator and the philosopher—a sagacious soul capable of a deep argument and a long, deep and hard thought. A healthy poetic nature 'wants no Moral Law, no Rights of Man, no Political Metaphysics. You might have added as well it wants no Duty, no Immortality, to stay and uphold itself withal' (xxvii, 213). Aurobindo has extended this issue a little further by suggesting that the artist has the ability to discover the 'all informing spirit' (*swayamprakash*) that bridges the hiatus between his understanding and execution. He reaches the spirit of things to create beauty out of the different inherent forces. The beauty leads to the aesthetic power of spirit. Entering the very centre of things, this gets identified with the 'stress and surge, taste and *rasa* of movement and creation'.[30]

Both Aurobindo and Carlyle believe that the poet may end up expressing precisely the same thing as the philosopher or the man of religion or the man of science unless he transmutes it (*nirmiti*) and abstracts something *more* from it. Carlyle observes:

> The prophet announces the Truth as the word of God or his command, he is the giver of the message, the poet shows us Truth in its power of beauty, in its symbol or image, or reveals it to us in the workings of Nature or in the workings of life, and when he has done that his whole work is done; he need not be its explicit spokesman. The philosopher's business is to discriminate Truth and put its parts and aspects into intellectual relation with each other; the poet's is to seize and embody aspects of Truth in their *living relations*. (Ibid., 42–3, italics mine)

He acknowledges these 'living relations' and underlines the complicity involved in the relation that the poet shares or chooses to share with the whole world. The 'true' poet manifests an awareness of the wholeness of things—an uncanny ability to grasp the organic unity (*totum*). In such a spirit and with an eye that takes in all provinces of human thought, feeling and activity into his viewing sweep, the poet stands forth as the true prophet of his time'—victorious over its contradiction, possessor of its wealth, embodying the nobleness of the past into a new whole, into a new vital nobleness for the present and the future.[31]

> So long as the several elements of Life, all fitly adjusted can pour forth their movement like harmonious tuned strings, it is a melody and unison; life, from its mysterious fountain, flows out as in celestial music and diapason. ... Thus too, in some languages, is the state of health denoted by a term expressing unity; when we feel our selves as we wish to be, we say that we are whole'. (xxviii, 2)

This is the overmind effect which Aurobindo believes, 'sees and thinks and creates in masses, which reunites separated things, which *reconciles opposites*'.[32] The overmind effectuates the working of the 'living relations'.

Combining the different traits—the touch of religion, science and philosophy—the poet-hero converts the *more* into the truth of poetry with the aid of a directly perceiving and interpreting eye. This validates a distinct right of the poet to think, feel and *see*—his right to dare to philosophise.

114   'Hero as Poet'

Carlyle's emphatic accent on the penetrating vision of the poet bears clear echoes of the Vedic concept of the 'seeing eye'. The *Rig Veda* points out that the 'wise' poets explore their hearts and by dint of their power of intuition come to know about the stages of origination—'Poets seeking in their heart with wisdom found the bond of existence in non-existence'.[33] It is only the power of the language of the poet that can stir the hidden universe to break forth with a meaning. If one can understand the language of the poet then he can also understand the 'mystery' of the universe, and Dirghatamas, one of the greatest poet-philosophers of the *Rig Veda*, appears to suggest that it is the poets who comprehend the mystery. Also, Sunahsepa, one of the prominent Vedic poets, finds himself in bondage and undertakes a self-exploration to discover the illumination that would provide him with the clue to the mystery of the world. An understanding of the mystery enables him to behold his father (wisdom) and mother (poetry). Carlyle's poet-hero, like his Vedic counterpart, is the 'wise poet' who is gifted with inner faculties that lets him see through the apparent opacity of things and understand their true laws (mystery): 'Let him who really knows proclaim here the *hidden* place of that beloved bird'.[34] The 'beloved bird', as mentioned in 1.164.7 of the *Rig Veda*, can come to mean truth or illumination that is concealed from the ordinary view. It is only the poet-hero who can, by an 'inner height', discern the position of the bird. So, 'unknowing, ignorant, I ask for knowledge about it from the *poets who know*'.[35] The omniscient 'knowing' intellect enables the poet to grasp the truth of the universe. In fact, the poets in *Atharva Veda* use the root *vid* about 250 times, *cit* about 35 times and *jna* about 80 times in the sense to know and *drs* about 80 times in the sense to *see*, to observe. They have the ability to realise the forces that guide the operations of nature and, endowed with this knowledge, they want to control and command them. It may be mentioned in this context that Dadhyane, an important poet of the pre-Rigvedic times, had an 'eye' for the *madhu* or honey—*madhu-vidya* or knowledge of the great mystery—which is close to what Carlyle points out as 'penetrating into the heart of things'.

> Thus have I, an illumined sage, by my thoughts and utterances spoken to thee, who knowest, O Fire, O Creator, secret words of guidance, seer-wisdom that speak out their sense to the seer.[36]

The poet-seer-hero has access to the *madhu-vidya*—knows the secret words that unveil the 'mystery'. Carlyle's poet-hero is the illumined *rishi* who has access to the secret words *ninyavacamsi* and possesses the wisdom to utter the hidden meaning—*kavyanikavayenivacana*.

This idea of the *kavyanikavayenivacana* underlines the importance that 'vision' holds for both Carlyle and Aurobindo. Acknowledging 'sight' as the 'essential poetic gift'[37], Aurobindo considers poetry to be a great formative and illuminative power. He insists that the native power of poetic creativity is in 'sight'. Sight shapes structure. It lends order, meaning and a measure of permanence to the incomprehensible flux of our 'perceptual persisting'. It is through the function of 'seeing' that all senses meet in a living relationship to generate the vision. It is in this sense that Carlyle's poet-hero becomes Aurobindo's 'archetypal poet'.

> The archetypal poet in a world of original ideas is, we may say, a Soul that sees in itself intimately this world and all the others and God and Nature and the life of beings and sets flowing from its centre a surge of creative rhythm and world images which become the expressive body of the vision; and the great poets are those who repeat in some measure this ideal creation, *kavayahsatyasrutah*, seers and hearers of the poetic truth and poetic word.[38]

Creativity is a mystery and Carlyle knows it. Creativity is the poet's ability to escape into life, and both Carlyle and Aurobindo are acknowledging of it. The life of the poet flows into the life of our existence. *Nirmiti* produces a world that exceeds the mere nature of *sukha–dukha–mohasvabhava* (pleasure–pain–infatuation), making reality *more* real. This helps both to see the native power of poetry which is not just constructed through intellectual thought-matter but is deeply informed by a vision. 'The poetic vision of life', for them, 'is not a critical or intellectual or philosophic view of it, but a soul-view, a seizing by the inner sense'.[39] Both the poet-hero and the archetypal poet connect their inner sense with the native power of poetry leading to *nirmiti*. Aurobindo argues:

> The prophetic or revealing power sees the substance; the inspiration perceives the right expression. Neither is manufactured; nor is poetry really a poiesis or composition, nor even a creation but rather revelation of *something that eternally exists*. The ancients knew this truth and used the same word for poet and prophet, creator and seer, *sophos, vates, kavi*.[40]

So poetry comes from inspiration and a sense of 'life' and not from the mere study of philosophy. The heightened consciousness in the poet-hero or the *kavi* generates an access to the *madhu-vidya* which is 'something that eternally exists'.

II

Dante, one of Caryle's poet-heroes (not the archetypal poet for Aurobindo, who considered him a grade lower than Shakespeare), is described as the saint of poetry whose greatness lies not in liberality but in fiery emphasis and depth. He is world-deep, not worldwide: 'The very movements in Dante have something brief; swift, decisive, and almost military. It is of the inmost essence of his genius, this sort of painting. The fiery, swift, Italian nature of the man, so silent, passionate, with its quick abrupt movements, its silent pale rages, speaks itself in these things' (273). He possesses the gifts of sympathy that enable him to grasp the essence of things—'an escape into life'. The moral nature—rigour, earnestness and depth—enables him to leave out the trivial and the worthless and seize upon the essentially noble and the worthwhile. From this arises the power of his immortal work. Dante's intensity gives him the intellectual insight that makes him a great painter as well as a great reasoner in verse. In fact, Carlyle's transcendentalism and his faith in a divine world of ideas inform his appraisal of Dante as one who had an intense perception of the other world and firmly believed in its reality and in the vividness of its presentation.

Shakespeare, Carlyle's ultimate poet-hero, is argued to be divinely inspired having a rare power of vision, keen insight, and felicity of thought, sympathy, understanding, joyous strength and a calm and tranquil soul:

> Perfect, more perfect than any other man, we may call Shakespeare in this: he *discerns, knows as by instinct*, what conditions he works under, what his materials are, what his own force and its relation to them is: It is not a transitory glance of insight that will suffice: it is *deliberate illumination of the whole matter*; it is a *calmly seeing eye*, a great *intellect* in short. (285; emphases added)

Nirmiti is the 'illumination of the whole matter'. Shakespeare's *nirmiti* comes from an inner harmony that enables him to discern the *madhu-vidya*—a faculty that exists not because of 'habits or accidents, but is the gift of Nature herself' and is 'the primary outfit for a Heroic Man' (287). He enjoys the intellectual and moral superiority that every 'true' poet experiences against the 'clanking of the world machine'. Shakespeare's intellect includes man's spiritual nature and his morality which is one and indivisible. The power of the intellect resides in a wholesome combination of the calmly seeing eye, intuitive reason and discerning intelligence. Gifted with an 'unconscious intellect', he discloses human nature in a fresh light and enhances our knowledge of the true nature of man and of the world.[41] Carlyle acknowledged the sovereignty of the unconscious in all literary, moral and political activity and argued that the immortal works of art are 'created' and not 'manufactured' in the dark mysterious depths of the unconscious.

Cultivating a similar line of thought, Aurobindo considers the poet as possessing the largest, widest and most comprehensive view of life; this is a life which the poet has to re-embody in the beauty of the word—a life which is all life, the infinite life of the spirit thrown out in its many creations (his version of the 'unconscious'). Aurobindo admires the predominance of the 'life element' in Shakespeare: 'it is its living interpretation of the truth and powers of the life-soul of man that are the core of greatness of his work and the rest without it would be a vain brute turmoil'. Shakespeare's creativity has a background of life and a mind and an imagination that has seen much and observed much; it is rich in what Aurobindo calls 'life-experience'—'no real portion of the function of art is to cut out palpitating pieces from life and present them raw and smoking or well-cooked for the aesthetic digestion'.[42] The creative essence of the poet-hero lies not in his reproduction of actual human events or men as they appear to us in life, but in bringing out the deeper reality of things—essential, universal, eternal in Man and Nature and Fate so that when we see them life may present to us something deeper than its actual present mask. This is the *more* in *nirmiti*. The poet's greatest work, says Aurobindo, with distinct Carlylean resonances, 'is to open to us new realms of vision, new realms of being, our own and the world's and he does it even when he is dealing with actual things'.[43]

Aurobindo attributes the supremacy of the poet to his complete hold on life, 'for life itself has taken hold of him in order to recreate itself in his image'; it results in the joy produced out of a 'multiple poetic vision of life and vital creation with no centre except the life-power itself'. He observes that Shakespeare stands apart from others in his method, quality and spirit for he is not primarily an artist but a vital creator with 'life-spirit' and a disseminator of *ananda* comparable with the Vedic sage Viswamitra who, in his sacred wrath, created a new heaven and earth: 'More than any other poet Shakespeare has accomplished mentally the legendary feat of the impetuous sage Viswamitra, his power of vision has created a Shakespearean world of his own. …' Aurobindo finds Shakespeare not just thinking for the sake of thought, but for the sake of life; his way indeed is not so much what the poet thinks about life; it is what life thinks out in him 'through many mouths, in many moods and moments, with a rich throng of fine thought-effect'. Aurobindo believed that Homer[44], Kalidasa, Virgil, Shakespeare, Dante, Valmiki, Vyasa, William Blake and Walt Whitman had a large and powerful interpretative and intuitive vision of nature and human Life.

Poet-heroes see the universe intimately—God, nature and the human life. This is what Carlyle calls the 'calmly seeing eye' in creativity. This sight sets flowing from its centre a surge of creative rhythm and word images which become the expressive body of the 'vision', marking out the 'learned men' from the 'common men'. The poet-hero's access to such a level of creativity does not enjoin him to spiritual experiences. Aurobindo warns the reader that spiritual experience by itself can never turn a person into a poet. Both Carlyle and Aurobindo see in such creative heights a combination of inspiration ('the gift of Nature' as Carlyle calls it), a 'vital' power, and the transmitting skill. The poet-hero is Rajasekhara's *sarasvata kavi*, a favourite of the goddess of learning, *abhyasika kavi* and not merely a poet by practise, *aupadesika kavi*, and a poet by instruction.[45] Shakespeare's creativity is a blessing of the Muse (*sarasvata*) and a blend of effort (*abhyas*) and study (*aupadesh*)—a synthesis of 'Nature's gift' and 'intellect'. Art involves more than art. It is a journey through *sadhanas*. That Shakespeare, as Carlyle points out, discerns and 'knows by instinct what condition he works under, what his materials are, what his own force and its relation to them is' (285) become a kind of *sadhana*. To put form on matter ('deliberate illumination of the whole matter', ibid.) and lend it an intellectual discipline is another form of *sadhana*. Committed to various levels of *sadhana*, the poet-hero discovers an intense illumination of speech—the inspired word—that helps a sublime level of rhythmic movement to meet with 'a depth of sense'. It is a dynamic and creative energy, a *chit-shakti*, the power behind all forms.

III

Aurobindo lays out five significant aspects for the poet-hero—inspiration, imitation, persuasion, communication and expression. Art cannot give what nature gives; it gives something *more* and reaches its peak at the stage of persuasion. At this stage, the artist is able to give his visionary spirit a suitable form through his superior sense of discrimination and inner power. Within the Carlylean aesthetic, the native power of *nirmiti* makes allowance for the intimations of the secrecy of the age which, in the smithy of the artist's understanding gets deeply integrated with the resultant aesthetic wholeness involving both the beauty and good in art. Within the ambit of such integration, true poets interpret facts and communicate them 'musically'. Goethe, Carlyle's true poet, is seen as the 'Uniter, and victorious Reconciler of the distracted, clashing elements of the most distracted and divided age that the world has witnessed since the introduction of the Christianity …'.[46] It is his *tapasya* and *sadhana* that opens him to an intensely large vision of the greatness of the world, the wonder of life, the self of man, the mystery of the spirit in him and the universe. But this is no mere intellect—both Carlyle and Aurobindo do not evince much faith in this faculty—that discloses a harmonic vision on the poet-hero. Aurobindo argues that 'intellect is an absurdly overactive part of the nature … it instinctively interferes with the inspiration, blocks half or more than half of it and labours to substitute its own inferior and toilsome productions for the truth speech and rhythm that ought to have come'.[47] The poet-hero's inner power of discrimination is not critical intellect. Aurobindo finds 'discrimination' as a strong repertoire in Shakespeare's life-mind—a discrimination that functions as creative, intuitive, a part of the vision, coming as part of that influx of 'power' and 'light' that lifts the faculties into their intense supra-rational working. The poet-hero has broken through the 'intellect's hard and lustrous lid'[48] to attune with the higher plane of consciousness resulting in 'vital poetry'.

What, then, does Carlyle mean when he considers Shakespeare's art as not artifice (291)? By accenting the 'unconscious intellect' and the 'unknown deeps' in the poet, Carlyle opens up the area of 'speaking silence'—the 'inarticulate deeps' (296)—in aesthetic creativity. The poet-hero creates 'silences' that are articulate and dynamic. Poets make us understand great many things, but a few things are to be understood in their silences: silences not in the sense of being unmentioned or elided, but in forms of meaning which words cannot always successfully communicate. Commenting on the limits of our knowledge, Carlyle notes:

> For the present, I will confess it, I scarce see how we can reason with absolute certainty on the nature of fate or anything; for it seems to me we only see our own perceptions and their relations; that is to say, our soul sees only its own partial reflex and manner of existing and conceiving.[49]

Certain things need not and cannot be explained with certainty and, hence, remain a mystery, a magic and maze at the hands of the poet-hero. The poet 'bodies forth the forms of things unknown' and there is always something unfathomable about his vision—a distance beyond distance, a depth beyond depth. In an inspired moment, the poet becomes the medium of an expression of spiritual truth which is beyond him and 'the expression as it is not that of his own mind, may be very powerful and living not merely aesthetically agreeable'.[50] What the poet writes cannot always be the 'fabrication of the brain-mind' but something more sovereign breathed or poured from 'above'—inspiration that descends from 'above' cooperates with his dynamic desire to make every line of his poetry a 'perfect perfection'. Carlyle believes, as does Aurobindo, that man's duty is to keep alive the 'aboriginal splendour of the soul'. So creativity for both is essentially the problem of harmony; it is an integration and evolution of several modes of consciousness—a formation that can reveal the 'indwelling spirit' and work on 'possibilities'. It points to a plasticity embedded in physical-vital tendencies and exists as the luminous medium that prepares the poet-hero for greater self-consciousness—'suprarational influx of light and power'. Aesthetic consciousness is 'creative knowledge': it is intuitive, alethic and encompassing of inner and exterior reality. Creativity ensures the harmonious possession and enjoyment of the power, beauty and 'delight of human existence': it inspires self-enlargement and liberation.

Aurobindo then implies, much in the same way that Carlyle has intoned, a poetic mind that combines a psychic and poetic intelligence—a 'sublimised vital'. It is a mind that is often illumined, intuitivised and intervening. Aurobindo mentions four distinct super-conscient or overhead regions, namely those of the Higher Mind, Illumined Mind, Intuitive Mind and the Overmind. The poet-mind that Carlyle implicates but struggles to envisage theoretically or conceptually in full measure is the Illumined Mind and the Intuitive Mind. Aurobindo writes,

> The outflow of the illumined mind comes in a flood brilliant with revealing words or a light of crowding images, sometimes surcharged with its burden of revelations, sometimes with a luminous sweep.[51]

The intuition is usually a lightning flash showing up a single spot or plot of ground or scene with an entire and miraculous completeness of vision to the surprised ecstasy of the inner eye; its rhythm, as Kaikhosru Sethna argues, 'has a decisive inevitable sound which leaves nothing essential unheard'.[52] Carlyle's Shakespeare combines both the 'illumined mind' and the 'intuitive mind' and can be appraised under the conditions of 'overhead poetry'.

Carlyle notes,

> it is only when the heart of him is *rapt into true passion of melody*, and the very tones of him, according to Coleridge's remark become musical by the greatness, depth and music of his thoughts, that we can give him right to rhyme and sing; that we can call him a Poet ... (270, emphasis added)

'False song' is not 'true passion of melody'; it can be hollow, superfluous and insincere. Creativity builds on the depth and musicality of thoughts and the inspiration of the inner eye: it is born into the music of visionary expression. This brings us close to what Aurobindo calls the *Mantra* (it does not have an adequate English equivalent). When the highest intensity of rhythmic movement, verbal form, thought and the soul's vision of the truth become indissolubly one, poetry emerges as *Mantra*. Aurobindo speaks of *Mantra* as 'the highest intensest revealing form of poetic thought and expression'.[53] What Carlyle attributes as 'rapt into' the true passion of melody with its internal manifestation in greatness and depths of thought becomes the *Mantra* of poetry for Aurobindo. Poetry is *Mantra* only when it is the voice of the inmost truth and is couched in the highest power of the very rhythm and speech of that truth. Here Aurobindo extends Carlyle's ideas on this subject by moving into a more fulfilling thesis on creativity. Aurobindo's poet-hero understands the true nature of *Mantra* as a direct, most heightened, an intensest and most divinely burdened rhythmic word (ibid., 280).[54] Ventriloquising Carlyle in more ways than one, Aurobindo argues that poetry then will be the 'voice and rhythmic utterance of our greater, our total, our infinite existence, and will give us the strong and infinite sense, the spiritual and vital joy the exalting power of a greater breath of life'.[55] The poet's art then becomes a heightened execution of life-values, mind-values and soul-values. What for Carlyle is 'expressing musically' becomes for Aurobindo the 'soul of rhythm' that poet-heroes are able to connect with and eventually master—'the unheard melodies'. Aurobindo's poet works under a deeper and more subtle music—a rhythmical soul-movement that meets the deeper aims of the creative spirit—'something within trying to bring out an echo of hidden meanings, a secret of rhythmical infinities within us'.[56] It is the sublime expression in *chhandas* (rhythms) where the creative sound grows conscious of the secret of its own power. It is about rendering greater attention to the suggestive force of the sound, its life, its power and the mental impressions that it carries. It is not the mere harmonious arrangement of sounds—'it is sound suggesting the hidden life throb of a thing as felt by a certain mode of consciousness'.[57]

So Carlyle's 'expressing musically' is Aurobindo's poetic rhythm and movement that lie awake when the inner ear begins to listen. It is the power of the soul-life and soul-emotion with a deep supra-intellectual resonance. This is the matrix of song-making and vision-making.

Heavily invested in antipositivism, both Carlyle and Aurobindo advocate the superrational and supranormal ways of knowing and understanding where the poet-hero as *rishi* or *yogi* ('A *yogi* who writes is not a literary man for he writes only what the inner Will and Word wants him to express. He is a channel and instrument of something greater than his own literary personality'[58]) remains always a 'possibility'—a transfigurative force in beauty and delight. Experiencing beauty is the 'aesthesis' and the poet is close to experiencing the spirit's delight in existence. Beauty is revealed only to the 'unsealed vision of the poet' that breaks into delight—a category that Aurobindo brilliantly interprets through his conflatory understanding of the 'delight of being' and 'delight of becoming'. The delight of being is 'supra-aesthetic'[59] which points to the subliminal nature of poetic creativity. The poet-hero attains supra-aesthetic qualities—the 'desire soul'. Aurobindo observes:

> The artist and the poet do it when they seek the *rasa* of the universal from the aesthetic emotion or from the physical line or form the mental form of beauty or from the inner sense and power alike of that from which the ordinary man turns away and of that to which he is attached by sense of pleasure.[60]

The poet, thus, is only a hero when he becomes the spokesperson of the eternal spirit of beauty and delight wholesomely aestheticised in *ananda*. The poet-hero develops a self-consciousness which is not different from self-delight—the 'being' which, by its power of transcendence, generates the 'becoming'. Reading the two thinkers trans-habitually we find how poetry is 'another cult and worship' and how the poet changes his 'robes of mind' and serves the 'rites of a different consecration',[61] generating life-values, mind values and soul-values into the emergence and sustenance of Art. Carlyle and Aurobindo then inaugurate 'future poetry'—a mind-spirit and poetic body—which is forever 'coming' and always steeped in the depths of one's being and whose form is 'touched by the sense of some nameless perfection'.[62] Both the thinkers welcome the emergence of a new poetic ego.[63]

Notes

1. Rabindranath Tagore, 'The Vision' in *The Religion of Man* (London: George Allen and Unwin Ltd., 1958), 95–6.
2. Ralph Ellison, *Invisible Man* (New York: Random, 1952), 4.
3. Thomas Carlyle, *Two Notebooks of Thomas Carlyle*, (ed.) Charles Eliot Norton (New York: The Grolier Club, 1898), 4.

4. As Teufelsdroeckh says 'All forms whereby Spirit manifests itself to Sense, whether outwardly or in the imagination, are Clothes' (1: 215).
5. D. J. Trela & Rodger L. Tarr (eds.) *The Critical Response to Thomas Carlyle's Major Works* (Westport, Conn.: Greenwood Press, 1997), 97.
6. Zhang Longxi, *Unexpected Affinites: Reading Across Cultures* (Toronto: University of Toronto Press, 2007), 11.
7. See J. A. Froude, *Thomas Carlyle: A History of the First Forty Years of His Life: 1195–1835*, 2 vols. (London, 1882), II, 267.
8. *On Heroes, Hero-Worship and the Heroic in History* (ed.) H. D. Traill (Centenary Edition; New York, 1897–1901), V, 157. All later references to Heroes are to this edition; volume and page numbers are given parenthetically unless otherwise stated.
9. *The Harmony of Virtue*, Vol. 3, (Pondicherry: Sri Aurobindo Birth Centenary Library, 1972), 105.
10. Aurobindo, *Life, Literature, Yoga* (Pondicherry: Sri Aurobindo Ashram, 1952), 28.
11. *Letters of Sri Aurobindo* (on Poetry and and Literature) Third Series (Bombay: Sri Aurobindo Circle, 1949), 101.
12. Aurobindo, *Savitri* (Pondicherry: Sri Aurobindo Birth Centenary Library, 1972), 126.
13. Bhavabhuti, *Uttara-rama-carita*, VII.
14. Emery Neff, *Carlyle and Mill: An Introduction to Victorian Thought* (New York: Columbia University Press, 1926), 220.
15. Charles Frederick Harrold, (ed.) *Sartor Resartus* (New York, 1937), 243. As a matter of fact, in the *Rig Veda* (X 91.3) God is depicted as a poet:.

    Most skilful with Thy powers, most wise with wisdom
    O God, Thou art a Poet knowing all with thy poetic wisdom.
    Master of good things, Thou, the One, art the Lord
    Of what the heaven and the earth produce.

    See A. C. Bose, *The Call of the Vedas* (Bombay: Bharatiya Vidya Bhavan, 1960), 119. It is to the poet alone that god is visible—'May my song be pleasing to the house of Zeus'. See Herman Frankel, *Early Greek Poetry and Philosophy* (Oxford: Basil Blackwell, 1975), 164.
16. See his essay in *Monthly Review*, 155 (May 1841): 1–21 in D. J. Trela & Rodger L. Tarr (eds.) *The Critical Response to Thomas Carlyle's Major Works* (Westport, Conn.: Greenwood Press, 1997), 96.
17. L R. Furst, *European Romanticism, An Anthology* (London and New York: Methuen, 1980),72.
18. *Savitri* 26–27.
19. A.M.D. Hughes, *Thomas Carlyle: Introduction and Notes* (London: Oxford University Press, 1957), 3. Carlyle nevertheless considered Goethe a great poet, who stood out more grandly as he himself increased: "yet stands out, as I might say, as an object finished, to which there will be no continuation made; like a granite Promontory, high and sheer, stretching far into the waste chaos; yet not thro' it; thro' it the world seems seeking itself another road, or losing all aim of any. To me most significant, forever bedeutungsvoll, verehrungswirdig! He thought that, with Goethe, his labors in the German field might well end or at least pause. The fire was kindled: "… and thou take thy bellows elsewhither!

This is one phase of the 'spiritual crisis' I spoke of...". (Thomas Carlyle, 'New Letters of Carlyle to Eckermann', edited by William A. Speck, reprinted from *The Yale Review*, July, 1926 [New Haven, 1926], 9–10).
20. See B. H. Lehman, *Carlyle's Theory of the Hero* (Durham: Duke University Press, 1928), 4.
21. Alexander Carlyle (ed.) *New Letters of Thomas Carlyle* (London and New York, 1904), 3. *New Letters*, i, 190.
22. David J. Delaura, 'Ishmael as Prophet: Heroes and Hero-Worship and the Self-Expressive Basis of Carlyle's Art' *Texas Studies in Literature and Language*, 11, no. 1 (Spring 1969), 720.
23. E. Jones, (selected and edited) *English Critical Essays (Nineteenth Century)* (Oxford: Oxford University Press, 1919). All quotations from 'Hero as Poet' are provided from this volume. The page numbers are given parenthetically in the body of the text.
24. *Letters of Sri Aurobindo*, 124, 127.
25. He is the 'Able Man'—close to Fichte's idea of the 'learned man'—who interprets the 'ideal' to men unable to discern it for themselves. Able Man is not to be limited to the role of the priest because Carlyle never recovered his faith in orthodox Christianity. The Able Man, as in *Sartor Resartus*, is still primarily the writer and teacher, as he is in Fichte; he can also be the king but his essence lies in being the messenger of the divine to men. He has insight into the ultimate spiritual reality to which most men are blind; all good men—in a good society, all men—will sense the fact, follow him willingly, because only in conformity to the dictates of that ultimate spiritual reality we can be in the midst of freedom. 'But in Carlyle's eyes, the "super-man" is not so much the product of a surplusage of force—in Nietzsche's sense of the word—as of "sincerity". Now sincerity, according to Carlyle, implies superior insight into truth and loyalty to it. Not the logical processes of the "Understanding", but the mystical perceptions of the "Reason", constitute the "hero's" superiority to other men, and establish his claim to true leadership among men. Thus our loyalty to the "hero" is in reality a loyalty to Truth itself, – that Truth first mystically perceived by the Hero, – and "this loyalty of all men to great men is a mystic bond."' See Bliss Perry, *Thomas Carlyle: How to Know Him* (Indianapolis: Bobbs-Merrill, 1915), 171.
26. Charles Frederick Harrold, 'Carlyle and Novalis' *Studies in Philology*, 27, no. 1 (Jan. 1930), 53, 56.
27. *The Hour of God*, Vol. 17, (Pondicherry: Sri Aurobindo Birth Centenary Library, 1972), 27.
28. Pt. Durgaprasad & P.W.L. Sastry (eds.), *Dhvanyaloka* IV (Bombay: Nirnayasagara, 1928), 4. While the *Brahma Sutra* refers to the creation of the world as an art of *lila*, play, the joy of the poet—eternally young—the *Upanishad* considers the *kavi* (poet-hero) as an artist, a maker or creator and not a mere imitator. Anandavardhana, quoting *Agnipurana*, compares the poet to the creator of the world. See R. Mitra, (ed.), *Agnipurana* Vol. III (Calcutta: Asiatic Society of Bengal, 1879), 339.10.
29. *Savitri*, 342.
30. Sri Aurobindo, *The Future Poetry* (Pondicherry: Sri Aurobindo Ashram, 1972), 343.
31. Hughes, *Thomas Carlyle*, 9.

124 'Hero as Poet'

32. See *The Human Cycle* (Pondicherry: Sri Aurobindo Birth Centenary Library, 1972), 130. Italics are mine.
33. D. W. O'Flaherty (trans.), *The Rig Veda* (New Delhi: Penguin, 1981), 25.
34. Ibid., 76. Italics mine.
35. Ibid., 1.164.6; emphases added.
36. Vamadeva's hymns, IV, 3.16. See S. Aurobindo, *Hymns to the Mystic Fire* (Pondicherry: Sri Aurobindo Ashram, 1991), 174.
37. *The Future Poetry*, 41.
38. Ibid.
39. Ibid., 46.
40. Aurobindo, *The Harmony of Virtue* Vol. III. (Pondicherry: Sri Aurobindo Ashram, 1972), 105. Emphasis added.
41. 'Shakespeare's intellect is still greater because unconscious; it is part of Nature; and his works grow up like the oak with the symmetry of Nature's laws. He is greater than Dante in that he fought truly and did conquer. He too knew deep sorrows, and yet he exaggerates only in mirthfulness and love of laughter. Of the man we get no full impress in his work, for he wrote under conditions for the Globe Playhouse. He was also a Prophet, but of the "Universal Church": indifferent to creeds, but no "Sceptic". He was greater for being *conscious* of no heavenly message; for all that Mahomet was conscious of was error, and the great in him was the unconscious. ... This Shakespeare, this Stratford peasant, is the grandest thing we have yet done. We would give up our Indian Empire rather than him. His voice will unite Saxondom scattered over the globe, as Dante unites dismembered Italy'. See Augustus Ralli, *Guide to Carlyle* Vol. 1, (London: G. Allen & Unwin Ltd., 1920), 284.
42. *The Future Poetry*, 323.
43. Ibid., 118.
44. Homer's poetry is endowed with the quality to reveal new beauties and enlarge the dimensions of the human spirit. Samuel Bassett notes: 'The Creator gave life and particular qualities to existing matter and brought our world into existence. The aim of the early poet is thus creating is also illustrated by the Hebrew account of Creation .... The only reason for the creative effort of the early "poet", as poet, was the joy in the making, which, because of his humanity or for some othe reason, he shared with his audience. There is strong evidence that Homer had no other purpose than this—a fact which, if established, gives to our oldest literary document the added value of being poetry in its pure state'. See his *The Poetry of Homer* (Berkeley: University of California Press, 1938), 8–9. Through a reading of the singer both in *Odyssey* and *Iliad* one may observe how the bard sings 'all too according to the order of things', *lien kata kosmon*, and knows *thelkteria*, 'enchanting things'. In *Illiad* (2,485) we are told that the Muses were the original poets who experienced the epic events as eye-witnesses and transmitted such knowledge to later men. The point is that, poetry is a sort of knowledge, and that the poet, when he is blessed by the Muses, comes to have a privileged access to knowledge. Homer, as much as Shakespeare, was blessed to have such access combining both *darshana* (vision) and *varnana* (power of description).
45. C. D. Dalal & B. Bhattacharya (eds.) *Kavyamimamsa* (Baroda: Oriental Institute, 1934), 13.
46. Hughes, *Thomas Carlyle*, 9.

47. *Letters of Sri Aurobindo*, 5.
48. *Savitri*, 123.
49. *Two Notebooks of Thomas Carlyle*, 97.
50. *The Future Poetry*, 524.
51. *Letters of Sri Aurobindo*, 116.
52. K. D. Sethna (ed.) *Overhead Poetry* (Pondicherry: SAICE, 1972), 10.
53. *The Future Poetry*, 280.
54. K. D. Sethna writes: 'The *mantra* arrives in utter authenticity on the pinions of a rhythm that seems to make each line a brief aureoled manifestation, so to speak, of its passage from infinite to infinite. A consciousness, sovereign and boundless, is at play in it, and the play is most vividly communicated through an immense unfathomable vibration…'. See *Inspiration and Effort* (Waterford, Conn.: The Integral Life Foundation, 1995), 39.
55. *The Future Poetry*, 329–30.
56. Ibid., 29.
57. Sethna, *Sri Aurobindo: The Poet* (Pondicherry: Sri Aurobindo Ashram, 1970), 42.
58. *Letters of Sri Aurobindo*, 285.
59. Ibid., 42.
60. Aurobindo, *The Life Divine* (New York: Sri Aubindo Library, 1949), 206.
61. *The Future Poetry*, 298.
62. K. D. Sethna, *Talks on Poetry* (Pondicherry: Sri Aurobindo International Centre of Education, 1989), 354.
63. 'The little ego is constituted by Nature and is at once a mental vital and physical formation meant to aid in centralizing and individualizing the outer consciousness and action. When the true-being is discovered the utility of the ego is over and this formation has to disappear—the true being is felt in its place'. *Letters on Yoga*, 238.

7 'O life unlike to ours!'
Matthew Arnold as an Indian Sage?

> The materia poetica is common to all writers as the materia medica to all physicians.
> —John Dryden[1]

> The poet's matter ... increases with every century.
> —Matthew Arnold[2]

> We all feed on others, though we must properly digest what we thus receive. Even the lion is nothing but assimilated mutton.
> —Paul Valery[3]

Matthew Arnold speaks about a 'world' that becomes a general expression of our humanity[4], a resetting of borders that urges our habits of interaction to change: 'The civilised world is to be regarded as now being, for intellectual and spiritual purposes, one great confederation, bound to a joint action and working to a common result; and whose members have for their proper outfit a knowledge of Greek, Roman, and Eastern antiquity, and of one another'.[5] This confederationist and disinterested endeavour, as I have argued elsewhere[6], to know the best that has been thought and known in the world cannot be left in the 'abstract' (confined to the 'athletes of logic'[7], systematic philosophy and dogmatic theologians) but must find a way to connect with life and become a criticism of life, generating a sense of creativity. Arnold was not committed to uphold British civility; instead he invested his life and thought into creating a culture. Unlike his German counterpart, Johann Gottfried Herder (*Kulturgeschichte*), for whom the self-sufficiency of a nationalist whole dominated the cultural-literary discourse, Arnold thought of a perfection where walking alone was courting anarchy and being *with* others organically and symbiotically spelt culture. A deep interest in comparative education—Arnold's reports on the education system in France, Italy, Germany, Holland and Switzerland are the work of an educational prophet—demonstrates his eagerness to know 'how others stand' and 'to know how we ourselves stand'.[8] Arnold writes:

> In short, it is expedient for the satisfactory resolution of these educational questions, which are at length beginning seriously to occupy us, both that we should attend to the experience of the Continent, and

that we should know precisely what it is which this experience says. Having long held that nothing was to be learned by us from the foreigners, we are at last beginning to see, that on a matter like the institution of schools, for instance, much light is thrown by a comparative study of their institution among other civilised states and nations. To treat this comparative study with proper respect, not to wrest it to the requirements of our inclinations or prejudices, but to try simply and seriously to find what it teaches us, is perhaps the lesson which we have most need to inculcate upon ourselves at present.[9]

A critical comparative negotiation between the self and the other, the native and the foreign, the insider and the outsider, is what forms 'culture'. Rhetoric and emotional exuberance over triumphalist racist, ethnic and nationalist braggadocio clogs the mind into an unvital space disabling all spiritual progression. Arnold points out that 'everywhere there is connexion, everywhere there is illustration: no single event, no single literature, is adequately comprehended except in its relation to other events, to other literatures'.[10] The ethics of thinking and doing is recognising the 'connection', the *sahit*, that contributes both to the idea of perfection and 'modernity'—the intellectual maturity and orientation to observe facts with a critical spirit, not prejudice or caprice. 'Tradition' is the word that holds the desired tenancy. Shirley Letwin explains that Arnold's thinking in terms of tradition can be illustrated through the example of Palladian architecture. Palladian buildings bear traces of classical tradition but Palladio maintained a certain sense of order, a sense of the parts connecting to the formation of the whole. Palladio learned a 'classical theory of proportion through his studies in the circle around the humanist, Trissino'. But he ensured that he added his own contribution, supplemented through his reading of Alviso Cornaro, the Bolognese theorist, Sebastiano Serlio, Italian designers like Bruneleschi and Michelangelo and others. Letwin argues that 'all this Palladio absorbed and reformulated so that out of a repertoire drawn from many diverse sources, he produced buildings that look as if they have grown out of the ground on which they stand. Though there is good reason for describing Palladio as classical, he was not classical in the same way as Bramante, Sangallo, Sansovino, or Raphael. He has created a style of his own, the Palladian building'.[11] This accent on 'comparison' and 'synthesis' leaves us to confront trans-habit in the understanding of art: the trans-habitual eros that does not stay immured in the nationalist bunkum but develops its travelling potential *across* systems, cultures and continents. This is not in being 'ought' but is in the 'is'; being British is becoming British with the German, Italians and the French.[12] There is a transpoetical hunger for the idea of wholeness but formed not with parts that are monochromatic and dogmatically affiliated to an inflexible core. Parts are distinct; they have their own hunger which combine cosmopolitically and transpoetically to produce an idea. This idea is the 'being with'—discovering oneself, not just 'how to live' but also what makes living. Tradition is a failure if deemed as rigid and transcendental;

tradition is life and 'sweetness' when it outlives any imposed dogmatism to start believing in 'incorporation', a connective momentum across borders. Trans-habit is the propriety of literary conduct which becomes both the authority and the order, transgression and culture. This chapter works on a trans-habitual moment of negotiation which tries to impotentialise Arnold as an Indian sage, working out of the sanctioned potentiality of his Victorian validation and sagist authority. The aesthetic moment of reinterrogation brings certain paradigms of Sanskrit poetics into a constellative reading of Arnold's poetics—a 'taking place'.

Talking about the formation of the poet, Arnold writes,

> Everything depends on the reality of a poet's classic character. If he is a dubious classic, let us sift him; if he is a false classic, let us explode him. But if he is a real classic, if his work belongs to the class of the very best …, then the great thing for us is to feel and enjoy his work as deeply as ever we can, and to appreciate the wide difference between it and all work which has not the same high character.[13]

The poet's attention should be fixed upon excellent models: the 'subject' must be human actions that appeal to elementary feelings, independent of time. The Greeks used 'great action' to control and govern the structure of poetry. Sanskrit literary theory in general also introduces the paradigm of *visaya* (subject) which determines the character of the artistic creation and aesthetic enjoyment (reference can be drawn to *Siddhantamuktavali* belonging to the Nyaya school). For Arnold, there is the relation between *visaya* (subject) and *proyojana* (another important paradigm in Sanskrit literary criticism) which means purpose. Anandavardhana and Abhinavagupta instruct the poets to be very careful in constructing their plot, character, situation and language following the principle of propriety. There are five successive stages in the entire plan of poetic composition: selection of the main plot, addition of sub plots, carrying the action toward fruition, concentration upon the sentiments (*rasa*) and arrangement of characters, situation, ornament, etc. proper to the desired sentiment. Arnold demonstrates similar principles of organisation and selects 'actions' that possess an inherent interest. This becomes the 'binding effect' of the final poetic discourse. *Visaya* in the Sanskrit poetical tradition is commonly held to mean something that regulates or directs; the prefix *vi* accordingly implies characteristics, and the root *si* is indicative of the sense of binding. Embedding the *visaya* in human action that appeals to elementary feelings (*sthayibhavas*) the poet is expected to provide the binding effect.[14]

The reasons that Arnold gives for excluding "Empedocles on Etna" from his collection of poems (1853) are pertinent. The poet should write to strengthen the individual. Poetry must do something for the reader and thereby for the society in which the poet is placed. It must cure him and society of 'sick hurry and divided aims', a kind of paralysis that results from the mind 'which has a sense of being divided within itself'. "Empedocles on Etna" is unrelieved by incident, hope, or resistance. Later, he raised the same question about the effect of "The Scholar-Gipsy" on the reader but he perhaps felt that it was more positive than "Empedocles". This crisis, in some form or another, troubled Arnold throughout his career. The poet is antagonistic to self-pity, enervation, immobilization caused by a mind divided against itself. In the 'Preface' Empedocles is seen to have had a mental spasm or self-schism. It was a malady from which the Spasmodics, as their name signifies, suffered as well—an over-morbid preoccupation with thought to the neglect of action. Representation to be poetical in the aesthetics of Arnold needs to interest, 'inspirit and rejoice the reader' and must 'convey a charm, and infuse delight'.[15] To Arnold, therefore, as to Aristotle, the joy that poetry imparts is dependent on its subject.[16] It is not merely the 'sheer penetrating power' that Wordsworth produced to impart joy; it also owes something to the 'profound sincereness with which Wordsworth feels his subject'.[17] Sanskrit poetics points out that poetry always and invariably gives us joy and the poet does not escape from life (it is important to note that Chaucer, even though he is not one of the great classics to Arnold, is a 'genuine source of joy and strength, which is flowing still for us and will flow always)'.[18] Rather, as the *Agni Purana* points out, the poet escapes into life. In the same register we find Rabindranath Tagore ascribing delight or joy as marks of creation of true art—the inner tumult of sentiments awaits a kind of organization and expression in beautiful and coherent forms where self-expressions are, on most occasions, self-realisations. For Tagore and Arnold, joy or *ananda* is not simply the product of a sense of coherence but it owes its manifestation to the poet's sense of life, the power to relate the inwardness of thought to the currents of outer life. Tagore himself points out in *Sahityer Pathe* that art does not aim at creating beauty but by creating forms that give us a sense of coherence or harmony (*sumiti*) it aims at giving us delight. The poet for Arnold generates *sumiti* by the proper choice of *visaya*—the premise from which discussion proceeds and argumentation emanates. The business of poets, Arnold writes,

> is not to praise their age, but to afford to the men who live in it the highest pleasure which they are capable of feeling. If asked to afford this by means of subjects drawn from the age itself, they ask what special fitness the present age has for supplying them: they are told that it is an era of progress, an age commissioned to carry out the great ideas of industrial development and social amelioration. They reply that with all this they can do nothing; that the elements they need for the exercise of their art are *great actions*, calculated powerfully and delightfully *to affect what is permanent in the human soul*.[19]

This mention of the 'permanent in the human soul' brings us to the subject of *bhava* (emotion/feeling) and the notion of *sthayibhava*. These emotions, as Abhinavagupta points out, are inborn impressions that are latent in our mind and help attain *rasa*. The poet should select actions of such nature that 'most powerfully appeal to those elementary feelings which are independent of time'.[20] Tagore, like Arnold, notes that 'emotional idea' (in his own words) expressed in art must be true and deeply felt and there needs to be a complete idea that animates a poem so that every part of the poem becomes radiantly significant by the light of the whole.[21] 'Elementary feelings' should form the deep core of art, and for Arnold and Tagore they also form the source of delight in art. One must look into Tagore's 'The Creative Ideal' to observe the process by which in 'great' art, deeply felt, elementary feelings become impersonal and universal. Thus Tagore's ideas on such permanently deep emotions—the notion of *sthayibhava* in Sanskrit poetics and Arnold's idea of 'elementary feelings'—help us to note that (and indeed Tagore makes us see) creation in Shakespearean plays 'throbs with Eternal Passion, Eternal Pain'. *Sthayibhava* are principal emotions in Arnold's poetic compositions and it is agreed that when these permanent emotions are invoked, a certain state of mind is achieved that communicates delight. The production of delight, the experience in art's completeness or totality, appeals to the intellect, the drive to sustain art through extraordinarily striking expression and the premium on form. Within a trans-(in)fusionist premise the major principles of Arnold's poetic art fall within the purview of *rasa* theory. For instance, in "The Scholar-Gipsy" there is the repeated heightening of the dominant mood centering on the Scholar-Gipsy in contrast to the life of the Victorians. Arnold avoids impropriety of expression by accentuating the presence of *rasa* and allows the emotions generated therein to have an obstructed growth and distillation. Abhinavagupta's identification of a few features that contribute to the unhindered *rasa* experience assists us to understand Arnold's thesis better: the use of disciplined imagination, the ability of the poet to exhibit a sense of time and place, moderate reliance on personal joys and tribulations, harmonising the dominant impulse of emotions and sentiments without losing clarity and a skilful subordination of the dominant emotion in the skein of the poetic tissue.[22] The poet needs to make his creation convincing, which, for instance, the symbolic portraiture of the Scholar-Gipsy or Thomas Arnold in "Rugby Chapel" has successfully accomplished. The emotions in the poem are adroitly subordinated to the dominant emotion that results in *rasa*. The importance to *sthayibhavas* is maintained throughout and poetic excellences are carefully attended to produce the aesthetic relish within the domains of propriety. It thus avoids *rasavighna* (*rasa*-rupture).

I

Arnold stands on the same ground as Anandavardhana and Mammata in his belief that the poet's art aims higher, is cathartic and the poet cannot conceal the ugliness of the substance of his art in the event of a compromise with subject (*visaya*). Such a compromise cannot be compensated by rhetorical embellishment.[23] The Greeks understood this better than others. The poetical character of the action in itself was their first consideration:

> with us, attention is fixed mainly on the value of the separate thoughts and images which occur in the treatment of an action. They regarded the whole; we regard the parts. With them action predominated over the expression of it; with us, the expression predominates over the action. Not that they failed in expression, or were inattentive to it; on the contrary, they are the highest models of expression, the unapproached masters of the grand style: but their expression is so excellent because it is so admirably kept in its right degree of prominence; because it is so simple and so well subordinated; because it draws its force directly from the pregnancy of the matter which it conveys.[24]

Passing actions possess so much that is of passing value that the Greeks wisely left them for the comic poets. For the Arnoldian poet expression is subservient to the excellence of action. In congruence with Arnold's principle of affiliation to a 'whole', Tagore sees a genuine work of art as much more than the 'emotional idea' expressed in it, just as a rose is much more than its substance. For both then, the ideal of art lies in the fusion of construction and emotional idea (cf 'The Realisation of the Infinite'). Tagore points out that in a work of art the handling of technique and the inspiration of vision are both necessary and his aesthetic commitment to blend the two paradigms is principally congruent with Arnold's view on the relation of the whole and the part. So it becomes an acknowledgement of the *sambandha* (relation) between the 'expressed whole' and the pregnancy of the *visaya*: *sadhya-sadhana-bhava* or *vacya-vacaka-bhava*.[25] This *sambandha* provides an insight into the relation between the poet and the *visaya* keeping delight and wisdom as its telos.

It is agreed then that the total impression or the *symmetria prisca* is the poet's prime concern—"Who saw life steadily, and saw it whole;" ("To a Friend" 12). His art should not influence in parts but should impact as a whole. However, without being a simple inevitable whole it must be an event that is guided by a deep internal law of development towards a necessary end. Certain dimness and indistinctness may impair the impression but a vigorous action has everything to it, the consolidated point of convergence. A poet has to develop situations stroke by stroke without wasting a word and freakishly throwing in a sentiment. The aesthetic finality is dependent on proportion (*sumiti*), coherence and organicity much like Tagore's metaphorical description of the rainbow in which the radiant manifestation of all colours are accommodated in their 'proper' places through an adjustment that articulates through totality. Sanskrit literary theorist Mammata sees this relation between the part and the whole as the root of *suddhalaksana* (the points that raise the levels of what can be ascribed as the *totum*); this relation is meaningfully aggravated—*avayava avayavibhava*—with the explanation of the term *agra-hasta* (forearm) in which *hasta* is meant only for a part of it. It is, thus, an acknowledgment of the *Riti* of the poet when

Riti, as Visvanatha points out, 'is comparable to the arrangement of the parts in relation to the whole'.[26] Arnold writes,

> ... modern poetry can only subsist by its contents: by becoming a complete magister vitae as the poetry of the ancients did: by including as theirs did, religion with poetry, instead of existing as poetry only, and leaving religious wants to be supplied by the Christian religion, as a power existing independent of the poetical power. But the language, style, and general proceedings of a poetry which has such an immense task to perform, must be very plain direct and severe: and it must not lose itself in parts and episodes and ornamental work, but must press forward to the whole.[27]

This is the attunement of outward expression with inward sense—the *Riti* which arises from the proper unification of *Gunas* or from a harmonious adjustment of sound and sense.[28] Here the true poet sees the segments of life in its totality—the Hellenic principles of subordinating expression to construction[29]—penetrating into the essential, underlying realities that help him to conjure a comprehensive vision:

> ...—he must life's movement tell!
> The thread which binds it all in one,
>   And not its separate parts alone.
>   ("Epilogue to Lessing's Laocoon" 140–43)

Based on philhellenistic tendencies where 'imaginative reason'[30] determines the tenor of poetic art, Keats and Shakespeare become bad models for younger poets to imitate. However, Shakespeare occurs to him as 'a name never to be mentioned without reverence' for he 'chose excellent subjects', 'had no theory of choosing subjects of present import', finding 'his best in past times', and he 'knew well what constituted a poetical action'[31]—all of which fits in well with Arnold's concept of the poet.

> ....Thou art free,
> We ask and ask—Thou smilest and art still,
> Out-topping knowledge.
>   ("Shakespeare" 1–3)

But Shakespeare has—it strikes Ben Jonson as well—such an unbridled expression, a gift of happy phrase, that he is unable to say a thing plainly, even when the weight of the action demands an uncomplicated expression. Arnold's poet knows 'how unspeakably superior is the affect of the one moral impression left by a great action treated as a whole, to the effect produced by the most striking single thought or by the happiest image'. He will cultivate, too, a respect for 'the wholesome regulative laws of poetry', which are threatened by 'their eternal enemy, Caprice'.[32] Toward the close of the preface he quotes Goethe[33] (clearly, Arnold is here under the spell of Goethe, who possesses the double notion of seeing the whole and seeing things as a whole about two kinds of dilettanti: 'he who neglects the indispensable mechanical part, and thinks he has done enough if he shows spirituality and feeling; and he who seeks to arrive at poetry merely by mechanism, in which he can acquire an artisan's readiness, and is without soul and matter'.[34] He says he would prefer to be the second kind since the first seems to do most harm to art). On such principles of creativity like 'avoidance of caprice', 'wholesome regulative laws of poetry' and the 'moral affect' we have a substantial diffractive correspondence with Bhamaha and Anandavardhana who see forcefulness and perspicuity as distinctive qualities of poetic activity and with Mammata for whom poetic creativity involves *dipti* which is expansion of mind.

About the importance of expression, Tagore writes: 'Unuttered poetry and self contained expression are two unmeaning phrases that have gained currency in certain quarters. But to call a person a poet, who may be gazing at the sky in rapture as silent as the sky itself, is like giving the name of fire to a piece of wood that is not alight. Poetry is expression; what is or is not silently passing through a person's mind matters little to others who are outside it'.[35] However, expression is not the 'whole' of art, for art needs to have a 'weighty' content. Expression is as important as how much is expressed and art for Tagore and Arnold cannot overlook the value of imagination as the living power and prime agent of all human perception. Both of them believe that the laws of poetic beauty and poetic truth are about comprehending and communicating the sense of the wholeness of life—'the fullness of being'. But there is a strong agreement on the principle of restraint in art and the internal law of development for untrained imagination, as Tagore points out, cannot hope to create beauty. It impedes the efficaciousness of *rasa* in art but judicious and productive functionality of imagination contributes to the notional profundity of *rasa* in art. However, a distortion of the central truth about the creative imagination has brought about confusion, and the emphasis has come to be laid on art as 'a true allegory of the state of one's own mind in a representative history'. This has notional proximity to the confusion resulting from a reliance on the inner voice against which Eliot had to protest later. Arnold realised that even Goethe's Faust was remembered more for its wonderful local felicities of expression (texture) than for its structure. But art for Tagore, as also for Arnold, is an expression of humanity; it is not identical with mere expression. Further, if expression is taken to mean internal expression only (Benedetto Croce's intuition) then art is not synonymous with it: art requires (besides intuition or internal expression) external or naturalistic expression.

II

The best poetry, Arnold professed, was a criticism of life under the conditions fixed for such a criticism by the laws of poetic truth and poetic beauty.

134 *'O life unlike to ours!'*

In fact, Sanskrit poetic theory evinces, as also do Tagore and Sri Aurobindo, the ontology and ramifications of poetic truth and beauty recommending a strength at the core of poetry. The poet should have for his subject some weighty idea or substantial action accompanied by a sense of architectonice. We can embed Arnold's sense of architectonice within the lineaments of Sanskrit poetical tradition which sees 'totality' as achieved through:

    i. Poetic configuration (*Rasa*)
    ii. Embellishment (*Alankara*)
    iii. Arrangement of words (*Riti*)
    iv. Strikingness of expression (*Vakrokti*)
    v. Propriety (*Aucitya*)
    vi. Charmingness in expression (*Camatkara*)
    vii. Aesthetic beauty (*Ramaniyata*)

The poet in Arnold combines the word and sense to a certain level of perfection.[36] Dandin notes that words characterised by an agreeable sense constitute the framework of poetry and, expression, thus, plays a dominant role in creation. It is to the credit of the poet to know that the charm of expression (*camatkara*) is what communicates delight.[37] In a poem such as "The Scholar-Gipsy", we find the poet's striking arrangement of words something that Vamana would see as a particularity that comes due to excellences in *riti* (modes of expression).[38] Vamana defines *sabda-gunas* (sound-attributes) as the *gunas* of the composition or the construction of the words. The two types of *gunas* fully explain the excellence of both: the word construction and meaning. The scope of *artha-gunas* is wide enough to include almost all the means of creating or producing poetic excellence, so much so that all the charms of *rasa* are included in the forms of striking expression: *uktivaicitrya* in the *madhurya* (charm of the artistic whole). It is through *riti* that the poet works on the levels of communication achieved, most often, through emotive mood.[39] For Arnold's poet the togetherness of sound (*sabda-gunas*) and sense (*artha-gunas*) is an intense point of engagement which a close look at these lines does not fail to reveal:

> The blackbird, picking food,
> Sees thee, nor stops his meal, nor fears at all;
> So often has he known thee past him stray,
> Rapt, twirling in thy hand a wither"d spray,
> And waiting for the spark from heaven to fall.
>   ("The Scholar-Gipsy", 116–20)

Word and sense have the harmony (*sumiti*) in these lines; the lines also exhibit the strikingness of expression (what Kuntaka call *vakrokti*)—'waiting for the spark from heaven to fall'—which creates delight in the connoisseur and introduces *sumiti* between the expression and the expressed. Arnold vindicates the necessity in the poet to grow a masterful control over *riti*; he sees the dynamism of the composition (*bandha*) subordinating the *gunas* into one composite whole. The sense of the presence of the scholar-gipsy, the proximity to nature and the meaningful contrast that he shares with the 'sick hurry' and 'divided aims' of the Victorians produce the *rasa* whose realisation comes to be legitimated within the aesthetic principle of propriety (*aucitya*). Arnold's poetics grant a rigorous consciousness of certain modes of expression, poetic configuration, embellishment and maturity (*paka*), contributing to the poetic charm (*camatkara*).[40] Arnold's evaluation of Chaucer highlights the 'lovely charm of his diction, the lovely charm of his movement'[41] and it is these *gunas* that produce the poetic appeal and the aesthetic delight towards the realisation of the *camatkara*. Milton, thus, qualifies as the model poet for he never departs from a style that is 'high and pure'—the 'discipline of respect for a high and flawless excellence' was his forte. So the poet needs to acknowledge the *kavyadosa* (poetic flaw) for 'best poetry will be found to have a power of forming, sustaining, and delighting us, as nothing else can'.[42] If that be true, then the poet needs to ensure an expression of thought and emotion that resists *arthadosa* (flaw in vague expression: incongruity and obstruction in comprehension of meaning and understanding giving rise to flaw of sense) and *rasadosa* (flaw in emotive mood). Poetry with high seriousness and 'penetrating power' of truth (in the words of Arnold) would avoid impropriety of sentiment (*rasavighna*) and cultivate, instead, as Anandavardhana notes, a remarkable proficiency, perspicuity (*prasada*), *arthavyakti* (clearness of expression), polish (*kanti* or brightness of style), and magnificence (*udarata*).[43] It is what Arnold qualifies as 'virtue'. Arnold's probing of Robert Burns' poetry manifests the emphasis on 'independence, equality, dignity of men' and an embellishment that acknowledges 'high seriousness which come from absolute sincerity' and the accent on the 'poetic virtue of the highest masters'[44]; the development of a poet hinges on the command over 'thorough truth of substance' and 'answering truth of style', which thereby gives us 'poetry sound to the core'.[45] It is what Kuntaka chose to identify as harmony—a sublime thought needs agreeable expression where sound and sense combine with a 'strikingness'.[46] Even Tagore acknowledges this strikingness which comes from a resonant integration where the truth of the content and technique come in for a close pairing up. Expressions produced through such an integration require, as Tagore observes, 'tune, gestures and postures. This idea has to be dressed, as the mother dresses her child, as the bridal chamber is decorated with garlands of flowers. The art of literature is in its rhythm, in the music of its sounds, in the choice and arrangement of words'.[47] For both Tagore and Arnold, art is the expression of a definite subject matter and not the expression of any and every subject: it is the adroit expression of a well-defined content. Arnold acknowledges how the form becomes the container into which the poet can pour the content. In Wordsworth, Arnold points out, the profound truth of subject and execution are balanced—the congruity between conception and expression, which is the result of the *trueness* of the poet.

When Arnold talks of congruence between sound and sense or form and content or expression and construction, the corresponding notion of *aucitya* (the principle of propriety) in Sanskrit aesthetics readily penetrates our discussion. *Aucitya* informs the viewing of a poetic composition as an entirety which, principally, comes close to Arnold's view of the 'whole' in art. Poetic beauty is dependent on *aucitya* and it is quite productive to see how *aucitya* in poetic composition relates to the *aucitya* of imagination, the *aucitya* of subject-matter, and the corresponding concept-formations in Arnold. Arnold's poetic art appreciates the combination of *sthyaibhava*, *rasa* and expression and, excels in the appropriate employment of such paradigms.[48] Ksemendra expounds how the principal and subordinate parts in emotion and construction are meaningfully harmonised; he writes beautifully:

> The girdle placed on the neck or the necklace on the waist make a body ridiculous. Similarly, anklets tied on the wrist and bracelet on the feet, valour shown to one who has already bowed down his head and compassion to an attacking enemy are fit to be laughed at. It is the same thing that happens in the case of *Guna* and *Alamkara* in poetry. Introduction of inappropriate figures and excellences becomes ridiculous.[49]

Aucitya in Arnoldian poetics stands to be realised through the congruity between emotions, the subordination of sentiments to the 'chosen' subject, the integration of the parts to the whole and the modes of expression. And poetry, as an expression hinging dominantly on *aucitya*, is an interpretation of life as the poet experiences and knows it, bringing into play the maturity of his intellect and mind brought about by experience and reading. Poetry is not, however, merely an intellectual exercise; it is subject to the laws of poetic truth and beauty. These laws insist on one condition: the poet's treatment of life. The recurrent stress on joy which is clarified by his addressing of poetry as speaking to the 'great primary human affection' and 'the elementary part of our nature' seems to refute an interpretation of 'high seriousness as churchyard solemnity'.[50] Indeed the quality of high seriousness comes out of the deepest sincerity that the poet feels for the subject. Arnold makes us aware that 'excellence is not common and abundant'; on the contrary, as the Greek poet long ago said, 'excellence dwells among rocks hardly accessible, and a man must almost wear his heart out before he can reach her'.[51] This accent on high seriousness can be found in the poetry of Dante, Homer, and Milton and this is what gives their poetry its power. It is this excellence that becomes the *nipunata* (loosely translated as proficiency) in art. *Nipunata* in Sanskrit poetics is interpreted as accruing from

i. Observation of the ways of the world,
ii. The study of various sciences (*sastras*),
iii. Study of poetical works of high merit.[52]

High seriousness and the style (poet is the man of industriousness and select reading)[53] in which it is clothed cannot be separated and the best way to define poetry is not to do it in the prose of a critic but to recognise it by feeling it in the verse of a master. Touchstones form a part of the *nipunata* of the poet.[54] The touchstones have all the characteristics one would expect in Arnold's poet—solemnity, sublimity, a melancholy reflection on life and its transience and a longing for the impossible. In Ksemendra's *Kavikanthabharana* the poet is expected to learn from 'touchstones'—'the study of poetical works of high merit'. Ksemendra shows us the necessity to pursue the study of the works of 'master poets' and how practise and understanding of the rhythm and skill of master poets help the aspirants to grasp the high seriousness of poetic art. So we cannot deny Arnold concurring with Ksemendra on the acquisitive dimensions of poetic art where all poetic virtues are not inborn (*sahaja*).[55] Consequently, we encounter *vyutpatti* which Rajashekhara sees as the 'discretion between proper and improper things or ideas'.[56] And it is through touchstones that Arnold's poet cultivates *vyutpatti* leading to *nipunata*.[57] Touchstones thus demand an alert mind: they demand what Dandin points out as a constant application of mind which tries to figure out the depth of thought, the range of emotion, and the finesse of construction.[58]

The sincerity of the poet comes from his speaking from the depths of his soul (the 'high-wrought mood'[59]) and this sincerity should be consistent and found uniformly throughout the poem. The soul of poetic power 'resides chiefly in the refining and elevation wrought in us by the high and rare excellence of the great style'.[60] The refinity and elevation are the products of *nipunata* in art. It is the poet's commitment—Aristotlean *spoudaiotes*—which gives authenticity to an order and vision of life behind the verbal:

> The poet to whose mighty heart
> Heaven cloth a quicker pulse impart,
> Subdues that energy to scan
> Not his own course, but that of man.
>
> ("Resignation" 144–47)

The poet cannot rest content with a romantic self-absorption for that would render his art weak much in the same way Keats's art for Arnold became enervated. With a quick internal impulse, the poet experiences the strong and beautiful forces of life and yet grows a detachment that whets his aesthetic appetite.[61] The poet must not stray into more than one sense because that precludes a disciplined accomplishment. This is another impediment to *rasa* in art—the *rasadosa*. Eschewing romantic excess the poet has the 'stream of life's majestic whole'[62] mirrored in the soul, manifesting, thereby, an untiring attendance on life's activity with the dual aim of combination and transcendence. This is the gift of 'fine balance':

> their eye
> Drinks up delighted ecstasy,
> And its deep-toned, melodious voice
> For ever makes their ear rejoice.

> They speak! the happiness divine
> They feel, runs o'er in every line;
> Its spell is round them like a shower—
> It gives them pathos, gives them power. (194–200)

III

The poet is expected to exude a kind of energy through each curve and angle of his art: the accent is on objectivity, 'steadiness' and joy in expression, which becomes the essential function of his art. Wordsworth, Arnold's model poet, 'has an insight into permanent sources of joy and consolation for mankind'.[63] In this context of the production of joy in art, Arnold writes: 'The source of joy from which he thus draws is the truest and most unfailing source of joy accessible to man. It is also accessible universally'.[64] He

> Sees his strong thought in fiery flood
> Roll through the heaving multitude;
> Exults—yet for no moment's space
> Envies the all-regarded place.
>
> ("Resignation", 155–58)

However, the poet, exulting in the 'heaving multitude', cannot afford to stand alone. He cannot say: 'I am alone' ("Resignation", 169). In a transpoetical momentum, he is one with Kahlil Gibran's poet who believes that in direct communication with the outer world lies the enrichment and extension of the inner self.

> Heaven fills my lamp with oil and I place it at my window to direct the stranger through the dark. I do all these things because I live in them; and if destiny should tie my hands and prevent me from so doing, then death would be my only desire. For I am a poet, and if I cannot give, I shall refuse to receive.[65]

The poet, for both Arnold and Gibran, mingles with the crowd, sees the gentle stir of birth, has the murmur of a thousand years in his ears, and with a Sophoclean breadth of vision, perceives life as a continuous whole that does not cease and 'whose secret is not joy, but peace'.[66] The poet achieves a superior self and a 'stillness' that the moonlight has, that the bee has while sucking honey from the chosen flower and which a wisdom-fed soul possesses. He is free from the accidents of the weary kingdom of time, imparting a new sense to men and making them find a world within their world. With his innate power,

> He read each wound, each weakness clear;
> And stuck his finger on the place,
> And said: Thou ailest here, and here!
>
> ("Memorial Verses", 20–22)

Arnold's poet needs to accomplish 'the noble and profound application of ideas to life', including his powerful application to his subject, of ideas 'on man, on nature, and on human life'. The primary concern of the poet is to rest his art upon that 'great and inexhaustible word life', dealing with it 'as a whole, more powerfully'.[67] In fact, in Arnold's aesthetic view no true greatness can be achieved when the poet's art is either a revolt against life or an indifference toward life. For Arnold poetry does not present life as it is, but rather adds something to it from the poet's own noble nature, and this *something* contributes to his criticism of life. The poet gives to his poetry what he really and seriously believes in; he speaks from the depths of his soul and speaks beautifully enough to create a perennial source of joy. Arnold observes that the poet's art must sustain and delight us as it answers the question, 'How to live?' by conforming to the ideals of truth and goodness. Similar thoughts on such moralistic and ethical underpinning in poetry can be noted in Bhamaha who points out that poetry facilitates four aims of human life (*caturvarga*): *Dharma* (virtue), *Artha* (material wealth), *Kama* (fulfillment of desire), and *Moksha* (salvation). Aesthetic delight apart, he notes, poetry deals with what Arnold qualifies as 'How to live?' and, thus, brings out the importance of 'virtue'.[68] This lends artistic sincerity and produces the finality of the aesthetic experience. Even sincerity for Tagore is the execution of his task in its essential nature and for Arnold it means a model of propriety and surrender to the fullness of expression where the ethical and the aesthetic happily meet.

Tagore feels that in art, communication is a conscious process:

> It was Tagore's considered opinion that the great authors never tried to be original at the cost of hampering communication; they took the most universal feelings and thoughts (which were also simple in character) for their subject matter. They consciously addressed the society, and expression was a conscious process.[69]

By describing a poem as a 'compromise of inspiration, taste, and judgment on one hand and public taste, past and present on the other', Tagore can be repremised within Arnoldian aesthetics. When expression is the primary truth about literature, Tagore believes that 'the chief indication of literature consists in its relationship with human life'. Quite relevantly, Dandin notes, too, that 'by all means life's journey in this world is carried on with the help of words imparted by the intelligent to the "enlightened" of society'.[70] So poetry leads to *lokayatra* (worldly dealings) and *vyavahanavida* (knowledge of the ways of the world.[71] In an aesthetic context, the poet's personality and nature/society do not exist opposed to each other but evince their complementarity. When the poet creates he writes for himself, for others, and for the society present or future. Here, in one respect, self-expression becomes self-socialization. The choosing of the content or the *visaya* is a matter of emotional and intuitive apprehension and in this apprehension the whole 'social mind' in seen to work. Both Arnold and Tagore declare a strong disavowal for 'pure' art, if by purity of art we mean the formalistic dimensions emptied of socio-ethical significance. Their humanism coloured their aesthetic creed and by keeping art free from the didactic and tendentious influences they ensured its protection from sterile purism.

So Goethe[72] emerges as the clearest, largest and the most helpful thinker of modern times—a 'physician of the iron age'. In the background of a soul-numbing age, Arnold accords Wordsworth a similar status:

> He too upon a wintry clime
> Had fallen—on this iron time
> Of doubts, disputes, distractions, fears.
> He found us when the age had bound
> Our souls in its benumbing round;
> He spoke, and loosed our heart in tears.
>
> ("Memorial Verses" 42–47)

He understands the real value of 'tears'—Arnold, it may be observed, harbors a complaint against the Carthusian monks. Through his sensibility, he combines light, wisdom, and freedom, evoking a power that makes the hitherto 'worn-out smile break forth with the freshness of a sun-lit field'. By his powers of receptivity he can grasp reality in all its grandeur, doling out installments of knowledge to the 'inconsummate' community.

So poetry as criticism of life would suggest that the poet's art is an interpretation and a healing representation of life. Dryden and Pope, as poets, lose the imaginative life of the soul as their criticism of life is not a 'poetic criticism'; their application of ideas to life may be powerful but proceeding principally from ratiocination, antithesis and clever craftsmanship it falls short of genuine poetry. Leopardi, whom Arnold admired highly, loses out against Wordsworth and Goethe because of his pessimism, and Coleridge is criticised for his lack of joy which seems to Arnold something unnatural and shocking. The poet's art then should touch some profound truth in man, enabling poetry to interpret and it is in this sense that life is the subject of interpretation. Criticism of life signifies evaluation and feeling for sympathetic 'sharing in' and Arnold believes, as I.A. Richards does, that poetry is sure to take the place of religion because it is in poetry that the religious, moral, and aesthetic elements coalesce. Poetry, for Arnold, has a twofold function: poetry as interpretation of the physiognomy and movement of the natural world, and poetry as the interpretation of the inward world of man's moral and spiritual nature. Arnold can only reject the poetry of Omar Khayyam which he says represents a revolt against moral ideas. His *weltanschauung* disclaims any dogmatic philosophy but stands as the convincing principle that has morality touched with emotion. However, Arnold is against direct moral teaching for he regards didactic poetry as the lowest kind of poetry. Without being simply didactic the poet needs to be concrete and Arnold criticises Emerson for lacking in concreteness and energy. Arnold and Tagore are one in agreeing that the poet's style has to have order, elegance, and charm. Style, here, could mean something moral and ethical as well: style could be the expression of the nobility of the poet's character. The true poet's work is a work of synthesis and exposition; his creative being lies in being happily inspired by a certain intellectual and spiritual milieu, and by a particular order of ideas. He presents the most effective and attractive combination without being analytical and exploratory, making, thus, his art survive as an interpretation of the natural world. Cultivating natural magic and moral profundity, the power of his art draws out an explanation of the 'mystery' of the universe, a strength that awakens in us a new, intimate, and wonderfully profound sense of things along with our relation to them.

Arnold, as I have tried to argue, has survived the anxieties of what I call transpoetical xenophobia: a survival that he himself would have loved to relish in a productive hyphen, in his own unmaking. The trans-habitual establishment, a reformulated address, in being an Indian sage comes with varying planes of interference. The transference that works upon Arnold's poetics is not wholly a decontextualised functionalism whose motive is mere comparison. This is the smooth space where Arnold's poetic theory, Tagore and relevant parameters of Sanskrit poetics co-evolve and mutually endow through co-particularity—'effective history is[73] efficacy at a distance'. Under the dynamics of trans-habit, no text can be read without interference and does profit from what Steven Yao call the 'gradient': it is 'a conception of difference that operates not through absolute, fixed distinctions, but rather by means of relative, phased dimensions. Instead of a radical discontinuity, such a model, or "figure" to use Spivak's terminology, imagines difference in a more complex and potentially useful way as a spectrum or a series of continua of variance, making it possible not only to undertake comparisons along any number of conceptual or material axes, but also to recognize gradations within and among those dimensions of difference. It makes the domain of comparison a space of potential relations, and a multi-dimensional one at that, instead of an indifferentiable accumulation of atomistic discontinuities. In doing so, the gradient enables nothing less than a reconfiguration of the very conditions of possibility for the act of comparison'.[74] Arnold, caught within the mediative space of trans-habit, teleiopoetically signals the crossing of distance with certain parameters of Sanskrit poetics, something of a co-evolutionary perspective that 'is imagining yourself, really letting yourself be imagined (experience the impossibility) without guarantees, by and in another culture, perhaps'.[75] Trans-habit draws both on close and distant reading which are heavily mediatory and contrastive—an activist philosophy in supplementation, differentiation and unveiling. If Arnold is our Indian sage, it is not a designation but a transubstantiation in habit, the projective power of habit, its 'taking place'.

Notes

1. John Dryden, *Of Dramatic Poesy and Other Critical Essays* (ed.) George Watson, 2 vols. (London: J.M. Dent and Sons, 1962), II, 49.
2. Howard F. Lowry (ed.) *The Letters of Matthew Arnold to Arthur Hugh Clough* (Oxford: Clarendon Press, 1932), 64–65.
3. Werner P. Friederich, preface to *Outline of Comparative Literature from Dante Alighieri to Eugene O'Neill* (Chapel Hill: University of North Carolina Press, 1954).
4. R. H. Super, *The Complete Prose Works of Matthew Arnold*, Vol. V, 94, 16–27.
5. Ibid., Vol. IV, 322.
6. See my Chapter 9 'Ethics of Reading Sahitya' in *Thinking Literature across Continents* (Durham: Duke University Press, 2016, co-authored with J. Hillis Miller).
7. *The Complete Prose Works of Matthew Arnold*, VI, 168.
8. Arnold, 'On the Modern Element in Literature', *The Complete Prose Works of Matthew Arnold*, Vol. I, 21. 'Dryden, Arnold and Eliot are deeply concerned with a European rather than merely an English literary tradition'. Robert D. Hume, in *Dryden's Criticism* (Ithaca, N.Y.: Cornell University Press, 1970), 19. In fact, all three were comparatists, who did not exhaust the potential of literary thinking within the confines of their culture and literature like most others. They believed in a life unlike ours—a life invested in the 'with' much in the spirit in which Dryden observed: 'no art or science is at once begun and perfected, but that it must pass first through many hands, and even through several ages' (*Of Dramatic Poesy and Other Critical Essays*, II, 139).
9. Quoted in Brendan Rapple, 'Matthew Arnold and Comparative Education', *British Journal of Educational Studies*, 37, no. 1 (Feb. 1989), 58.
10. See Donald D. Stone, 'Matthew Arnold and the Pragmatics of Hebraism and Hellenism', *Poetics Today*, 19, no. 2 (Summer 1998), 185. Jan M. Ziolkowski observes that the 'French basis for the English expression "comparative literature" dates back to 1816 (and think what unsettled years preceded this one) in the title *Cours de Litterature comparee* attached to a series of anthologies used for the teaching of literature. From there the phrase, literally meaning "compared literature" and modelled on sciences such as comparative anatomy, seeped into wider currency over the next two decades, despite the illogic of the singular literature: If comparison is going on, then there should be more than one (Weisstein 9).Yet the collective noun is revealing, since for more than a century and a half the French tradition of comparative literature contained a presumption that the comparing would involve, de rigueur one might say, French literature as either the source or destination of the comparison. In 1835, Philarete Euphemon Chasles (1798–1873) attempted to define "Litterature etrangere compare" with an unabashedly Gallocentric viewpoint: "France is the most sensitive of all countries. What Europe is to the rest of the world, France is to Europe." Other Romance languages followed suit later, such as Spanish with "literatura comparada," Portuguese with "litteratura comparada," and Italian with "letteratura comparata." German has the corresponding expression "vergleichende Literatur," which becomes established in the second half of nineteenth century. Its first attestation is in a book which refers to "vergleichende Literaturgeschichte." The peculiarity of the German formulation and the corresponding Dutch one ("vergelijkend literatuuronderzoek") is that they convey the idea of

'O life unlike to ours!'   143

comparing literature, but in such a way almost as to imply that the literature itself is doing the comparing. The most common German term, "vergleichende Literaturwissenschaft," could be translated as "comparative study of literature." In English, the first usage involves the plural "comparative literatures," recorded in a letter written in 1848 by none other than Matthew Arnold (1822–1888), the English poet and critic'. See 'Incomparable: The Destiny of Comparative Literature, Globalization or Not' *The Global South*, 1, no. 2, (Fall 2007), 16–44.

11. Shirley Robin Letwin, 'Matthew Arnold: Enemy of Tradition' *Political Theory*, 10, no. 3 (Aug. 1982), 338.
12. Arnold's deep interest in French literature and thought inspired Sainte-Beuve to write to Arnold (25 January 1863): 'Vous avez traversé notre littérature … par une ligne intérieure, profonde, qui fait les initiés et que vous ne perdrez jamais'. See G. W. E. Russell, *Matthew Arnold* (New York: Haskell House Publishers Ltd, 1904), 193; also, see Iris Sells Esther, *Matthew Arnold and France:The Poet* (Cambridge, 1935). For greater elaboration of Arnold's French connection, especially an interesting section on *Bhagavadgita* and orientalism of Arnold and Senancour, see pages 58–80.
13. Matthew Arnold, *Essays in Criticism* First and Second Series (London: J.M. Dent & Sons Ltd., 1964), 239.
14. See Raja Radhakantadeva (ed.) *Sabdakalpradruma* (Delhi: Motilal Banarasidass, 1961).
15. Edmund Jones, *English Critical Essays (Nineteenth Century)* (Oxford: Oxford University Press, 1919), 357.
16. For similar ideas, see Bharata's *Natyasastra*; M.R. Kavi, (ed) *Natyasastra* (Baroda: Oriental Research Institute, 1934).
17. Arnold, *Essays in Criticism*, 309.
18. Ibid., 246.
19. Jones, *English Critical Essays (Nineteenth Century)*, 372–73; italics added.
20. Ibid., 360.
21. Tagore, *Sadhana* (Madras: Macmillan, 1979), 40.
22. R. S. Tripathi, (ed.) *Dhvanyaloka* (Delhi: Motilal Banarasidas, 1963), 280.
23. Rhetorical embellishment (*alamkara*) is an important segment in Sanskrit poetics and indeed the *madurya* (charm in poetic art) is fructified through the combination of the subject (*visaya*) and *alamkara*. This combination works effectively in Arnold, bringing him closer to his purposes (*prayojana*) in aesthetic rendition/experiences. I stress the congruence in thought between Arnold, the Sanskrit aesthetic tradition, and the Hellenic concept of *collacatio*.
24. Jones, *English Critical Essays (Nineteenth Century)*, 362; italics added.
25. See M. Hiriyana (ed.) *Vedantarasa of Sadananda Yati* (Poona: Oriental Book Agency, 1929).
26. Pt. Durgaprasada (ed.) *Sahityadarpana* (Bombay: Nirnayasagara Press, 1931), 4.
27. G. Robert Stange, *Matthew Arnold The Poet as Humanist* (Princeton University Press, 1967), 35.
28. S. K. De, *History of Sanskrit Poetics* (Calcutta: K.L. Mukhopadhyay, 1960), 72.
29. Architectonice reminds me of Lu Chi's assertion that poetry shall be 'exquisite as fine patterned silk'. It is worthwhile to mention a few lines from his *Exposition on Literature*: 'As an object, literature presents many appearances;/ As form, it undergoes constant changes./ In joining ideas together one should esteem skill;/ In choosing words, one should value beauty. As for the alternation of sounds and tones,/ They should be like the five colors enhancing each other'.

See James J.Y. Liu, *Chinese Theories of Literature* (Chicago: University of Chicago Press, 1975), 102.
30. Lionel Gossman, 'Philhellenism and Antisemitism: Matthew Arnold and His German Models' *Comparative Literature* 46, no. 1 (Winter 1994), 1–39.
31. Jones, *English Critical Essays (Nineteenth Century)*, 366, 367.
32. Ibid,. 371, 375.
33. Helen C. White, 'Matthew Arnold and Goethe', *PMLA* 36, no. 3 (Sep. 1921), 436–53.
34. Jones, *English Critical Essays (Nineteenth Century)*, 374.
35. Prabas Jiban Choudhury, *Tagore on Literature and Aesthetics* (Calcutta: Rabindra Bharati, 1965), 123.
36. On this issue of the combination of sense and words, see Bhamaha's *Kavyalankara* (ed.) P.V. Sastry Naganath (Delhi: Motilal Banarsidass, 1970). For similar ideas, see Rudrata's *Kavyalankara*, (ed.) Pt. Durgaprasada (Bombay: Nirnayasagar Press, 1928).
37. For more details, see R. C. Mishra (ed.) *Kavyadarsha* I (Varanasi: Chowkhamba Vidyabhavana, 1958).
38. N. R. Acharya, (ed.) *Kavyalankarasutravritti* (Bombay: Nirnayasagara Press, 1953), 6–8.
39. It may be noted that the sound element is significant in the Vedic texts and in the case of *Itihasa* (history) and Puranic texts the element of sense seems to hold sway.
40. For more elaboration on this issue we can see *Camatkaracandrika* of Visvesvara, which is an interesting treatise on literary criticism in Sanskrit. See P. Shriramamurti (ed.) *Camatkaracandrika* (Waltair: Andhra University, 1969).
41. Arnold, *Essays in Criticism*, 247.
42. Ibid., 237.
43. See Pt. Durgaprasada and W.L. Sastry Panashikar, (eds.) *Dhvanyaloka* L (Bombay: Nimayasagar Press, 1928), 68–69.
44. Arnold, *Essays in Criticism*, 255–57.
45. Ibid., 258.
46. See K. Krishnamoorthy (ed.) *Vakroktijivita* (Dharwad: Kamataka University, 1977), 10–21.
47. Prabas Jiban Choudhury, *Tagore on Literature and Aesthetics* (Calcutta: Rabindra Bharati, 1965), 137.
48. Anandavardhana devotes enough space to discuss propriety and how it enables the artist in the formation of *rasa* and in the enhancement of the aesthetic relish. He mentions propriety of figures of speech, propriety of excellences, propriety of arrangement, propriety of long composition, propriety of poetic configuration, and propriety of style. Honouring *aucitya* at all these levels helps to produce works of excellence that stand the test of time and ultimately emerge as "touchstones". See R.S. Tripathi, ed., *Dhvanyaloka* (Delhi: Motilal Banarasidas, 1963).
49. Brajmohan Jha, (ed.) *Aucityavicaracarca* (Varanasi: Chowkhamba Vidyabhavana, 2000), 6.
50. Arnold, *Essays in Criticism*, 165.
51. Ibid., 261–62.
52. Even Mammata notes that poet's preparation must include (i) observation of the world (ii) the study of the works of other great poets. This is another

'O life unlike to ours!' 145

endorsement of *nipunata* and these trains of thoughts ably enucleate Arnold's *nipunata* in relation to his art.
53. Arnold, *Essays in Criticism*, 265.
54. The touchstone passages are eleven in number; three each from Homer, Dante, and Milton; two from Shakespeare. They are 'lines and expressions of the great masters,' 'short passages, even single lines', 'the poet's comment,' 'the address of Zeus,' 'the words of Achilles,' 'Ugrolino's tremendous words,' 'the lovely words of Beatrice,' 'the simple, but perfect, single line,' 'Henry the Fourth's expostulation,' 'Hamlet's dying request,' 'that Miltonic passage,' 'the exquisite close'. We now come to the generalization which purports to unite these fragments. Though differing widely from one another they have, we are told, a common poetic cement.

   i They have in common the possession of the very highest poetical quality; a quality revealed in matter, substance, manner, and style.
   ii In substance and matter they are characterized by an eminent degree of truth and seriousness.
   iii The special character of the style and manner is given by diction and movement.
   iv Two and three are inseparable.

   See John Shepard Eells Jr., *The Touchstones of Matthew Arnold* (New York: Bookman Associates, 1955), 17.
55. V. K. Lele (ed.) *Kavikanthabharana* (Delhi: Motilal Banarasidas, 1967), 45–54.
56. C. D. Dalal and Benoytosh Bhattacharya (eds.) *Kavyamimamsa* (Baroda: Oriental Institute, 1934), 16. Can we not assume that Arnold's note on 'touchstone' is an invitation to poets to embark on *abhyasa* (practise), which in due course can get them closer to the perfection in execution and *rasa* that Arnold heavily emphasises? *Abhyasa* (practise) as a principle of poetic composition is the equipment of the poet that assists in avoiding 'poetic flaws' and inspires poetic excellences. Rudrata, Namisadhu and Mammata believe in the creative process that combines poetic intuition, scholarship, internal coordination, and practise.
57. In fact, an understanding of the various principles of Arnold's notion of creativity and the poet brings us strikingly close to Vamana's thoughts in his *Kavyalankarasutravritti*: he points out the principles that an aspiring poet should be alert about—acquaintance with poetic creations of other poets, practise in composing poetry, attendance upon seniors, insertion and rejection of words, poetic faculty, and concentration. In fact, in many ways, as I have shown through this paper, Arnold's ideas on 'composition' are perceptively close to these Sanskrit theoreticians.
58. R. C. Mishra, (ed.) *Kavyadarsa* (Varanasi: Chowkhamba Vidyabhavana, 1958), 103.
59. Arnold, *Essays in Criticism*, 299.
60. Ibid., 264.
61. It is the 'aesthetic disinterestedness'. Tagore, in fact, emphasises that in all art and, most importantly, in poetry, the mind of the artist must achieve a 'certain degree of aloofness'; the 'creator' within man must be given the liberty to have sole control where the subject matter need not get the better of the creation. Tagore underlines the importance of this process because without it, the result will only be a mere replica of the event, not a reflection of it through the artist's

146 *'O life unlike to ours!'*

mind. Both Tagore and Arnold believe that art is the emotional incarnation of facts and ideas. For both, artistic vision is essentially a unified one.
62. "Epilogue to Lessing's Laocoon", 187.
63. Arnold, *Essays in Criticism*, 329.
64. Ibid., 307.
65. Andrew Dib Sherfan, *A Third Treasury of Kahlil Gibran* (Philosophical Library, 2011), 242.
66. "Resignation", 192.
67. Arnold, *Essays in Criticism*, 301, 302, 304.
68. P.V. Naganath Sastry, (ed.) *Kavyalankara* (New Delhi: Motilal Banarasidas, 1970), 2.
69. S. K. Nandi, *Studies in Modern Indian Aesthetics* (Shimla: Indian Institute of Advanced Study, 1975), 61.
70. Mishra, *Kavyadarsa*, 3.
71. For more on the 'purposes' (*prayojana*) of poetry primarily in relation to poetry's integral connection with the world and explanation of human nature, see Kuntaka's *Vakroktijivita* and Mammata's *Kavyaprakasa*. Kant in his third *Critique* mentions that art presupposes the social spirit of humanity. Humaniora is the necessary condition of the culture of mental powers, and humanity entails the universal feeling of sympathy or communication. Tagore mentions that the will to communicate goes hand in hand with the will to create. The artist inhabits a non-solipsistic world, and self-expression is self-socialization as well. The word *sahitya*, which Tagore uses for art, indicates that the artist and his audience together constitute the domain of creativity, even as the moral action presupposes a world of other free selves, besides the moral agent. The moral world, as well as the aesthetic, is the world of humanity. It is true of Arnold as well. For the poet, what remains significant is a faith in the future of humanity.
72. Arnold's faith in Goethe reminds me of Sri Aurobindo's "Goethe":

    A perfect face amid barbarian faces,
    A perfect voice of sweet and serious rhyme,
    Traveler with calm, inimitable paces,
    Critic with judgment absolute to all time,
    A complete strength when men were maimed and weak,
    German obscured the spirit of a Greek. ("Goethe" 26).

    Arnold and Aurobindo believed that Goethe as a true poet bears a proximity to Truth; he is the gifted soul in whose hands God has placed a viola to soothe the spirit and bring his fellow men close to life and the beauty of life. See Aurobindo, *Collected Poems* (Pondicherry: Sri Aurobindo Ashram, 1994).
73. Paul Ricoeur, *From Text to Action: Essays in Hermeneutics*, II (trans.) Kathleen Blamey and John B. Thompson (Evanston, IL: Northwestern University Press, 1991), 281.
74. Steven G. Yao, 'The Unheimlich Maneuver; or the Gap, the Gradient, and the Spaces of Comparison' *Comparative Literature*, 57, no. 3 (2005), 251.
75. See Jacques Derrida, *Politics of Friendship* (trans.) George Collins (New York: Verso, 1997), quoted in Corinne Scheiner, 'Teleiopoiesis, Telepoesis, and the Practice of Comparative Literature', *Comparative Literature*, 57, no. 3 (Summer 2005), 23–25.

8 The 'Platinum' Poet and the Trans-Habitual Making of a Poem

> A thought is a tremendous mode of excitement. Like a stone thrown into a pond it disturbs the whole surface of our being.
> —A. N. Whitehead[1]

> Tradition is not but episodes of extended benefits that learners get and learn from teachers.
> —Salah Abdel-Sabour[2]

> When I was working in Peking at *Mencius on the Mind* about 1930, he [Eliot] wrote to me …that reading in a remote text is like trying to be on both sides of a mirror at once. A vivid and a suitably bewildering image. To ask how exact it may be would be to raise the prime question "What is understanding?" anew.
> —I. A. Richards[3]

T. S. Eliot's poet is en-*transed* because Eliot is a vexed victim of trans-habit. Deeply committed to a perception of tradition or a historical sense which 'is a labile, self-transformative organism extended in space and time, constantly reorganized by the present'[4] and which involves not just the 'pastness of the past but of its presence' and the 'sense of the timeless and of the temporal, and of the timeless and the temporal together',[5] Eliot addresses the existence of the poet in a planetarity, in diffracted modes of association and interference. Dissatisfied with the vagueness of impressionistic criticism, he institutes a scientific inquiry into the process by which a work is produced to account for its effect. In spite of sharing a common Modernist elitism, he, quite often, files an apology for traditional hierarchical values. In spite of his classicist leanings, he did not intend to arrange and systematise his ideas into a coherent theory of poetry; he was not interested in the formal definitions of poetry. What he sincerely attempted is to push the cause of his own new kind of writing: 'I believe that the critical writings of poets, of which in the past there have been some very distinguished examples, owe a great deal of their interest to the fact that the poet, at the back of his mind, if not as his ostensible purpose, is always trying to defend the kind of poetry he is writing, or to formulate the kind that he wants to write'.[6] Eliot's trans-habits of creativity do not throw the poet over-indulgently into the muddle of materials—chaotic, shifting and fluid. It points to a critical sensibility, ensures a growth of consciousness of a 'living past'—the entire pattern of emotion, feeling, moral, forms, rhythms and words is modified by the existing or contemporary pattern. He observes that 'we need an eye which can see the past in its place with its definite differences from the present, and yet so lively that it shall be as present to us as the present. This is the creative eye'.[7] The creative eye, I would like to argue, owes its figurations and configurations to Eliot's deeply intricate trans-habitations.

I

Trans-habit, as I have already argued, is multivoiced and Eliot's poetic creativity cannot do without invisible voices with 'no ascertainable past and no particularized present,' existing mostly, as Hugh Kenner notes, as 'congeries of effects'[8]. Without the error of pure contemporaneity, the poet is himself the invisible poet who builds a poetics of resurfacement under the F. H. Bradleyian arch.

> The study of Bradley ... may be said to have done three things [for Eliot]. It solved his critical problem, providing him with a point of view towards history ...; it freed him from the Laforguian posture of the ironist with his back to a wall, by affirming the artificiality of all personality, including the one we intimately suppose to be our true one; not only the faces we prepare but the "we" that prepares; and it released him from any notion that the art his temperament bade him practice was an eccentric art, evading for personal and temporary reasons a more orderly, more "normal" unfolding from statement to statement.[9]

The trans-poetics have a creative eye for the eccentric—'heap of broken images'[10]—but not without its order, 'a self among others', a 'construction in space and time' whose existence is never possible outside a common world.[11] The eccentricity with an undertow of the Joycean idea of 'retrospective arrangement' contributes to a sense of the past: 'It seems, as one becomes older, / That the past has another pattern, and ceases to be a mere sequence'.[12] The metic man and his trans-habits needed an apology as is evident in a letter he wrote to Mary Hutchinson explaining the nature of his impetus to write the 'Tradition and Individual Talent':

> I have now got started on a long subject which I have not now either time or energy to carry out — instead of replying simply to a question of civilisation and culture. I think two things are wanted – civilisation which is impersonal, traditional (by "tradition" I don't mean stopping in the same place) and which forms people unconsciously ... and culture— which is a personal interest and curiosity in *particular* things —I think it is largely the *historical sense,* which is not simply knowledge of history, a sense of balance which does not deaden one's personal taste, but trains one to discriminate one's passions from objective criticism.[13]

The seeds of trans-habit lie in Eliot's meticism. This turns poetic creativity into a product of an astute poetics of relationality. The accidental, consequential, peripheral, elemental and the circumstantial all roll into an instant of knowledge which is both conscious and unconscious, getting and taking shape. Eliot's trans-habituality recognises the invisible voices in the formation of a poem, the unnamed and uncanny voices which break through the curtain of habitual poetic understanding. The catalyst of the poet's mind is the intriguing category which traverses borders without citizenship, immigrates territories of thoughts and meanings without much of a compromise on its strangerhood.

Maud Ellmann makes an interesting observation:

> Tradition has no outside. Patiently digesting differences, the old incorporates the new. In fact, the search for novelty strikes Eliot as a perilous pursuit, more likely to 'discover the perverse' than the 'really new'.... The presence of the past has now become authoritarian, though Eliot conceals its iron hand by sentimentalizing its paternalism. If he suggests that literary history is a play of differences with no fixed terms, no stable legislature, he now submerges his suspicion in the rhetoric of organicism. He speaks as if tradition had emerged according to the laws of nature, rather than through the social, economic and political exclusions which institute the canon by expelling any works that challenge its hegemony. Spongeous and capacious, tradition absorbs all friction into the serenity of its organic form.[14]

Tradition is organic, dialectical and reflexive wherein 'we grasp hold of what has been as being something else, which while being something else is at the same time our own and nothing but our own. In tradition we experience ourselves as something else, i.e., as something which we emphatically define as not being ourselves'. Here we experience the phenomenon of both the 'not yet' and 'otherwise' in a kind of recreation involving 'the identity of identity and non-identity'.[15] In the section on memory, in his dissertation on F. H. Bradley, Eliot writes: 'Ideas of the past are true, not by correspondence with a real past, but by their coherence with each other and ultimately with the present moment; an idea of the past is true, we have found, by virtue of relations among ideas'.[16] Eliot knows that a poet, like a scientist, contributes to the development of culture and 'it is just as absurd for him not to know the work of his predecessors or of men writing in other languages as it would be for a biologist to be ignorant of Mendel or de Vries'.[17] He observes further that 'the point of view (or finite centre) has for its object one consistent world, and accordingly no finite centre can be self-sufficient, for the life of a soul does not consist in the contemplation of one consistent world but in the painful task of unifying (to a greater or less extent) jarring and incompatible ones, and passing, when possible, from two or more discordant viewpoints to a higher which somehow shall include and transmute them'.[18] Here one finds Eliot struggling with a sort of Hegelian inheritance. Gregory Jay points out that the 'key to Hegel's idealism and to his narrative of Spirit's inevitable Unity in History is the sublation, or *Aufhebung*, the critical motion that somehow both negates and preserves the past, controlling the lineage of generation in a restricted economy of ever more proper identities. This conceptual structure yields the Word that recovers the dead and saves the wasted, leaving no remainder... the program of the *Aufhebung* defines logocentrism and constantly tempts Eliot's divided soul with a promise of redemptive synthesis'.[19] However, such synthesisations speak of 'peculiar personal intimacy', a close kinship with dead authors, which, as Eliot argues in 'Reflections on Contemporary Poetry', 'may overcome us suddenly, on first or after long acquaintance; it is certainly a crisis; and when a young writer is seized with his first passion of this sort he may be changed, metamorphosed almost, within a few weeks even, from a bundle of second-hand sentiments into a person. The imperative intimacy arouses for the first time a real, an unshakable confidence. That you possess this secret knowledge, this intimacy, with the dead man, that after few or many years or centuries you should have appeared, with this indubitable claim to distinction; you can penetrate at once the thick and dusty circumlocutions about his reputation, can call yourself alone his friend: it is something more than encouragement to you.... The use of such a passion is various... [Ultimately,] we are broadened. We do not imitate, we are changed; and our work is the work of a changed man; we have not borrowed; we have been awakened; and we become bearers of a tradition'.[20]

The poet then has the subtle sense to create a conformity between the old and the new work of art where the supervention of novelty need not impair the delicate configuration but, only slightly, alters the existing order; with an auditory imagination the poet's mind draws the principles whereby the 'relations, proportions, values of each work of art toward the whole are readjusted'.[21] The irresistible and relentless noise of tradition produces the sound of a text—conversations built on different wavelengths, noise-effect and soundscapes. The potential for 'happening' is enormous as a text becomes an emergent organism that is both self-directive and other-directed. Poetic creativity has the contributing specificity of an aggregative and archaeological mind and an organismic evolution that builds on the radical and adventitious root of the 'contemporary'. Analogising a cellular growth, I am tempted to correspond with Hans Driesch's way of looking at organismic formations:

> ...in each of the n cells the same great number of possibilities of becoming is physico-chemically prepared, but checked, so to say, by entelechy. Development of the system DOW depends according to our assumption, upon the fact that entelechy relaxes its suspensory power and thus ...in cell a one thing is allowed to occur, in cell b another, and in cell c something else; but what now actually occurs in a might also have occurred in b or c; or each one out of an enormous number

of possibilities may occur in each cell thus, by the regulatory relaxing action of entelechy in a system in which an enormous variety of possible events had been suspended by it, it may happen that an equal distribution of possibilities is transformed into an unequal distribution of actual effects.[22]

Tradition is not formed mechanically working on the stimuli and radiation of the past—events and dead poets. The past is dead but beyond death which is a way of saying that it is most often non-entelechic, having what Driesch calls 'general stock of possibilities and Kant calls 'purposive dispositions', *anlagen*. The poetic mind finds its own correspondence with inward-irectiveness of tradition and its own organic exfoliation. Despite its platinum analogy, the mind is not a mere physico-chemical agent; the mind is intrusive, borderbashed, and restorative, and its negotiations with historical sense have a 'vital energy', an 'energetical order'[23] and a troubled intimacy. Tradition has a kind of impersonality to it: a stock, a receptacle and repertoire that resists being overpowered by the creative mind or appropriately exhausted. Eliot knew that tradition's ways of worlding are not compulsively submitted to the moral and ethical agency of the poet. If the poet lives in the 'dead', in his relation with the 'dead', it speaks of both a performativity and preformed possibilities that mesh and morph creative products.

The poetic mind *orders* and yet lives the life of the uncanny. It forms out of the dialogism inherent in trans-habit. Mikhail Bakhtin's scepticism about poetry's ability to dialogise, unlike what the novel is able to achieve, is well known: 'Contradictions, conflicts and doubts remain in the object, in thoughts, in living experiences—in short, in the subject matter—but they do not enter into language itself. In poetry, even discourse about doubts must be cast in a discourse that cannot be doubted'.[24] However, such criticism is difficult to accept when one tries to construct a narrative on the internal dialogic ability of poetry, its multiple voices, and non-conservatism in expression and existence. Heteroglossia is integral to the novel and monologism peculiar to poetry implies that 'all fully signifying authorial interpretations are sooner or later gathered together in a single speech center and a single consciousness; all accents are gathered together in a single voice'.[25] The poet is formed out of dialogic relationality made possible through life-giving ethical encounters across paradigms, cultures and civilisations. Donald Wesling sees Bakhtin's poetry-over-prose prejudice as a notably Russian one 'that still haunts the minds of critics and writers on that territory, because it is rooted in the Russian Orthodox trust in the Word'.[26] But poetic doing or activity is exotopic, and its telos of synthesis or a resolution, as is primarily the achievement in dialectical systems, is contradictious, intersubjectively vibrant and transdiscursively productive. Admitting of Bakhtin's ambiguity about poetry's dialogic potential, Michael Eskin finds in it the ethics of producing mutual understanding and 'concomitantly, the subversion of sociopolitical, potentially repressive, authority'.[27] Eskin further argues that poetry 'palpably instantiates the existential clashes between homogenizing and oppositional discourses in its very construction, by imposing a unifying—though not necessarily regular—organisation on the voices of potential others, which is (quantitatively and qualitatively) less determinant in (non-"poeticized") novelistic discourse'.[28] However, my understanding of the answerability of poetry extends beyond its ability to construct communal language, allowing, thus, for socio-political critique. Eliot's opposition to the monologicity of poetry is legitimised in his construction of the historical sense where oscillation among paradigms and congeries of thoughts and, polysemous texturing leading to clash of epistemes, generate an ambiguity of reading that promotes radical otherity.

A poet, thus, cannot have a life without others—being with others and constituted by others. The classic poet is aware of his past, his predecessors, has a self that is 'conscious of being several selves' in what Frank Kermode would describe as a 'Cubist historiography, unlearning the trick of perspective and ordering history as a system of perpetually varying spatial alignments'.[29] If the argument as to his contradictory engagement with Victorians demonstrates an unconscious doing of tradition, Eliot's connection with Cubism is surely a manifestly conscious working of poetic execution. The poetic mind is cubist in its dispensation with conventional perspectives, transgressive and relational modes of presentation, parallelism and the acute angularities of thinking. In a Bergsonian way the mind of the poet lives 'among a multiplicity of interpenetrating processes of change'. Bergson points out that

> there is no state of mind, however simple, which does not change every moment, since there is no consciousness without memory, and no continuation of a state without the addition, to the present feeling, of the memory of past events. It is this that constitutes duration. Inner duration is the continuous life of a memory which prolongs the past into the present, the present either containing within it in a distinct form the ceaselessly growing image of the past, or, more probably, showing by its continual change of quality the heavier and still heavier load we drag behind us as we grow older. Without this survival of the past into the present, there would be no duration, but only instanteity.[30]

The poet's historical situatedness is diffractive in that history does not impose absolutes or universals to determine poetic creativity; instead, creativity has the measure of its own time, not essentially a linear variable of time, not a Euclidian perspective that pins down understanding to fixed coordinates of time progression. Absolutes cohabit the synchronic: the defined and directed are simultaneous with the unpredictable and serendipitous. Eliot vouchsafes for a temporal parallelism existing alongside isomorphic perceptions. The singularity of a poet's existence is not in recognising what is out there, but in us, growing and living with us. Trans-habit of the poet then is both an act and event, inhering in the singularity of creation and principles of unconscious and alert accommodation. When tradition is not inheritance and achieved through labour, the voices *trans*forming poetic creativity are often unfamiliar spots of interaction and negotiations. Breaking away from tradition is welcoming tradition, 'connecting with' is about knowing what and when to disconnect. Creativity is change of order, mending walls and about cannibalising the other. Derek Attridge writes:

> If one is able to break down the old in a creative and not just a negative manner (and at the time it is not possible to be sure which of these one is doing), the new comes into being; at the same time, the breakdown of the old is produced by the pressure of its internal contradictions—which, since its contradictions are a function of what it excludes, is the same as saying that it breaks down under the pressure of the other. Since the other is manifested only in a dynamic process, there would be some justification for jettisoning the noun in favor of a verb; even the terms "event" and "eventness" are misleadingly nominal, abstracting away from the happening they name. Otherness exists only in the registering of that which resists my usual modes of understanding, and that moment of registering alterity is a moment in which I simultaneously acknowledge my failure to comprehend and find my procedures of comprehension beginning to change.[31]

The poet's historical sense—staying alive with and because of the dead—is not built exclusively on clock time without, however, being expressly relational, relative, unpredictable and completely non-objectifiable. It is not predominantly transitive and relative. 'To use an old metaphor', as Kenneth Inada argues, 'events are taking place like waves in the vast ocean. In mid-ocean the myriad waves are appearing and disappearing as if each is independent of each other but in truth there are many factors and conditions at play which make it possible for each wave to appear and disappear thus and so. Such is also the nature of the rise and subsidence of consciousness. All this goes to show that relational-origination is a conditioning or compounding phenomenon; it is exhibiting the complex but unique way in which an experiential event transpires'.[32] The poet is the product of this compoundness which has at once a rational analytic and a 'play'. In the pastness of the past and the presence of the past the poet is premised within a *family* by which Eliot meant 'a bond which embraces a longer period of time than this: a piety towards the dead, however obscure, and a solicitude for the unborn, however remote'.[33] This is apparently non-Nietzschean in that Eliot cannot do without historical sense, a sort of monumental view of history. If Eliot is proposing a recreative and transformative use of history, Nietzsche is for active forgetting, enabling him to remain in the proper service of life (*Nutzen*). But Eliot's historical sense has the power of 'presence' as its formidable other half of the story which collapses the temporal and the timeless and repremises our understanding of the 'contemporary'. Epistemological understanding builds around the antagonism between the past and the present, the dead and the living, the conscious and the unconscious, the present and the presentified. Both the thinkers develop closer points of contact when Nietzsche argues that living outside history is a difficult act to perform because 'human existence is merely an uninterrupted past tense [*ein ununterbrochenes Gewesensein*], a thing that lives by denying and consuming itself, by opposing itself'.[34] The dialectic bred thereof between living unhistorically and the impossibility of unhistoricalness point to a 'future past' which essentially defines constellative poetic creativity.

Does Eliot's historical sense promote a 'rechewing' of other literatures across traditions, devouring and cannibalising a variety of texts, breaking borders and setting up new orders? The complex dynamics between tradition and the *other* throw us into the fury and force of literary cannibalism. Brazilian modernist poet Oswald de Andrade's 'Manifesto da Poesia Pau-Brasil' ['Manifesto of Brazilwood Poetry', 1924] and *Manifesto Anthropofago* (1928) talk about a deep tension that 'challenges the dualities civilisation/barbarism, modern/primitive, and original/derivative, which had informed the construction of Brazilian culture since the days of the colony'. The import of modernist esthetic projects and national and nativist identities are held in a 'playful, polemical theory of cultural cannibalism' where the cannibal metaphor develops the idea of devouring—the consuming of the other—in that one's literature adapts the strength of the other and incorporates them into the native self.[35] The ethics of anthropophagy brings into play 'participatory consciousness'—'I am only concerned with what is not mine. Law of Man. Law of the cannibal'[36]; an implicit refigurative spirit constructed as a challenge to authority and authenticity is revealed in expressions like: 'the world's single law. Disguised expression of all individualism, of all collectivisms. Of all religions. Of all peace treaties'.[37] Kenneth Jackson observes that 'from Freud, Oswald absorbed the transformation of tabu into totem and blended the concept with Nietzsche's metaphor (in *A Genealogy of Morals*) of man as an animal that assimilates interior and exterior conflicts. From Keyserling the idea of technological savagery would be mixed with Spengler's conclusion about the victory of the machine and lead Oswald to the theory of a 'revolucao caraiba' ['supernatural and indigenous revolution']. This Brazilian revolutionary synthesis would replace indigenous originality and pau-brasil [Brasilwood] simplicity with the cannibalistic instinct of rebellion'.[38] So anthropophagus reason makes allowance for the continual 'chewing' and mastication of the other to produce what I may argue as the regurgitated aesthetics of reading which is about setting new *trans*-poetical orders, politics of relationality and planetization. Pointing to the new literary combinatorics, Rachel Galvin notes that 'the poetics of cannibalism have pointed politico-aesthetic implications: ingesting and devouring describe the ludic recombination of preexisting cultural elements—or what might be called, more neutrally, innovation through engagement with tradition'.[39] Poetic creativity is about 'displacement' where a text or a thought of the other disposes oneself 'to accept the principle of alterity'. It is the consciousness of the other and tradition in its varying articulation and reticulation does not make the other change 'myself' but enables the other to dwell within oneself without violating him or her.[40] Cutting up tradition, caring for discourses of thought and knowledge and constructing fresh literary capital are operations that invent the sacred of recombinatory poetics. Eliot's poet refigures the notion of private literary property where rights are built in allowing others to devour oneself and claims are forged to poach and hunt on other's property to build an assertive enterprise of one's own. Such a property becomes mine in being founded on others. Poetic creativity, thus, raises the complexity and anxiety of a creative act which cannot exist inviolably in a compositional quarantinity. The displeasure of self-satiety translates to a radical hunger of literary ingestion and astute gormandising. It bears mention that the mystery of the poet's formation is not conformity but rearrangement and accommodation en route to creative order. This again is not a collapse to relativism; it must, as Noel-Tod argues, 'retain the agency of a transcendent entity, evolving in conformity with itself, like Novalis' "infinite structure of the Universe." With the revelatory advent of the new work of art, it is "the whole existing order" which must be "readjusted" by some inherently wise guiding purpose. This is Tradition's holy plan, as communicated by its prophet, the great poet-critic—a heroic role that Eliot would later make explicit in his 1932 essay on 'Matthew Arnold': "From time to time, every hundred years or so, it is desirable that some critic shall appear to review the past of our literature, and set the poets and the poems in a new order. The task is not one of revolution but of readjustment."'[41] However, the provocation of anthropophagia disembeds what stays latent in the philosophy of revisionism and *across*. The literary capital built out of such transcreative hunger has its own power and politics of insertion, interference and assimilation. Historical sense conceals a hunger that inspires recycling, reimagining and recombinatory energy.[42]

Poetic creativity is the product of a journey through ruins: an archaeology of thoughts, ideas, 'sinking to the most primitive and forgotten, returning to the origin and bringing something back, seeking the beginning and the end'; the poet 'fuses the old and obliterated and the trite, the current, and the new and surprising, the most ancient and the most civilized mentality' to create a poetry, as Charles Martindale notes, 'at once modern and, in Eliot's sense, classical'.[43] Working on the logic of the ruin as having the evocative potential for a poet, Martindale observes that a 'ruin is evidence of decay, of transience, of the power of time to weaken and destroy'; it is the 'site of recovery' and reendowment, as Hegel observes, in the *Philosophy of History*:

> The sight of the ruins of some ancient sovereignty directly leads us to contemplate the thought of change in its negative aspect. What traveller

> among the ruins of Carthage, of Palmyra, Persepolis, or Rome, has not been stimulated to reflections on the transiency of kingdoms and men, and to sadness at the thought of a vigorous and rich life now departed. …But the next consideration which allies itself with that of change, is that change, while it imports dissolution, involves at the same time the rise of a new life that while death is the issue of life, life is also the issue of death.[44]

Poetry cannot reach a state of purity for pure literature is a 'chimera of sensation'.[45] So, in an intricate and intensive poetics of listening, the trans-habitual capital of poetic formation is located. Eliot's poet listens to the historical sense, the murmur and fervor of tradition, in a way where listening is dialogue. He wants accentuated listening that makes possible a certain engagement across genre, canon, culture and inheritance with assertiveness, approbation and ingenuity. Tradition produces its own music and creates music too. Listening at the appropriate points of communication and active conversation across cultures and times produces its own harmonies—listening-in-conversation, a transactional exchange integral to the initiation of poetic creativity. Speaking about the personal impact of LaForgue on him, Eliot writes:

> It may overcome us suddenly, on first or after long acquaintance; it is certainly a crisis; and when a young writer is seized with his first passion of this sort he may be changed, metamorphosed almost within a few weeks, even, from a bundle of second hand sentiments into a person. The imperative intimacy arouses for the first time a real, an unshakeable confidence. This process occurred both with Fitzgerald's Omar Khayyam and LaForgue. In the absence of a present teacher, the elder poet fills the role as teacher who is also friend. That you possess this secret knowledge, this intimacy, with the dead man, that after few or many years or centuries you should have appeared, with the indubitable claim to distinction; who can penetrate at once the thick and dusty circumlocutions about his reputations, and call yourself alone his friend: it is something more than encouragement to you. It is a cause of development, like personal relations in life. Like personal intimacies in life, it may and probably will pass, but it will never be ineffaceable.[46]

Eliot and LaForgue are caught in a dynamical listening: across and within each other, rescribing premises, reshaping the inside and the outside, waking up and getting drowned in the other. When Eliot emphasises tradition as an object awaiting to be labored upon, achieved laboriously, we can confidently argue its listening-potential (I-them exchanges). This potential builds the hybrid character of the text growing separate altitudes through processes of remonumentalisation. Does the poet's formation then owe to the hybridity

The 'Platinum' Poet and the Trans-Habitual Making of a Poem 157

that Eliot's historical sense generates? Caught amidst the dialectic of tradition and inheritance, in a separate order of things, the poet submits to a continual self-sacrifice, an extinguishment that, ironically, builds fresh self-other equations. Foucault writes:

> And the imaginative values then assumed by the past, the whole lyrical halo that surrounded the consciousness of history at that period, the lively curiosity shown for documents or for traces left behind by time—all this is a surface expression of the simple fact that man found himself emptied of history, but that he was already beginning to recover in the depths of his own being, and among all the things that were still capable of reflecting his image (the others have fallen silent and folded back upon themselves), a historicity linked essentially to man himself. But this historicity is immediately ambiguous. Since man posits himself in the field of positive knowledge only in so far as he speaks, works, and lives, can his history ever be anything but the inextricable nexus of different times, which are foreign to him and heterogeneous in respect of one another?[47]

Premised in a hybrid poetics, confrontation becomes colloquy and encounter turns into genesis. Eliot's poet builds its formative force around folds and transgressions resulting in an empathetic and astute dialogue with literature and the world around us. Somewhere it removes romantic egocentricism to construct a separate vocabulary and valence of creative ego for whom experiencing fragments is not epistemic seclusion but mediation. This builds a sense of meaning, a circulation of sense whose world formation is also in unworlding. I see in this a Martin Buberian love which is a reciprocity between what the poet writes and what the dead authors have written: accessibility combines with responsibility that conjoins with answerability. Eliot's inclusivist politics is also exclusionary in that the poet is not formed through random pickings and carvings. The constitutive properties of the poet are labored upon for a just selection that provides a new order: discriminative appropriations that aggravate textual density and resonance.

Here a trans-habitual understanding of the platinum poet opens us onto the artful power of plagiarism as conceptualised by several critics in medieval Arabic literary criticism. *Al sariqa* is a special kind of 'literary theft'—sometimes 'euphemized by the word *akhdh* meaning taking, or taking over'—distinguished from *al-intihal* which denoted deception, explains Esad Durakovic.[48] There was no stratagem or deception among poets when they borrowed from their predecessors; rather, they enriched the 'taking over'—synthesis as *experience* which in turn became tradition. The classical poet needed a vast knowledge of tradition, a fine sensibility to make discrimination among genres and motifs. Literary theft then was a demonstrative art and philologists like al-Askari and al-Amidi look for the individuality in such creative stealing—the *akhdh* establishing a 'listening' that speaks of the continuity of tradition. What Eliot sees as positive borrowing—the fecund 'take over'—can be qualified by some critics of classical Arabic literature as the power that comes from 'idiosyncrasy'. In his *Umdah*, Ibn Rashīq talks about creative thievery which involves the transformative or idiosyncratic appropriation of conceptual content, emphasising that no poet can claim to be free from any sort of plagiarism.[49] Ibn Rashīq points out that *tawlid* [procreation] which is about 'letting the motifs breed'[50] is between original creation (*ikhtira*) and plagiarism (*sariqa*)—a re-creative use of ideas by poets from the past, Eliot's 'dead poets'. *Sariqat* is allusiveness and such persistent and unavoidable allusiveness with its politics of adaption and adoption can have *muwallad* (invention) where the poet is 'a stallion (*fahl*) who opens a path, and, in a word, deflowers the idea'.[51] In his *Kitab al-Sina'atayn*, Abu Hilal Al-'Askari notes the near impossibility of staying free from borrowing (*akhdh*) concepts of one's predecessors—approximating a skilful instance of 'beautiful plagiarism'. In fact, blame-worthy plagiarism cannot reveal idiosyncrasy, but praise-worthy plagiarism 'does alter the text and attempts to differentiate it from the verses he [poet] plagiarizes. In that case, the new verse is not considered pure imitation, or pure theft, and classical critics would point out some aspects of idiosyncrasy in it'.[52] Abu Hilal suggests that a resemblance, either in form or content, between two different works should not always be taken as plagiarism. Originality should not be understood as a continuous introduction of new themes into literature. It is not the quality of individual talent but is realised in tradition through submission of poets and rediscovery of poetic motifs, images, concepts, style, and various other aspects of poetic thought and thinking. Originality relates to inventing a new *ma'na* (idea, motif), working on and improving a borrowed *ma'na* through adroit formulations and enlarging upon a borrowed *ma'na* by adding one's own themes to it (*lafz*).[53] It is artful thievery—an interpretive assimilation or intermeshing—of the good poet and not the imitation that Eliot associates with the bad poet. The good poet is Ibn Rashiq's *mukhtari* (the innovative poet), who develops his uniqueness but does not lay down an inflexible standard of creative principle for others to follow. The poetic art of a *mukhtari* can discover more innovative interest in generations to follow, and develop more idiosyncrasies through beautiful plagiaristic appropriations. So the borrowing here for both Eliot and his Arabic counterparts is implicated in bearing out a *debt* to the past or the poet's predecessors. Traditions are indeed built through such recompositions. Existence is co-existence; experience is inherence; inclusivism is co-extensivity.

II

Eliot distinguishes between the poet who 'thinks' and the poet who does not. The former is capable of expressing the emotional equivalent of thought. One can argue that it is the presentation that matters for the poet does not allow 'thought' to remain as it is in the product; he transmutes it into a complex experience suitably contained in a verbal structure. The true poet, for Eliot, develops a mechanism of sensibility (infusion of intellect and emotion) that can devour any kind of experience. Donne is the representative poet here, for whom thought was an experience; his sensibility was modified by it: as metaphysicians make metaphysics, the bee makes honey, the spider secretes filament, the poet makes poetry. The poet does not have the mandate on him to believe. His job is to *do*. Donne did not have to believe. Like a magpie, he culled various shining fragments of ideas that caught his eye and *laid them* in the various rooms and spaces of his verse. In fact, the concern of the classic poet is not with a narrow range of sensibility of thought and feeling. The classic poet

> must within its formal limitations, express the maximum possible of the whole range of feeling which represents the character of the people who speak the language. It will represent this at its best, and it will also have the widest appeal: among the people to which it belongs, it will find its response among all classes and conditions of men.[54]

Besides, the classic poet, being universal, sets the standard and serves as a yardstick to measure the attainments and deficiencies of other poets. Virgil, the classic poet in Eliot's concept, is not provincial and insular. He is a poet who possesses the highly essential attribute of Universality—'It is the importance of that civilization and of that language, as well as the *comprehensiveness* of the *mind* of the poet, which gives the universality'.[55] To Eliot the whole of European literature is one whole, and its blood-stream is Greco-Roman. He claims Virgil as the standard of the whole of Europe—irrespective of all its diversity of languages, literatures, national cultures and traditions. He is 'the classic of all Europe'[56], declares Eliot, without any reservations. It is not necessary that the production of a classic should be repeated because a classic is a permanent touchstone. This standard set by the classic poet frees the European literatures from 'chaos' and helps establish 'order'. However, the poet needs to be intelligent for the more intelligent he is the more varied will be his interest—intelligence leading to order. So Eliot is suspicious of poetry that attracts or appeals to a crowd of people. Ezra Pound who found the method of Chinese ideogram very interesting, considered poetry as 'a sort of inspired mathematics which gives us equations, not for abstract figures, triangles, spheres and the like, but equations for the human emotions'.[57] The complexity of the emotion is not an instance of abstraction; transmutative principles of art create aesthetic or art emotions that are generally not vague and vapid. Eliot points out that in the 'common mind all interests are confused, and each degraded by the confusion. And where they are confused, they cannot be related; in the common mind any specialized activity is conceived as something isolated from life….To maintain the autonomy, disinterestedness, of every activity, and to perceive it in relation to every other, require a considerable discipline'.[58]

The ontologics of poetic creativity is complex; expressions 'become an "intolerable wrestle with words and meanings", a hauling and straining, a racking of the mind's power of comprehension'. There is as much a consciousness in expression as there exists a necessity. So the obsessive attempts to say 'the unsayable' can be genuinely exacting on the elasticity of the poet's mind. Mind-stretching and, hence, experiments beyond the conventional limits of human understanding bring us before the febrile axes of creativity and the ambiguity of language.[59] So,

> Words strain,
> Crack and sometimes break, under the burden,
> Under the tension, slip, slide, perish,
> Decay with imprecision, will not stay in place
> Will not stay still
>
> ("Burnt Norton" V 149–53)

This closely resembles T. E. Hulme's poet who is engaged in 'a terrific struggle with language'.[60] The highest form of poetic activity is 'the avoidance of conventional language in order to get the exact curve of the thing'.[61] Eliot observes that

> a language is always changing; its developments in vocabulary, in syntax, pronunciation and intonation—even, in the long run, its deterioration—must be accepted by the poet and be made the best of. He in turn has the privilege of contributing to the development and maintaining the quality, the capacity of the language to express a wide range, and subtle gradation, of feeling and emotion; his task is both to respond to change and make it conscious, and to battle against degradation below the standards which he has learnt from the past. The liberties that he may take are for the sake of order.[62]

It is this order that the true poet is capable of maintaining—striking the balance between the fixity and flux in language and holding the strength, subtlety and the quality of feeling. The poet knows the purity he has to maintain, combining vigour, sensitivity, resilience with clarity, stability and order.

When Eliot noted that an 'identical spoken and written language would be practically intolerable', claiming that the 'spoken and the written language must not be too near together, as they must not be too far apart'[63], he was ensuring the musicality of language the vitality that poetic language is capable of bringing; the poet must 'like the sculptor, be faithful to the material in which he works; it is out of sounds that he has heard that he must make his melody and harmony'.[64] Wary of the encroachment of abstractions, the poet is expected to inject suppleness and variety and through rhythmic modulation align the principles of stability and order. He observes that 'words too familiar, or too remote, defeat the purpose of the poet. From those sounds which we hear on small or on coarse occasions, we do not easily receive strong impressions, or delightful images; and words to which we are nearly strangers, whenever they occur, draw that attention to themselves which they should transmit to things.[65] It is the music of the words that concerns the poet—the music of a word arising from 'its relation first to the words immediately preceding and following it, and indefinitely to the rest of its context; and from another relation, that of its immediate meaning in that context to all other meanings which it has had in other contexts, to its greater or less wealth of association'. Eliot argues that 'not all words, obviously, are equally rich and well-connected: it is a part of the business of the poet to dispose the richer among the poorer, at the right points, and we cannot afford to load a poem too heavily with the former—for it is only at certain moments that a word can be made to insinuate the whole history of a language and a civilization'.[66] The process has the control of reason and subtle ability for selection that coordinates and discriminates between alternative possibilities and resources of language, form and technique for the purpose of finding the appropriate verbal shape for the impulse. Here, under creation, the poet is in labour which Stephen Spender points out as 'the hard race, the sweat and toil'.[67] Through the 'technique of feeling' the poet develops his form through the right verse pattern and speech. He incorporates, remodels, adapts or invents as occasion suggests.

This gets us closer to Eliot's realisation that feeling for rhythm is 'far below the conscious levels of thought', which is why 'poetry can communicate before it is understood'. Francis Matthiessen explains that 'Eliot's enumeration of so many qualities inhering in the pattern of the syllables reveals how much he implies when asserting that the primary means of testing a new poet is by whether or not he possesses an individual rhythm'.[68] However, for the rhythm to be significant, one must embody a significant mind and 'must be produced by the necessity of a new form for a new content'. The poet's rhythm involves a particular union of past and present, 'his double possession of "the most ancient and the most civilized mentality" in his awareness of the primitive magic of sound joined with his quickening sense of the new manifestation of life in his own day. His rhythm, therefore, must embody an acute feeling both for the music of words, and for their richly varied connotations'.[69] This defines 'sensibility' and reemphasises the necessity of learning as much language as possible because 'every vital development in language is a development of feeling as well', enabling a word-thought conjugation. Eliot notes that 'it is a commonplace to observe that the meaning of a poem may wholly escape paraphrase. It is not quite so commonplace to observe that the meaning of a poem may be something larger than its author's conscious purpose, and something remote from its origins.... If, as we are aware, only a part of the meaning can be conveyed by paraphrase, that is because the poet is occupied with frontiers of consciousness beyond which words fail, though meanings still exist'.[70] Eliot's poet, then, is faced with the difficulty that language presents. Maria Frendo rightly observes that the poet 'finds himself less free of the riches of the past than the painter and musician are, if only because most of the poems of the past are written in languages he does not understand' and so the 'transfiguration of the dead and the re-writing of their literature require of the poet countless deaths, his present self always under revision in a dialogue with compound ghosts. This self-erasure and wounding, this ascesis of impersonality, is central to Symbolist thought. However, it also seems to be a dangerously ironic way of arriving at creative potency. One may well argue that nothing can stop the influence of the dead from silencing the nascent voices of those who turn to the past in the hope of recollecting a language for the living. It may also be difficult to believe that the nightmare of history can be transformed into dawn, when one knows that every day begins as the knowledge of night. Poetics-as-inheritance has to devise solutions to these riddles'.[71]

Absolute freedom means absolute chaos and the poet's art has limitations within which he is to work—limits which do not just confine but also sustain and preserve. Graham Clarke notes that not 'only is art a "transmutation" of suffering and passion, Eliot suggests, but the better the art, the more complete the transmutation. This is an artist's catharsis to match Aristotle's audience-catharsis and is actually, although Eliot seems never to have noticed it, the very quintessence of romantic individualism and Protestantism, a utilitarianism that finds the value of art in its services to one superior individual, the artist, and thus the farthest extreme from the tradition and from Catholic criteria of 'communion'.[72] This is close to what Paul Valery interprets as the 'drama of creation'. In 'The Creation of Art', Valery points out the investment that a poetic process requires: 'I have sometimes imagined constructing a literary work in a completely theoretical way; a work manufactured out of the whole cloth, planned in its most minute details like a highly complex machine'.[73] If Eliot's poet is the platinum, catalysing the process of creation through a careful arrangement of disparate items, Valery's token of image is the dark room where a film is developed with infinite care. Both the poets lead us to a finished product brought about through intellectual exercise, care, chance, and a desired development. Valery observes:

> In another case a line came to me, obviously engendered by its sound, its timbre. The meaning suggested by this unexpected element of a poem, the image is evoked, the syntactical figure it presented (an apposition), acted like a little crystal in a supersaturated solution and led me as though by symmetry to expect and to construct according to my expectation a beginning before my line to prepare the way for it and justify its existence, and after it a continuation to round out its effect. Thus from a single line there developed, little by little, all the elements of a poem, the subject, the tone, the type of prosody, etc.[74]

This is 'theoretical meditation'.[75] The poet waits for the impressions to join together at the right time. Valery thinks, as Ince points out 'words are subject to laws and combinations quite different from those characterising ordinary states of mind and body...it is to be noted that the state of exalted inspiration, particularly in the form of improvisation *de degree superieur*, is not seen as reducible to formulae or rules which can be transmitted to be applied to another person; it is rather, in E. Noulet's phrase, '*la transformation de l'intelligence en instrinct*', a method made flesh and only so made by dint of long meditation, training and effort. Each poet has to perform the task for himself. These qualifications do not alter the interest for us and the reality for the poet of this striving towards the ideal state where something like the internal mechanism indicated does exist'.[76] If Coleridge was fully conscious of poetry being a deliberate art, Valery admits of poetry's sensational foundations, and Eliot acknowledges the unconscious in poetic creation. The artist then is seen both as primitive and civilised—a combination wrought through the 'auditory imagination' which is the 'feeling for syllable and rhythm penetrating far below the conscious levels of thought and feeling, invigorating every word; sinking to the most primitive and forgotten, returning to the origin and bringing something back, seeking the beginning and the end'.[77] This privileges a process which is opposed to any attempt to fix the content of experience[78]—not a circularity of thinking but spatialising of thought, we-ing of thoughts to produce a verticality of understanding.

III

Talking of the modernist mind, James McFarlane observes:

> A sense of the total *relatedness of things*, altogether different from those tightly drawn casual links by which the positivist world had together, stimulated a search for that mystic 'world of relationships'—Hofmannathal's *Welt der Bezuge*—in which the role of the poet was that of 'silent brother of all things', who saw the world ...as an infinitely complex lattice of relationships, personal to him, of which his mind was the centre and *coordinator*....the poet was able to *coordinate, in patterns appropriate to the new thinking, those disparate elements* which, following the fragmentation of the positivistic world, would otherwise have remained merely chaotic and unrelated.[79]

A poet's 'platinum' mind destroys only to create, building on an inherent chaos: 'poet's mind is in fact a receptacle for seizing and storing up numberless feelings, phrases, images, which remain there until all the particles which can unite to form a new compound are present together'.[80] The mind of the poet, says Eliot,

> would be magnetised in its own way, to select automatically in his reading (from picture papers and cheap novels, indeed, as well as serious books, and least likely from works of an abstract nature, though

even these are ailment for some poetic minds)—an image, a phrase, a word—which may be of use to him later. And this selection probably runs through the whole of his conscious life. There might be the experience of a child of ten, a small boy peering through sea-water in a rock-pool, and finding a sea-anemone for the first time: the simple experience (not so simple experience for an exceptional child as it looks) might lie dormant in his mind, for twenty years, and reappear transformed in some verse-context charged with great imaginative pressure.[81]

However, on the 'platinum' analogy, Jeremy Noel-Tod sees Eliot as losing control over the metaphor—beginning with the poet's mind as a catalyst and not a chamber but in analysing the last quatrain of Canto XV of Dante's *Inferno*, he points out that the poet's mind is a receptacle. The poet's mind, thus, is both a shred of platinum and a container and this metaphoric slack 'betrays the fact that the poet—full of "numberless" pieces of data—is not the scientist in this scenario, but the mysterious creature under investigation. Like Carlyle's Shakespeare, he is an "unconscious intellect" whose creative process is a process of Nature'.[82] The dominant yet subtle, mysterious yet synthetic, mind of the poet looks into finding a rhythm which is fundamental to poetry, the seed that helps in the 'taking place'—the coming into existence of a new order. Rhythm brings poetry into an intricate and intense contact with music. Creation in both emphasises an anonymity which is tensional and impersonal.

Although Eliot cites the chemical analogy in the production of a poetic product and poesis we encounter two forces in the creative process: one is the principle of duration and the other is the creative instant. In trying to connect creativity with tradition, I see in Eliot a Bachelardian notion of time. This is a somewhat audacious rewriting given the association that one knows Eliot had with Bergson and the disagreement that Bachelard had with Bergson over the notion of duration. If tradition is a continuum that environs a poet, it cannot do without interruptions or ruptures which are, in fact, bridges in their own right. The artificiality of breaking time into the present and past simplifies the notion of understanding creativity which builds in an instant through selection and appropriations that are splits in the process—schisms not wholly disruptive but are gaps that the creative mind leaps over in discretion and discrimination. So Bachelard points out that 'if we felt the sudden mutation where the creative acts are occurred, how is it possible not to understand that the new era is always opened up by abruptness? Thus every evolution, if it is important, is punctured by the creative instants'.[83] However, in my view, Eliot's historical sense and its pregnant connect with poetic creativity are both indebted to Bergson, Bachelard and Gaston Roupnel's theory of art—'a blurred heterogeneity'[84] combining with a redoing of the idea of the contemporary. What cannot go amiss is the quotient of 'accident' or distraction that tradition imports into poetic creativity—the dialectic of duration that comes from *le groupement*, thumps of triggers that facilitate dechronologised reading. If Tiresias, the Holy Grail, Fire Sermon, *Brihadaranyak Upanishad* and other epistemological units walk into the formation of "The Waste Land" it cannot simply be a mathematical precision of referential architecture. Duration, rather, the collapse of time, is built of hatches of discontinuity, the thoroughfares of distractions which build the creative instant. Interestingly, continuity conceals the instants, the accidents that overcome apparent aporetic challenges. Eliot's powerful imagination produces creative instants which is as much the flow of time as it is about temporal interruptions—not the romantic imagination of Wordsworth but, perhaps, one can indulgently see Coleridge's penchant for abstruse researches, his investments in contradictions and the muddle in the way metaphors are built, images are constructed and, somewhat unconsciously, epistemes are forged. Creativity comes out of a break in the flow, just as a chemical product is not merely a fruition of a flow chart but a part and a break from the continuity of its evolution. This again is not temporal segregation but quantumisation of a fluidity whose origins are as suspect as its telos. Creativity is projection.

Diffractive or quantum entanglement then is enabled by an impersonality, a sudden, though certain, demise of the autonomy of doing, a kind of unselfing that happens through the empowerment of other not without the expense of extirpation of the self. The hermit's poetic creativity is deeply meshed in such formations and constellations. The sacred of poetic production has its intra-active consequences where the source is not simply about the documented, materially realised and the educatively settled. The source is formed through an intra-active motor that writes its own text in unapprehendable ways. The sacred of formation is in realising this submission to ruin—a chemical reaction, I would like to argue, does not appropriately analogise poetic production because a product is simply the accumulated and formally cohered units of a process which never considers the loss, the deficit, the unattended energies and vibrations. A poetic product surely and secretively exceeds its own annotation. It is born beyond its processes of birthing.

Eliot's understanding of poetic creativity through a chemical analogy speaks of a pattern, a process whose definitiveness at certain levels of operation cannot be denied. However, historical sense implicates a non-linearity and an expansiveness which, again, at some levels of understanding, discounts strictness of design. But rewriting Eliot is in resettlement within such moments of ambiguity. Eliot's rejuvenation as a poet-thinker is in such contradictions, in being lost in spaces of innate antagonism. It is poetic creativity that brings partial ordering in the organisation of thought-loops. Creativity is entanglement but not without a development of sensibility and free intelligence. Tradition for Eliot's poet has this sacred of sensibility in it. The past as wave-packets collapses in the present, rather, the instant. "The Waste Land", for instance, is an indeterministic event which, however, fructifies through the possible histories of thought and tradition but in an outcome which is more diverging in nature. Eliot's sense of tradition and the point of creativity are modalities in 'splits'—'counterparthood'.[85] The creative mind is quantum evolution of point particles in time and history, in cultures and heritage, in epistemology and existence. The creative moment—the separation between suffering and poetic creation—is the measurement of various frequencies of thought, the collapse of wave packets, deterministic points of convergence before the inevitable divergence and decoherence. So "The Waste Land" is always in ruin, in dissipation, is radioactive.

If selections, pickings and assortments form part of poetic consciousness as much as sudden revelations, irruptions, and intertextual peepings which are not always nominated by the poet's conscious aesthetic callings, the fact that sometimes the poet's areas of theoretical commitment are intriguingly undercut by a countercurrent not endorsed by the conscious sensibility of the poet himself comes to trouble his aesthetic. This diffractive dimension in Eliot's understanding of the poet is evident in how his continued avowed dissociation from the Victorians—Tennyson, Browning and the rest—is associatively entangled with certain principles of Victorian poetics. Eliot's moving away from the Victorians through a particular 'dissociation of sensibility' programme undercuts the very principles that make his historical sense an encompassive power.[86] Labouring for a tradition is working into a provenance of thinking, preferred and privileged, and, being worked upon by a few things that our conscious creative commitments choose to ignore and are protective against. I find Carol Christ's critical insight into Eliot's connection with the Victorians a powerful exemplification of this problematic paradigm of trans-habit. Christ points out that Eliot's description of the process of composition has remarkable parallels with Walter Pater's description of the process of criticism in the preface to his *The Renaissance*. Whereas Pater speaks about the mind of the critic who can distinguish, analyse, and separate from its adjuncts, the virtue by which a picture, a landscape, a fair personality in life or in a book, produces this special impression of beauty or pleasure, to indicate what the source of that impression is, and under what conditions it is experienced, Eliot through the platinum analogy speaks about the ability of the poetic mind to seize and store up feelings, phrases and images to form a new order, a distinct event and experience.[87] Eliot's committed attempt to distance his concept of the poet from the Victorians is intriguingly belied through Tennyson's use of the picturesque which leads directly to Eliot's own use of symbolism, the Victorians' concern over the romantic ego resulting in alienation, solipsism and madness, the haunting influence of Matthew Arnold on him, his learning the technique of dramatic monologue from Tennyson, and in his finding 'in the dramatic monologue [like Tennyson and Browning] a poetic form that enables him to efface himself, to transcend his own personality'.[88] This is the diffractive formation of a poetic mind.

Eliot's proposition to consider the poet as a 'popular entertainer' and poetry not as a career but a 'mug's game'[89] need not make us diagnostic about any romantic fantastical play. Poetry produces refined and intellectual pleasure and such production maintains causal connection with a certain kind of activity—the rapprochement between the reward and the rigour. The entertainment comes with seriousness and only seriousness, as Gadamer notes, 'in playing makes the play wholly play. One who doesn't take the game seriously is a spoilsport'.[90] Pleasure of poetry is not the facile receptionist entertainment but an appreciative, non-impressionistic understanding stemming from complicated modes of communication—'fresh understanding of the familiar, or the expression of something we have experienced but have no words for, which enlarges our consciousness or refines our sensibility'.[91] A poem cannot have any other end than itself—autotelic without being art for art's sake—and cannot afford to have naked emotions, spontaneous and surplusive. Like Baudelaire's aesthetic penchant for the strange and the familiar, the beautiful and the grotesque, the ugly and elegant (elegiac poets then, for Baudelaire are canailles), Eliot's poetic art and the concept of the poet too saw such contrastive and contradictious correspondences among disparate and discordant things and dimensions. But the game of poetic experience has more to it than rules that come from curiousness, uncanniness and penchant for the peculiar and the unfamiliar. Tradition sets up a rule bound game which, however, does not forbid *gaming* where tradition intensifies its existence in putting the rules under revision, its existence under peril—the intimation of ruin as the promise of creation. The poet needs to have a wide range of interest and sympathy for nothing is simple: there is always a *complexity* that the poet through his understanding and intelligence can and has to unravel.[92]

The ability of the poetic mind to put disparate things together is not mere orderly arrangement: rather, *agencement*, Deleuze's assemblage. It is more of a process, putting together as an act, under continual revision and vitality. Eliot would rightly decry any random in creative assemblage and, also, a staid and solemn fitting together of parts or pieces of observation and experiences. Tradition conceals thoughts and ideas as fossils and the poet draws the fossil-fuel out without always being alert to every paleontological and archaeological detail and specificity. Deleuze observes that 'we will call an assemblage every constellation of singularities and traits deducted from the flow—selected, organized, stratified—in such a way as to converge (consistency) artificially and naturally; an assemblage, in this sense, is a veritable invention'.[93] Eliot's poet invents and the act of invention is not romantic agency but reterritorialisation of space and strata, making creativity one's *home*. The neoclassicists teach how a house can be turned into a home; the poet here sees a home being formed out of a gaming, a force that works 'in terms of speeds and slownesses, of frozen catatonias and accelerated movements, unformed elements, nonsubjectified affects'.[94] The 'dramatology' of tradition shuts out any binaric bind without losing the relevance of the limit, the commensurability that legitimises artistic creation. What Eliot might agree with is the conative dimension to creativity given the implicit truth of tradition's *appetitio*. For instance, "The Waste Land" is built on intensities that underwrite codes which interrupt meaning-generation only to remind us that our state of experience of creativity has not come to a halt. Poetic creativity through its trans-coding is both the effect and effectuating power. Somewhat lost to time, poetic production then is mostly 'untimely'.

IV

The concept of the 'poet' for all the thinkers discussed in this book is predominantly carnivalised in three Ts—tradition, theft[95] and time. The poet's aesthetic circle functions under the dialectic of two hemispheres—one is the actual life which is always his 'material', and the other is the abstraction from actual life which is the necessary condition to the creation of a work of art. His circumference is symptomatic of his range, the extent of the area of experience he has explored and the formal technical and linguistic resources he has exploited. Armed with 'scrupulous attention' a 'great poet should not only perceive and distinguish more clearly than other men, the colours or sounds within the range of ordinary vision or hearing; he should perceive vibrations beyond the range of ordinary men, and be able to make men see and hear more at each end than they could ever see or hear without his help'.[96] Such delicate and diverse comprehensive finesse produces 'some new experience, or some fresh understanding of the familiar or the expression of something we have experienced but have no words for, which enlarges our consciousness or refines our sensibility'.[97] It is the real poet who is never unconscious where he ought to be conscious and conscious where he ought to be unconscious.[98]

Trans-habit is about accepting the opposition in habitual modes of seeing, doing and thinking—the refigurative dynamics in time and history. It is a way of creating dissonances, the struggle to negotiate between opposites not hopelessly irreconcilable always. Without getting heavily into the grammar about apparent and real time (the distinctions solicited in our reading of Henri Bergson and Ezra Pound), trans-habit reframes our ways of doing literature: literature living with change and changelessness with the changing world. It changes its pattern, modalities of manifestation but not its essential habit of *connecting* without prejudice and ideological embargo. Pound notes that all 'ages are contemporaneous'. That the 'future stirs in the minds of the few' is particularly true of literature, 'where the real time is independent of the apparent, and where many dead men are our grandchildren's contemporaries, while many of our contemporaries have been already gathered into Abraham's bosom, or some more fitting receptacle'.[99] This gathering or the ingathering speaks of a love for the real poet—a friendship that believes in love and averting love, in acquisitions, in learning about its origins and endings. So having a view is *crossing* points of view. This leaves

The 'Platinum' Poet and the Trans-Habitual Making of a Poem 169

us 'broadened': 'we do not imitate, we are changed; and our work is the work of the changed man; we have not borrowed, we have quickened, and we have become bearers of a tradition'.[100] Eliot's poet, much like the poet of all the thinkers discussed in the book, lives with others, and has others to help him know who he is, his essential operative identity, his power to make a difference. Poets are trans-beings, daemonised; they emerge and are preformed in the trans—victims of diffraction and parallax. Poetic creativity then, as this book tries to demonstrate has a very long history of trans-habit.

Notes

1. Alfred North Whitehead, *Modes of Thought* (Cambridge: Cambridge University Press, 1938), 50.
2. Salah Abdel-Sabour, *Aqoolo Lakom a'n Al-She'r*. I Tell You about Poetry (Cairo: The Egyptian Book House, 1992), 400.
3. I. A. Richards, *So Much Nearer: Essays Toward a World English* (New York: Harcourt Brace, 1968), 202.
4. Terry Eagleton, *Criticism and Ideology* (London: New Left Books, 1976), 147.
5. Eliot, *Sacred Wood* (London: Methuen and Co., 1960), 49.
6. Eliot, *On Poets and Poetry* (London: Faber and Faber, 1957), 26.
7. Eliot, *Sacred Wood*, 77.
8. See Matthew Hart, 'Visible Poet: T. S. Eliot and Modernist Studies', *American Literary History*, 19, no. 1 (Spring 2007), 175.
9. Ibid., 176.
10. Eliot, "The Waste Land", 135.
11. Eliot, "Leibniz", 204. Quoted in Hart, 'Visible Poet', 177.
12. Jean Michel Rabate, 'Tradition and T S Eliot', *Cambridge Companion to Eliot*, 210.
13. Ibid., 211.
14. Graham Clarke (ed.) *T. S. Eliot: Critical Assessments*, Vol. IV (London: Christopher Helm Ltd., 1990), 206. This points to a collective mind that is not based solely on the poet's ego. 'In this way', argues D. E. S Maxwell, 'the poet becomes a medium capable of relating, "the accumulated wisdom of time" to the problems of this unsettled age, and will be better able, because of this, to see the pattern into which the chaos may be resolved'. Maxwell notes further that a 'theory laying such importance on tradition must have something in common with Augustan literary doctrine. The differences, however, are more revealing, as they help to define the exact nature of Eliot's view. The eighteenth century made little attempt to analyse the nature of the tradition to which they delegated such authority. For them there was no question of arguing terms with the past, of deciding which of a variety of directions should be taken. But then they did not have so wide and so confusing a choice of traditions. Nor, in an age of comparative certainty, were they so troubled by social and artistic insecurity, by the prospect of gods become "a heap of broken images"'. D. E. S. Maxwell, *The Poetry of T. S. Eliot* (London: Routledge, 1960), 22–23.
15. Hans Heinz Holz, *Vom Kunstwerk zur Ware* (Neuwied and Berlin, 1972) in Jürgen Kramer, 'T. S. Eliot's Concept of Tradition: A Revaluation', *New German Critique*, no. 6 (Autumn 1975), 21.

16. *Knowledge and Experience in the Philosophy of F. H. Bradley* (New York, 1964), 54, quoted in Gregory S. Jay, *T. S. Eliot and the Poetics of Literary History* (Baton Rouge: Louisiana State University Press, 1983), 32–33. Also see J. E. Mallinson, *T. S. Eliot's Interpretation of F. H. Bradley: Seven Essays* (Amsterdam: Springer Science and Business Media, 2013).
17. P. G. Ellis, 'The Development of T. S. Eliot's Historical Sense' *The Review of English Studies*, 23, no. 91 (Aug. 1972), 297–98.
18. Bradley, *Knowledge and Experience in the Philosophy of F. H. Bradley*, 147–48. Brian Glaser observes that 'read as such a post-philosophical movement in his ongoing investigation of the self, one of Eliot's first critical formulations, "Tradition and the Individual Talent" can be seen as a corrective to [Rudolf] Eucken's insistence that there are no private truths, which takes the form of an original theory of how such truths do in fact become part of the public character. Among its rhetorical functions, the central metaphor of this essay— that the sensibility of the artist is like a filament of platinum which catalyzes a reaction between oxygen and sulfur dioxide without coming into contact with either of them—offers a way to think about the usefulness of language in communicating transpersonal significance without any reliance on the idea of truth. For the illuminating perspective on selfhood offered by the poet, in Eliot's view, is evidenced by the perceptibility of his alienation from the voices he creatively combines. The art work is the sign of some experience of his own continuity through relation that he has had the discipline to force into intelligibility, though for precisely that reason it means the work will express a self in an ultimately negative way'. 'F.H. Bradley: A Hegelian Reading of T. S. Eliot's Negativity', *Cercles* 12 (2005), 33. It is useful to see Meyrick Booth, *Rudolf Eucken: His Philosophy and Influence* (Leopold Classic Library, 2016) & W. Tudor Jones, *An Interpretation of Rudolf Eucken's Philosophy* (Leopold Classic Library, 2016).
19. Jay, *T. S. Eliot and the Poetics of Literary History*, 36. The Hegelian departure is built around Eliot's annihilation of self but not its destruction. Jewel Spears Brooker notes that there is a dynamic and continuous dialectical process through 'self-annihilation', 'self-sacrifice' and 'self-surrender': 'what is annihilated is the autonomous self, the self as an all-sufficient whole. The death of the self, moreover, is not an end in itself, but a means to the greater end of realizing the self in writing. To be more specific: these metaphors refer to the middle term in a dialectical process that involves the experience of passion, the death of that passion (as an absolute, entire of itself) and the emergence of a stringer passion—a dialectics that can be redescribed as involving personal experiences, the relativization of that experience in a system and the emergence in art of a more genuinely personal experience. This process accommodates (indeed, depends upon) the existence and the interplay of opposites or "contradictions"'. 'Dialectic and Impersonality in T. S. Eliot' in *T. S. Eliot and the Concept of Tradition* (ed.) Giovanni Cianci & Jason Harding (Cambridge: Cambridge University Press, 2007), 43.
20. See T. S. Eliot, 'Reflections on Contemporary Poetry [IV],' *Egoist*, VI (1919), 39. See Armin Paul Frank, 'T. S. Eliot's Concept of Tradition and the American Background', *Jahrbuch fr Amerikastudien*, 16 (1971), 151–161. Peter White argues that 'Modern Tendencies in Poetry', in most other respects 'seems to echo the conclusions of its more famous counterpart essay', although the word tradition is used not once. 'Indeed, at various points in his lecture', White argues,

'Eliot seems positively to cast about for alternatives, preferring at one moment the somewhat less economical phrase our "heritage of literature", at another, the similarly wordy expression "the whole history of Poetry". In another paragraph he teeters on the verge of tautology with the assertion that "[g]reat poetry... is something which is a part of Poetry" in which, again, the poetry with a capital p seems to some extent to be standing in for tradition, and doing some of its work. These vaguely inelegant and uncomfortable substitutions tend to confirm that Eliot actively avoided this term in re-casting his theoretical pronouncements for the lecture platform. It would be a mistake, however, to see the non-appearance of the word tradition in 'Modern Tendencies in Poetry' as evidence merely of a shift in terminology. The temporary elimination of this word from Eliot's critical vocabulary is arguably only the most tangible sign of an intriguing reticence in this piece about the very idea of tradition as this is elaborated in the first part of 'Tradition and the Individual Talent'. 'Tradition and the Individual Talent' Revisited', *The Review of English Studies*, 58, no. 235 (Jun. 2007), 373.
21. Eliot, *Sacred Wood*, 50.
22. Quoted in Jane Bennett, *Vibrant Matters: A Political Ecology of Things* (Durham: Duke University Press, 2010), 74.
23. Ibid., 75.
24. Mikhail Bakhtin, 'Discourse in the Novel' in The *Dialogic Imagination* (ed.) Michael Holquist, (trans.) Caryl Emerson and Michael Holquist (Austin: University of Texas Press, 1981), 286.
25. Bakhtin, *Problems of Dostoevsky's Poetics* (ed. and trans.) Caryl Emerson (Minneapolis: University of Minnesota Press, 1984), 204.
26. Donald Wesling, *Bakhtin and the Social Moorings of Poetry* (Lewisburg, Pa.: Bucknell University Press, 2003), 21; quoted in Mary Scanlon, 'Ethics and the Lyric', *College Literature*, 34, no. 1, Winter 2007, 1–22.
27. Michael Eskin, 'Bakhtin on Poetry' *Poetics Today*, 21, no. 2 (Summer 2000), 390.
28. Ibid., 390–391.
29. See Charles Martindale, 'Ruins of Rome: T. S. Eliot and the Presence of the Past', *Arion*, Third Series, 3, no. 2/3 (Fall 1995–Winter 1996), 102–140.
30. Bergson, *Introduction to Metaphysics*, 40; quoted in David Tomlinson, 'T. S. Eliot and the Cubists', *Twentieth Century Literature*, 26, no. 1 (Spring 1980), 69.
31. *Singularity of Literature*, 26–27. Eliot's intra-active poetics in its vastly inclusive and complex sensibility finds its 'vibrations' in modern Arab poets who were deeply influenced by his notion of tradition, intertextuality and mythic method of poetry-writing. Abdel-Sabour and his contemporaries find productive aesthetic connection through a fresh understanding of tradition and mythopoetics where the conservative and common 'poetic dictionary' reinvented. Eliot combines, as Moody rightly notes, both the 'simple, direct and even austere manner of speech to the phantasmagoric and the visionary'. See David Moody, *Thomas Stearns Eliot: Poet* (Cambridge: Cambridge University Press, 1980), 79. The connection between Eliot's concept of tradition and modern Arabic poetics is potentially intriguing. Muhsin Jassim al-Musawi helps us to see that Eliot's 'writings on tradition and his use of myth drew attention to pre-Islamic mythology, especially in its Babylonian and Phoenician manifestations. Tradition was manipulated, as well, in search of its dynamic impulse for innovation and change. Both al-Ma'arri and al- Mutanabbi were re-discovered beyond their

other attributes. Both foreshadow the modernist impulse for change, dissent, thought, reason and morality. Both make high claims for poetry. Although modern poets developed different commemorative strategies, recollection undergoes re-tailoring in view of each poet's commitment at a certain time'. See his 'Engaging Tradition in Modern Arab Poetics' *Journal of Arabic Literature*, 33, no. 2 (2002), 172, 172–210. Also see Muhammad Shaheen, 'Eliot in Modern Arabic Poetry,' in *T. S. Eliot.: Man and Poet*, vol. 1 (ed.) Laura Cowan (Orono, Maine: National Poetry Foundation, 1990), 151–64, and Terri De Young, 'T. S. Eliot and Modem Arabic Poetry,' *Yearbook of Comparative and General Literature* 48 (2000), 3–21. On the intricate connection between Eliot and Egyptian poet and dramatist Çalāh 'Abd al-Çabur see Khalil I. H. Semaan, 'T. S. Eliot's Influence on Arabic Poetry and Theater' *Comparative Literature Studies*, 6, no. 4 (1969), 472–89. Also one can look up the excellent essay by Muhsin Jassim al-Musawi, 'The Edge of Rejection and Rejection: Why T. S. Eliot?' in *Arabic Poetry: Trajectories of Modernity and Tradition* (New York: Routledge, 2006), 218–36. For more see Salma Khadra Jayyusi, 'Contemporary Arabic Poetry: Visions and Attitudes,' in *Studies in Modern Arabic Literature* (ed.) R. C. Ostle (Wilts, England: Aris & Phillips Ltd., 1975), 46–68; also of interest is Aida O. Aouqa, 'Defamiliarisation in the Poetry of Abd al-Wahhb al-Bayt and T. S. Eliot: A Comparative Study', *Journal of Arabic Literature*, 32, no. 2 (2001), 167–211.
32. Kenneth K. Inada, 'Time and Temporality: A Buddhist Approach' *Philosophy East and West*, 24, no. 2 (April 1974), 176.
33. Rabate, *Cambridge Companion to Eliot*, 220.
34. See John Zilcosky, 'Modern Monuments: T. S. Eliot, Nietzsche, and the Problem of History' *Journal of Modern Literature*, 29, no. 1 (Autumn 2005), 26.
35. 'Cannibalist Manifesto', Oswald de Andrade & Leslie Barry *Latin American Literary Review*, 1, no. 38 (Jul.–Dec. 11), 36.
36. Ibid., 38, 39.
37. Ibid., 38.
38. Kenneth David Jackson 'A View on Brazilian Literature: Eating the Revista de Antropofagia' *Latin American Literary Review*, 7, no. 13 (Fall–Winter 178), 3.
39. Rachel Galvin, 'Poetry Is Theft', *Comparative Literature Studies*, 51, no. 1 (2014), 20.
40. Edouard Glissant, *Poetics of Relation* (trans.) Betsy Wing (Ann Arbor: University of Michigan Press, 1997), 154.
41. Jeremy Noel-Todd, 'The Hero as Individual Talent: Thomas Carlyle, T. S. Eliot and the Prophecy of Modernism', *The Review of English Studies*, 64, issue 265 (2013), 484.
42. See my *Thinking Literature across Continents* (Durham: Duke University Press, 2016, with J. Hillis Miller).
43. Charles Martindale, 'Ruins of Rome: T. S. Eliot and the Presence of the Past', *Arion*, Third Series, 3, no. 2/3 (Fall 1995–Winter 1996), 116.
44. Ibid., 121.
45. Ibid., 123.
46. See John J. Soldo, 'T. S. Eliot and Jules LaForgue', *American Literature*, 55, no. 2 (May 1983), 139.
47. Michel Foucault, *The Order of Things* (London: Routledge, 2002), 402–403.
48. Esad Durakovic, *The Poetics of Ancient and Classical Arabic Literature: Orientology* (trans.) Amila Karahasanovic (London: Routledge, 2015), 208.

The 'Platinum' Poet and the Trans-Habitual Making of a Poem 173

49. Abdelfattah Kilito, *The Author and His Doubles: Essays on Classical Arabic Culture*, (trans.) Michael Cooperson (Syracuse: Syracuse University Press, 2001), 18. Also see Gustave von Grunnebaum, 'The Concept of Plagiarism in Arabic Literary Theory', *Journal of Near Eastern Studies*, Vol III (1944), 234–53. The dissertation titled 'Al-Sharif Al-Murtada's Contribution to the theory of Plagiarism in Arabic Poetry' by Ahmad Muhammad Al-matouq (January 1, 1987). Paper AAI8713997. http://repository.upenn.edu/dissertations/AAI8713997 is an interesting addition on this subject. Accessed 23.2.2016.
50. Julie Scott Meisemi & Paul Starkey (ed.) *Encyclopedia of Arabic Literature* Vol. 1 (London: Routledge, 2004), 82.
51. Kilito, *The Author and His Doubles*, 19.
52. See Ali A. Hussein, *The Lightning-Scene in Ancient Arabic Poetry Function, Narration and Idiosyncrasy in Pre-Islamic and Early Islamic Poetry* (Weisbaden: Otto Harrassowitz GmbH, 2010), 21. Also on this subject see George J Kanazi, *Studies in the Kitab As-Sina'Atayn of Abu Hilal Al-'Askari* (Leiden: Brill, 1989); for more intensive and informed discussion around the debate between *taqlid* and *ijtihad* see Khaled El-Rouayheb, *Islamic Intellectual History in the Seventeenth Century* (Cambridge: Cambridge University Press, 2015). Wen-chin Ouyang's *Literary Criticism in Medieval Arabic-Islamic Culture: The Making of a Tradition* (Edinburgh: Edinburgh University Press, 1997) can be of abiding interest also.
53. George Kanazi, 'Literary theory of Abu Hilal Al-'Askari' in *Studies in Medieval Arabic and Hebrew Poetics* (ed.) Sasson Somekh (Leiden: Brill, 1991), 29.
54. Eliot, *On Poetry and Poets*, 69.
55. Ibid., 55. Italics are mine.
56. Ibid., 73.
57. Ezra Pound, *The Spirit of Romance* (London: 1910), 5.
58. 'Purpose of a Literary Review', *The Criterion* I (July 1923), 421.
59. See Malcolm Bradbury & James McFarlane (eds.) *Modernism* (London: Penguin Books, 1976), 72.
60. T. E. Hulme, *Speculations* (London: Routledge and Kegan Paul, 1936), 132.
61. Ibid., 137.
62. Eliot, *On Poetry and Poets*, 37–8.
63. Eliot, *Selected Essays* (London: Faber and Faber, 1951), 497.
64. Eliot, *On Poetry and Poets*, 24; also see Sourindra Mitra, *T S Eliot the Critic: A Study in Critical Ideology and Method* (Nataraj Books, 1985) for further elaboration.
65. Ibid., 185.
66. Ibid., 32–33.
67. Stephen Spender, *The Making of a Poem* (London: Hamish Hamilton, 1955), 52.
68. F. O. Mattheissen, *The Achievement of T. S. Eliot: An Essay on the Nature of Poetry* (New York: Oxford University Press, 1947), 81–82.
69. Ibid., 82.
70. 'The Music of Poetry', in *On Poetry and Poets*, 30.
71. Maria Frendo, (1999) T. S. Eliot and the Music of Poetry, Durham theses, Durham University. Available at Durham E-Theses Online: http://etheses.dur.ac.uk/4565/, 23–24. Accessed 16.10.2015.
72. Clarke, *T. S. Eliot: Critical Assessments*, 124.
73. Jackson Mathews (ed.) *Paul Valery: Collected Works* (London: 1964), 137.

74. Mathews, *Paul Valery*, 131. Edouard Roditi points out that 'Eliot and Valery both understand the significance of associations of ideas and are both equally conscious of their existence and nature: Valery wants to conceal them and absorb them by a conscious act of will whereas Eliot, just as conscious and with as much will-power, calls attention to them and wants to clarify them and make his reader as conscious of them as he is. Not content with quoting texts which he had perhaps remembered, at first, only unconsciously, Eliot adds, at the end of his poem, a whole critical apparatus of notes which refer the reader to most of the literary sources of the poem. Valery offers a rare example, in our age of doubts and sudden conversions, of consecutive thought, indeed of a thought which has not changed much through the years and their events. It is therefore almost unnecessary to indicate historically or biographically the significance of experience and chronology in his works; time is actually reduced there to the mere function of a clock whose ticking barely accompanies the various movements of a mind which has liberated itself of almost everything that could obstruct its development, more logical than chronological'. 'Paul Valery's Poetics as an Exact Science' *The Kenyon Review*, 6, no. 3 (Summer 1944), 401.
75. Also see Sourindra Mitra, *T S Eliot the Critic: A Study in Critical Ideology and Method* (Nataraj Books, 1985) for further elaboration.
76. W. N. Ince, *The Poetic Theory of Valery* (Leicester: Leicester University Press, 1970), 146–147.
77. Richard Chase, 'The Sense of the Present' *The Kenyon Review*, 7, no. 2 (Spring 1945), 226.
78. M. A. R. Habib, 'The Prayers of Childhood: T. S. Eliot's Manuscripts on Kant' *Journal of the History of Ideas*, 51, no. 1 (Jan.–Mar. 1990), 93–114.
79. *Modernism*, 83; italics are mine.
80. Eliot, *Sacred Wood*, 55; emphases are mine.
81. *The Use of Poetry and the Use of Criticism* (London: Faber and Faber, 1959), 78–9.
82. 'Hero as Individual Talent', 483.
83. Hashizume Keiko, 'Bachelard's Theory of Time: Missing Link Between Science and Art', *Aesthetics*, no. 13 (2009), 2.
84. See Gaston Bachelard, *Dialectic of Duration* (Clinamen Press, 2000).
85. Jeremy Butterfield, 'On Time in Quantum Physics' in *A Companion to the Philosophy of Time*, (ed.) Heather Dyke and Adrian Bardon (John Wiley & Sons, Inc., 2013), 224.
86. Eliot is not wholly correct when he points out that in the seventeenth century a dissociation of sensibility set in, from which we have never recovered. Wordsworth, Coleridge, Yeats in many instances repudiate such claims.
87. Carol T. Christ, 'T. S. Eliot and the Victorians', *Modern Philology* 79, no. 2 (November 1981), 162.
88. Christ, 'T. S. Eliot and the Victorians', 163.
89. *The Use of Poetry and the Use of Criticism*, 154.
90. Gadamer, *Truth and Method* (New York: Crossroads, 1982), 92.
91. *On Poetry and Poets*, 18.
92. Richard Shusterman, 'T. S. Eliot on Reading: Pleasures, Games and Wisdom' *Philosophy and Literature*, 11, no. 1 (April 1987), 1–20.
93. *A Thousand Plateaus*, (trans.) B. Massumi (Minneapolis: University of Minnesota Press, 1987), 406.

94. *Spinoza: Practical Philosophy* (trans.) R. Hurley (San Francisco, Calif.: City Light Books, 1988), 129.
95. One of the surest of tests is the way in which a poet borrows. Immature poets imitate, mature poets steal; bad poets deface what they take, and good poets make it into something better, or at least something different. The good poet welds this theft into a whole of feeling which is unique, utterly different from that from which it was torn; the bad poet throws it into something which has no cohesion. A good poet will usually borrow from authors remote in time, or alien in language, or diverse in interest. 'Philip Massinger', 1928, 125.
96. John Hayward (ed.) *T. S. Eliot: Selected Prose* (London: Penguin Books, 1955), 100–1.
97. Eliot, *On Poetry and Poets*, 18.
98. There is a great deal, in the writing of poetry, which must be conscious and deliberate. In fact, the bad poet is usually unconscious where he ought to be conscious, and conscious where he ought to be unconscious. Both errors tend to make him *personal* (Eliot, *Sacred Wood*, 58; italics mine). Here Eliot is close to Coleridge for whom the poet's art needs to involve an interpenetration of passion and will, spontaneous impulse and voluntary purpose.
99. Louise Blakeney Williams, *Modernism and the Ideology of History: Literature, Politics and the Past* (Cambridge: Cambridge University Press, 2002), 104.
100. 'Reflections on Contemporary Poetry', *Egoist*, VI (July 1919), 39.

Bibliography

Abdel-Sabour, Salah. *AqooloLakoma'n Al-She'r*. I Tell You about Poetry (Cairo: The Egyptian Book House, 1992).
Abrams, M. H. *The Mirror and the Lamp* (New York: Oxford University Press, 1953).
Acharya, N. R. (ed.) *Kavyalankarasutravritti* (Bombay: Nirnayasagara Press, 1953).
Aden, John M. 'Dryden and the Imagination: The first Phase' *PMLA*, 74, no. 1 (Mar. 1959): 28–40.
Agamben, G. *Potentialities: Collected Essays in Philosophy* (ed. & trans.) D. Heller-Roazen (Stanford, Calif.: Stanford University Press, 1999).
———. *Idea of Prose* (trans.) M. Sullivan & S. Whitsitt (Albany: State University of New York Press, 1995).
———. *The Coming Community* (trans. M. Hardt) (Minneapolis: University of Minnesota Press, 1993).
Aitkin, J. W. H. *English Literary Criticism* Vol. II, (Jaipur: Surabhi Publications, 1999).
Àjami, Mansour. *The Alchemy of Glory: The Dialectic of Truthfulness and Untruthfulness in Medieval Arabic Literary Criticism* (Washington, D.C.: Three Continents Press, 1988).
Albrecht, W.P. *Hazlitt and the Creative Imagination* (Lawrence: University of Kansas Press, 1965).
Alhadeff-Jones, Michel. 'Three Generations of Complexity Theories: Nuances and ambiguities', *Educational Philosophy and Theory*, 40, 1, (2008): 66–82.
Allen, Kristie M. *Second Nature: The Discourse of Habit in Nineteenth-Century British Realist Fiction*, A Dissertation submitted to the Graduate School-New Brunswick Rutgers, The State University of New Jersey, 2008.
Allen, Roger. *The Arabic Literary Heritage: the Development of its Genres and Criticism* (Cambridge: Cambridge University Press, 1998).
Al-matouq, Ahmad Muhammad. 'Al-Sharif Al-Murtada's Contribution to the theory of Plagiarism in Arabic Poetry' (Dissertation Paper) (January 1, 1987). AAI8713997. http://repository.upenn.edu/dissertations/AAI8713997.
Al-Musawi, Muhsin Jassim. 'The Edge of Rejection and Rejection: Why T. S. Eliot?' in *Arabic Poetry: Trajectories of Modernity and Tradition* (New York: Routledge, 2006): 218–236.
———. 'Engaging Tradition in Modern Arab Poetics' *Journal of Arabic Literature*, 33, no. 2 (2002): 172–210.
Ames, Roger T. & David L. Hall (trans.) *Daodejing: Making This Life Significant* (New York: Ballantine Books, 2003).

Andrade, Oswald de & Leslie Barry 'Cannibalist Manifesto', *Latin American Literary Review*, 1, no. 38 (Jul.–Dec., 11): 38–47.
Aouqa, Aida O. 'Defamiliariation in the Poetry of Abd al-Wahhb al-Bayt and T. S. Eliot: A Comparative Study', *Journal of Arabic Literature*, 32, no. 2, (2001): 167–211.
Arieh Sachs, 'Generality and Particularity in Johnson's Thought', *Studies in English Literature, 1500–1900*, 5, no. 3, (Summer, 1965): 491–511.
Arieti, Silvano. *Creativity: The Magic Synthesis* (New York: Basic Books, 1976).
Aristotle. *The Metaphysics* (Dover Publications, 2008).
———. *Nichomachean Ethics* (translated with introduction) Terence Irwin (Indiana: Hackett Publishing Company, 1999).
Arnold, Matthew. *Essays in Criticism* First and Second Series (London: J.M. Dent & Sons Ltd., 1964).
Ashfield, Andrew and Peter de Bolla (ed.) *The Sublime: A Reader in British Eighteenth-Century Aesthetic Theory* (Cambridge: Cambridge University Press, 1996).
Atkins, J. W. H. *English Literary Criticism: The Renascence* (London, 1947).
Auerbach, Erich. 'Philology and Weltliteratur,' (trans.) Marie and Edward Said, *Centennial Review*, 13, no. 1 (Winter 1969): 1–17.
Austen, Gillian. *George Gascoigne* (Cambridge: D. S Brewer, 2008).
Bachelard, Gaston. *Dialectic of Duration* (Manchester: Clinamen Press, 2000).
———. *L'Eauet les Re'ves, Essaisur V'imagination de la matiere* (Paris: Corti, 1942).
Bain, Alexander. *Emotions and the Will* (London, 1859; 4th ed. 1899).
Bakhtin, Mikhail. *Problems of Dostoevsky's Poetics* (ed. and trans.) Caryl Emerson (Minneapolis: University of Minnesota Press, 1984).
———. *The Dialogic Imagination* (ed.) Michael Holquist (trans.) Caryl Emerson and Michael Holquist (Austin: University of Texas Press, 1981).
Barnouw, Jeffrey. 'The Morality of the Sublime: To John Dennis', *Comparative Literature*, 35, no. 1, (1983): 21–42.
Bassett, Samuel. *The Poetry of Homer* (Berkeley: University of California Press, 1938).
Bataille, G. *Eroticism* (trans.) M. Dalwood (London: Marion Boyers, 1987).
———. *Literature and Evil* (trans.) A. Hamilton (London: Calder and Boyars, 1985).
———. *Visions of Excess* (trans.) A. Stoekl (Manchester: Manchester University Press, 1985).
Battestin, Martin C. (ed.) Preface to *Henry Fielding's Joseph Andrews and Shamela* (Boston: Houghton Mifflin, 1961).
Batteux, Charles. *The Fine Arts Reduced to a Single Principle* (translation with an introduction) James O Young (Oxford: Oxford University Press, 2015).
Beach, D. M. 'The Poetry of Idea: Sir Philip Sidney and the Theory of Allegory', *Texas Studies in Literature and Language*, 13, no. 3 (Fall 1971): 365–389.
Beardsley, Monroe C. *Aesthetics from Classical Greece to the Present: A Short History* (New York: The Macmillan Company, 1966).
Behrendt, Stephen C. 'The Best Criticism: Imitation as Criticism in the Eighteenth Century', *The Eighteenth Century*, 24, no. 1 (Winter 1983): 3–22.
Benjamin, Walter. *Walter Benjamin: Selected Writings 1931–34* Vol. 2, (Cambridge, Mass.: Harvard University Press, 1999).
Bennett, Jane *Vibrant Matters: A Political Ecology of Things* (Durham: Duke University Press, 2010).

Bernard, J. H. (trans.) *Immanuel Kant, Critique of Judgment* (New York: Hafner Publishing Company, 1951).
Bhamaha, *Kavyalankara* (ed.) P.V. Sastry Naganath (Delhi: Motilal Banarsidass, 1970).
Bhavabhuti, *Uttara-rama-carita*, VII (Nirnaya-Sagara Press, 1903).
Biran, Maine de. *The Influence of Habit on the Faculty of Thinking* (trans.) Margaret Donaldson Boehm (Westport, Conn: Greenwood Press, 1970).
Bloom, Harold (ed.) *The Art of the Critic*, Vol. II (New York: Chelsea House, 1986).
Bose, A. C. *The Call of the Vedas* (Bombay: BharatiyaVidya Bhavan, 1960).
Boswell, James. *Life of Johnson* (ed.) G. B. Hill, rev. L. F. Powell (Oxford, 1934).
Bouhours, Dominique, *The Art of Criticism*, Philip Smallwood (ed.) (Delmar, N.Y.: Scholar's Facsimiles & Reprints, 1981).
Bradbury, Malcolm & James McFarlane (eds.) *Modernism* (London: Penguin Books, 1976).
Brady, Jennifer. '"Beware the Poet": Authority and Judgment in Jonson's Epigrammes', *Studies in English Literature, 1500–1900* 23, no. 1 (Winter 1983): 95–112.
Brett, R. L. *The Third Earl of Shaftesbury: A Study in Eighteenth-Century Literary Theory* (London: Hutchinson's University Library, 1951).
———. 'The Third Earl of Shaftesbury as a Literary Critic', *The Modern Language Review*, 37, no. 2 (Apr. 1942): 131–146.
Bronson, Bertrand H. (ed.) *Samuel Johnson: Rasselas, Poems, and Selected Prose* (New York: Rinehart Press, 1952).
Buelow, George J. 'Originality, Genius, Plagiarism in English Criticism of the Eighteenth Century' *International Review of the Aesthetics and Sociology of Music*, 21, no. 2 (Dec. 1990): 117–128.
Burik, Steven. *The End of Comparative Philosophy and the Task of Comparative Thinking Heidegger, Derrida, and Daoism* (Albany: SUNY, 2009).
Burkhardt, Frederick H., Fredson Bowers & Ignas K. Skrupskeli (eds.) *The Works of William James* (Cambridge, Mass.: Harvard University Press, 1975–1988).
Butterfield, Jeremy. 'On Time in Quantum Physics' in *A Companion to the Philosophy of Time*, (ed.) Heather Dyke and Adrian Bardon (John Wiley & Sons, Inc., 2013), 220–241.
Caciarri, Massimo. *Architecture and Nihilism: On the Philosophy of Modern Architecture* (trans.) Stephen Sartarelli (introduction) Patrizia Lombardo (New Haven: Yale University Press, 1993).
Cantarino, Vicente. *Arabic Poetics in the Golden Age* (Leiden: E. J. Brill, 1975).
Carli, Silvia. 'Poetry is more Philosophical then History: Aristotle on Mimesis and Form', *The Review of Metaphysics*, 64, no. 2 (December 2010): 303–336.
Carlyle, Alexander. (ed.) *New Letters of Thomas Carlyle* (London: John Lane, 1904).
Carlyle, Thomas. *Past and Present* Vol. 10 (New York: Charles Scribner's Sons, 1904).
———. *Two Notebooks of Thomas Carlyle* (ed.) Charles Eliot Norton (New York: The Grolier Club, 1898).
Cassirer, Ernst. *The Philosophy of the Enlightenment* (Boston: Beacon Press, 1955).
Cassirer, H. W. *A Commentary on Kant's Critique of Judgment* (New York: Barnes & Noble. Inc., 1938).
Chapman, Emmanuel. 'Some Aspects of St. Augustine's Philosophy of Beauty', *The Journal of Aesthetics and Art Criticism*, 1, no. 1 (Spring 1941): 46–51.
Chatterjee, Visvanath (ed.) *An Apology for Poetry* (London: Sangam Books, 1975).

Chaudhury, Prabas Jiban. *Tagore on Literature and Aesthetics* (Calcutta: Rabindra-Bharati, 1965).
Christ, Carol. T. 'T. S. Eliot and the Victorians', *Modern Philology* 79, no. 2 (November 1981): 157–165.
Clarke, Graham (ed.) *T. S. Eliot: Critical Assessments*, Vol. IV (London: Christopher Helm Ltd., 1990).
Class, Monika *Coleridge and Kantian Ideas in England 1796–1817* (London: Bloomsbury, 2012).
Clements, Robert J. *Pictapoesis* (Rome, 1960).
Coburn, Kathleen. *Inquiring Spirit: A New Presentation of Coleridge from His Published and Unpublished Prose Writings* (New York: Pantheon Books, 1951).
Coleridge, Samuel Taylor. *Biographia Literaria* (ed.) James Engell and W. Jackson Bate (Princeton: Princeton University Press, 1983).
———. *Aids to Reflection* (Grant, Edinburgh, 1905).
Cooper, John Gilbert. *Letters Concerning Taste* (London: R. and J. Dodsley, 1755).
Coste, Didier. 'Is a Non-Global Universe Possible? What Universals in the Theory of Comparative Literature (1952–2002) Have to Say about It' *Comparative Literature Studies*, 41, no. 1 (2004): 37–48.
Daiches, David. *Critical Approaches to Literature* (Calcutta: Orient Longman, 1998).
Dalal, C. D. and Benoytosh Bhattacharya (eds.) *Kavyamimamsa* (Baroda: Oriental Institute, 1934).
D'Alembert, Jean le Rond 'Discourspreliminaire des editeurs,' *Encyclopedie, ou Dictionnaire Raisonne des Sciences, des Arts et des Metiers, Par uneSociete de Gens de Lettres*, 17 vols. (Paris, 1751–65).
Das, B. B. & J. M. Mohanty (eds.) *Literary Criticism: A Reading* (New Delhi: Oxford University Press, 1985).
De, S. K. *History of Sanskrit Poetics* (Calcutta: K.L. Mukhopadhyay, 1960).
Delaura, David J. 'Ishmael as Prophet: Heroes and Hero-Worship and the Self-Expressive Basis of Carlyle's Art' *Texas Studies in Literature and Language*, 11, no. 1 (Spring 1969): 705–732.
Deleuze, Gilles. *Difference and Repetition* (New York: Routledge, 1994).
———. *The Logic of Sense* (New York: Columbia University Press, 1990).
———. *Spinoza: Practical Philosophy* (trans.) R. Hurley (San Francisco, CA: City Light Books, 1988).
Deleuze, Gilles and Felix Guattari. *A Thousand Plateaus*, (trans.) B. Massumi (Minneapolis, MN: University of Minnesota Press, 1987).
Derrida, Jacques. *Politics of Friendship* (trans.) George Collins (New York: Verso, 1997).
Dewey, John. *Human Nature and Conduct* (New York: Dover Publications Inc., 2002).
Dieckmann, Herbert. 'Diderot's Conception of Genius', *Journal of the History of Ideas*, 2, no. 2 (April, 1941): 151–182.
Doherty, M. H. *The Mistress-Knowledge: Sir Philip Sidney's Defence of Poesie and Literary Architectonics in the English Renaissance* (Nashville, Tenn.: Vanderbilt University Press, 1991).
Donaldson, Ian. *Jonson's Magic Houses* (Oxford: Clarendon Press, 1997).
Dryden, John. *Of Dramatic Poesy and Other Critical Essays*, (Edited with an Introduction) George Grimes Watson, (London, 1962).
Du Bos, Jean-Baptiste. *Critical Reflections on Poetry, Painting and Music*, (trans.) T. Nugent (London: John Nourse, 1748).

Durakovic, Esad. *The Poetics of Ancient and Classical Arabic Literature: Orientology* (trans.) Amila Karahasanovic (London: Routledge, 2015).
Durgaprasada, Pt. (ed.) *Sahityadarpana* (Bombay: Nirnayasagara Press, 1931).
Durgaprasada, Pt. and W.L. Sastry Panashikar, (eds.) *Dhvanyaloka L* (Bombay: Nimayasagar Press, 1928).
Eagleton, Terry. *Criticism and Ideology* (London: New Left Books, 1976).
Eells Jr., John Shepard. *The Touchstones of Matthew Arnold* (New York: Bookman Associates, 1955).
Eidson, John Olin. 'Dryden's Criticism of Shakespeare', *Studies in Philology*, 33, no. 2 (Apr. 1936): 273–280.
El-Rouayheb, Khaled. *Islamic Intellectual History in the Seventeenth Century* (Cambridge: Cambridge University Press, 2015).
Eliot, T. S. *Sacred Wood* (London: Methuen and Co., 1960).
———. *On Poets and Poetry* (London: Faber and Faber, 1957).
———. *Selected Essays* (London: Faber and Faber, 1951).
———. *The Use of Poetry and the Use of Criticism* (London: Faber and Faber, 1933).
Ellis, P. G. 'The Development of T. S. Eliot's Historical Sense' *The Review of English Studies*, 23, no. 91 (Aug., 1972): 291–301.
Ellison, Ralph. *Invisible Man* (New York: Random, 1952).
Engell, James. *The Creative Imagination: Enlightenment to Romanticism* (Cambridge, Mass,: Harvard University Press, 1981).
Enright, D. J. and E.D. Chickera (ed.) *English Critical Texts: 16th to 20th Century* (Oxford: Oxford University Press, 1962).
Eskin, Michael. 'Bakhtin on Poetry' *Poetics Today*, 21, no. 2, (Summer 2000): 379–391.
Esther, Iris Sells. *Matthew Arnold and France: The Poet* (Cambridge: Cambridge University Press, 1935).
Fakhreddine, Huda J. 'Defining Metapoesis in the ʿAbbāsid Age', *Journal of Arabic Literature* 42 (2011): 205–35.
Farmer, Norman. 'Fulke Greville and the Poetic of the Plain Style', *Texas Studies in Literature and Language*, 11, no. 1 (Spring 1969): 657–70.
Fellows, Otis E. 'The Theme of Genius in Diderot's Neveu de Rameau' *Diderot Studies*, 2 (1952): 168–99.
Felski, Rita & Susan Stanford Friedman. (ed.) *Comparison: Theories, Approaches, Uses* (ed.) (Baltimore: Johns Hopkins University Press, 2013).
Fish, Stanley. 'Author-Readers: Jonson's Community of the Same', *Representations* 7 (Summer 1984): 26–58.
Flatley, Jonathan. *Affective Mapping: Melancholia and the Politics of Modernism* (Cambridge, Mass.: Harvard University Press, 2008).
Follet, Mary Parker. *Creative Experience* (New York: Peter Smith, 1951).
———. *The New State: Group Organization the Solution of Popular Government* (New York: Longmans, Green and Co., 1918).
Ford, Andrew. *The Origins of Criticism: Literary Culture and Poetic Theory in Classical Greece* (Princeton: Princeton University Press, 2002).
Foucault, Michel. *The Order of Things* (London: Routledge, 2002).
Frank, Armin Paul. 'T. S. Eliot's Concept of Tradition and the American Background', *Jahrbuchfr Amerikastudien*, 16 (1971): 151–61.
Frankel, Herman. *Early Greek Poetry and Philosophy* (Oxford: Basil Blackwell, 1975).
Friederich, Werner P. *Outline of Comparative Literature from Dante Alighieri to Eugene O'Neill* (Chapel Hill: University of North Carolina Press, 1954).

Frendo, Maria. *T. S. Eliot and the Music of Poetry*, Durham theses, Durham University. Available at Durham E-Theses, 1999. Online: http://etheses.dur.ac.uk/4565/.
Froude, J. A. *Thomas Carlyle: A History of the First Forty Years of His Life: 1195–1835*, 2 vols. (London, 1882).
Fujimura, Thomas H. 'Dryden's Poetics: The Expressive Values in Poetry', *The Journal of English and Germanic Philology*, 74, no. 2 (Apr., 1975): 195–208.
Furst, L R. *European Romanticism, An Anthology* (London and New York: Methuen, 1980).
Gadamer, Hans-Georg. *Truth and Method* (New York: Crossroads, 1982).
———. *Philosophical Hermeneutics* (trans & ed.) David E. Linge (Berkeley: University of California Press, 1977).
Galvin, Rachel. 'Poetry Is Theft', *Comparative Literature Studies*, 51, no. 1, (2014): 18–54.
Garrison, Jim. 'A Deweyan Theory of Democratic Listening', *Educational Theory* 46, no. 4, (1996): 429–51.
Gelder, G.J.H. Van *Classical Arabic Literary Critics on the Coherence and Unity of the Poem* (Leiden: Brill, 1982).
Gerard, Alexander. *An Essay on Genius* (ed.) Bernhard Fabian (Munchen: Wilhelm Fink Verlag, 1966).
Ghosh, Aurobindo. *Collected Poems* (Pondicherry: Sri Aurobindo Ashram, 1994).
———. *Hymns to the Mystic Fire* (Pondicherry: Sri Aurobindo Ashram, 1991).
———. *Savitri* (Pondicherry: Sri Aurobindo Birth Centenary Library, 1972).
———. *The Future Poetry* (Pondicherry: Sri Aurobindo Ashram, 1972).
———. *The Harmony of Virtue* Vol. III. (Pondicherry: Sri Aurobindo Ashram, 1972).
———. *The Hour of God*, Vol. 17, (Pondicherry: Sri Aurobindo Birth Centenary Library, 1972).
———. *The Human Cycle* (Pondicherry: Sri Aurobindo Birth Centenary Library, 1972).
———. *Life, Literature, Yoga* (Pondicherry: Sri Aurobindo Ashram, 1952).
———. *The Life Divine* (New York: Sri Aubindo Library, 1949).
———. *Letters of Sri Aurobindo* (on Poetry and and Literature) Third Series (Bombay: Sri Aurobindo Circle, 1949).
Ghosh, Ranjan and J. Hillis Miller. *Thinking Literature across Continents* (Durham: Duke University Press, 2016).
Ghosh, Ranjan and Ethan Kleinberg. (ed.) *Presence: Philosophy, History and Cultural Theory for the 21st Century* (Ithaca, N.Y.: Cornell University Press, 2013).
Gilman, Margaret. 'Imagination and Creation in Diderot,' *Diderot Studies*, 2 (1952): 200–20.
Gilpin, George H. 'Coleridge and the Spiral of Poetic Thought' *Studies in English Literature*, 12, no. 4, (Autumn 1972): 639–52.
Glissant, Edouard. *Poetics of Relation* (trans.) Betsy Wing (Ann Arbor: University of Michigan Press, 1997).
Gossman, Lionel. 'Philhellenism and Antisemitism: Matthew Arnold and His German Models' *Comparative Literature* 46, no. 1 (Winter 1994): 1–39.
Grassi, Ernesto. 'Humanistic Rhetorical Philosophizing: Giovanni Pontano's Theory of the Unity of Poetry, Rhetoric, and History', *Philosophy & Rhetoric*, 17, no. 3 (1984): 135–55.
Graves, Robert. *The Common Asphodel* (London: Hamish Hamilton, 1949).

Griggs, Earl Leslie. (ed.) *Collected Letters of Samuel Taylor Coleridge* (Oxford: Clarendon Press, 2000).
Grunnebaum, Gustave von 'The Concept of Plagiarism in Arabic Literary Theory', *Journal of Near Eastern Studies*, Vol. III (1944): 234–53.
Habib, M. A. R. *A History of Literary Criticism and Theory: From Plato to the Present* (Oxford: Blackwell, 2005).
——. 'The Prayers of Childhood: T. S. Eliot's Manuscripts on Kant' *Journal of the History of Ideas*, 51, no. 1 (Jan.-Mar. 1990): 93–114.
Halliwell, Stephen. *The Poetics of Aristotle* (Duckworth: London: 1987).
Hamilton, A. C. 'Sidney's Idea of the "Right Poet"', *Comparative Literature*, 9, no. 1 (Winter, 1957): 51–9.
Hamilton, Paul. *Coleridge's Poetics* (Oxford: Blackwell, 1983).
Hardikar, A. R. 'The Aesthetic Appreciator or *Sahridaya*', *Annals of the Bhandarkar Oriental Research Institute*, 75, no. 1/4 (1994): 265–72.
Harrold, Charles Frederick. (ed.) *Sartor Resartus* (New York: Odyssey Press, 1937).
——. 'Carlyle and Novalis' *Studies in Philology*, 27, no. 1 (Jan., 1930): 47–63.
Hart, Matthew. 'Visible Poet: T. S. Eliot and Modernist Studies', *American Literary History*, 19, no. 1, (Spring 2007): 174–89.
Havens, Raymond D. 'Johnson's Distrust of the Imagination' *ELH*, 10, no. 3 (Sep. 1943): 243–55.
Haven, Richard. *Patterns of Consciousness: An Essay on Coleridge* (Amherst: University of Massachusetts Press, 1969).
Hayot, Eric 'Bertrand Russell's Chinese Eyes' Modernisms' *Chinese Literature and Culture* 18, no. 1 (2006): 120–54.
Hayward, John (ed.) *T. S. Eliot: Selected Prose* (London: Penguin Books, 1955).
Hazard, Mary E. 'The Anatomy of Liveliness as a Concept in Renaissance Aesthetics', *The Journal of Aesthetics and Art Criticism*, 33, no. 4 (Summer 1975): 407–418.
Helgerson, Richard. *Self Crowned Laureates: Spenser, Jonson, Milton and the Literary System* (Berkeley: University of California Press, 1983).
Heninger Jr., S. K., Susan C. Staub, John T. Shawcross and Anne Lake Prescott, 'The Interface between Poetry and History: Gascoigne, Spenser, Drayton' *Studies in Philology*, 87, no. 1 (Winter 1990): 109–35.
Herford, C. H. & Percy and Evelyn Simpson, (ed.) *Ben Jonson* 11vols (Oxford: Clarendon Press, 1925–1952).
Hess, Jillian M. 'Coleridge's Fly-Catchers: Adapting Commonplace-Book Form', *Journal of the History of Ideas*, 73, no. 3 (July 2012): 463–83.
Hillyer, Richard. *Sir Philip Sidney: Cultural Icon* (New York: Palgrave Macmillan, 2010).
Hipple, Jr. Walter John. *The Beautiful, The Sublime, & the Picturesque in Eighteenth-Century British Aesthetic Theory* (Carbondale: The Southern Illinois University Press, 1957).
Hiriyana, M. (ed.) *Vedantarasa of Sadananda Yati* (Poona: Oriental Book Agency, 1929).
Hooker, E. H. *Critical Works of John Dennis* (Baltimore: Johns Hopkins University Press, 1943).
Hughes, A.M.D. *Thomas Carlyle: Introduction and Notes* (London: Oxford University Press, 1957).
Hulme, T. E. *Speculations* (London: Routledge and Kegan Paul, 1936).
Hume, Robert. 'Dryden on Creation: Imagination in the Later Criticism', *The Review of English Studies*, 21, no. 83 (Aug., 1970): 295–314.
Hume, Robert D. *Dryden's Criticism* (Ithaca, N.Y.: Cornell University Press, 1970).

———. 'Kant and Coleridge on Imagination', *The Journal of Aesthetics and Art Criticism*, 28, no. 4 (Summer 1970): 485–96.

Hussein, Ali A. *The Lightning-Scene in Ancient Arabic Poetry: Function, Narration and Idiosyncrasy in Pre-Islamic and Early Islamic Poetry* (Weisbaden: Otto Harrassowitz GmbH, 2010).

Inada, Kenneth K. 'Time and Temporality: A Buddhist Approach' *Philosophy East and West*, 24, no. 2 (April 1974): 171–79.

Ince, W. N. *The Poetic Theory of Valery* (Leicester: Leicester University Press, 1970).

Ingalls, Daniel H. H., Jeffrey Moussaieef Masson, & M. V. Patwardhan (trans.) *The Dhvanyaloka of Anandavardhana with the Locana of Abhinavagupta*, (Cambridge, Mass.: Harvard University Press, 1990).

Isler, Alan D. 'Heroic Poetry and Sidney's Two "Arcadias"' *PMLA*, 83, no. 2 (May 1968): 368–379.

Jackson, J. R. de J. (ed.) *The Collected Works of Samuel Taylor Coleridge* Vol. 1 (Princeton, N.J.: Princeton University Press, 1975).

———. *Method and Imagination in Coleridge's Criticism* (London: Routledge & Kegan Paul, 1969).

Jackson, Kenneth David. 'A View on Brazilian Literature: Eating the Revista de Antropofagia' *Latin American Literary Review*, 7, no. 13 (Fall-Winter 178): 1–9.

Jacobson, Daniel. 'Sir Philip Sidney's Dilemma: On the Ethical unction of Narrative Art', *The Journal of Aesthetics and Art Criticism*, 54, no. 4 (Autumn 1996): 327–36.

Jaffe, Kineret S. 'The Concept of Genius: Its Changing Role in Eighteenth-Century French Aesthetics', *Journal of the History of Ideas*, 41, no. 4 (Oct.-Dec., 1980): 579–99.

Jay, Gregory S. *T. S. Eliot and the Poetics of Literary History* (Baton Rouge: Louisiana State University Press, 1983).

Jayyusi, Salma Khadra. 'Contemporary Arabic Poetry: Visions and Attitudes,' in *Studies in Modern Arabic Literature* (ed.) R. C. Ostle (Wilts, England: Aris & Phillips Ltd., 1975), 46–68.

Jefferson, Ann. *Genius in France: An Idea and its Uses* (Princeton, N.J.: Princeton University Press, 2015).

Jenkins, Patricia Mavis. 'Coleridge and the Perils of the Unbridled Imagination', *Philosophy and Literature*, 1, no. 2, (Spring 1977): 192–200.

Jha, Brajmohan (ed.) *Aucityavicaracarca* (Varanasi: ChowkhambaVidyabhavana, 2000).

Jones, Edmund. *English Critical Essays (Nineteenth Century)* (Oxford: Oxford University Press, 1919).

Joyce, Michael. *Othermindedness: The Emergence of Network Culture* (Ann Arbor: The University of Michigan Press, 2000).

Kaiser, Birgit Mara. 'WorldingCompLit: Diffractive Reading with Barad, Glissant and Nancy', *Parallax*, 20, no. 3, (2014): 274–87.

Kanazi, George J. *Studies in the Kitab As-Sina'Atayn of Abu Hilal Al-'Askari* (Leiden: Brill, 1989).

Kaplan, Edward K. 'Gaston Bachelard's Philosophy of Imagination: An Introduction' *Philosophy and Phenomenological Research*, 33, no. 1 (Sep. 1972): 1–24.

Karakayali, Nedim. 'The Uses of the Stranger: Circulation, Arbitration, Secrecy, and Dirt' *Sociological Theory*, 24, no. 4 (Dec. 2006): 312–30.

Katona, Gábor. 'The Cultural Background of Sir Philip Sidney's "Defence of Poesy"', *Hungarian Studies in English*, 22 (1991): 89–108.

Kavi, M.R. (ed) *Natyasastra* (Baroda: Oriental Research Institute, 1934).
Kearney, Richard. *Poetics of Imagining* (Edinburgh: Edinburgh University Press, 1998).
Keast, W. R. 'Johnson's Criticism of the Metaphysical Poets,' *ELH*, XVII (1950): 59–70.
Keiko, Hashizume. 'Bachelard's Theory of Time: Missing Link Between Science and Art', *Aesthetics* no. 13, (2009): 1–9.
Kelley, Donald R. and David Harris Sacks, (eds.) *The Historical Imagination in Early Modern Britain: History, Rhetoric, Fiction, 1500–1800* (Cambridge: Cambridge University Press, 1997).
Ker, W. P. (ed.) *The Essays of John Dryden* (Oxford: Clarendon Press, 1900).
Kewes, Paulina. *The Uses of History in Early Modern England* (Berkeley: University of California Press, 1994).
Keynes, Geoffrey. (introduction and commentary) *The Marriage of Heaven and Hell* (New York: Oxford University Press, 1975).
———. *The Complete Writings of William Blake* (Oxford: Oxford University Press, 1966).
———. (ed.) *Poetry and Prose of William Blake* (London, 1948).
Kilito, Abdelfattah. *The Author and His Doubles: Essays on Classical Arabic Culture*, (trans.) Michael Cooperson (Syracuse: Syracuse University Press, 2001).
Kipperman, Mark. *Beyond Enchantment: German Idealism and English Romantic Poetry* (Philadelphia: University of Pennsylvania Press, 1986).
Kishler, Thomas C. 'Aristotle and Sidney on Imitation' *The Classical Journal*, 59, no. 2 (Nov. 1963): 63–64.
Koestler, Arthur. *The Act of Creation* (London: Macmillan, 1975).
Kramer, Jürgen, 'T. S. Eliot's 'Concept of Tradition: A Revaluation', *New German Critique*, no. 6 (Autumn, 1975): 20–30.
Kraus, Hans-Joachim. *Theology of Psalms* (Minneapolis: Fortress Press, 1992).
Krishnamoorthy, K. (ed.) *Vakroktijivita* (Dharwad: Kamataka University, 1977).
Lamb, Mary Ellen. 'Apologising for Pleasure in Sidney's "Apology for Poetry": The Nurse of Abuse Meets the Tudor Grammar School', *Criticism*, 3, no. 4 (Fall 1994): 499–519.
Landa, Jose Angel Garcia. '"The Enthusiastick Fit": The Function and Fate of the Poet in Johnson's *Rasselas*', 1991, https://dialnet.unirioja.es/descarga/articulo/69021.pdf.
Lefebvre, H. *Rhythmanalysis: Space, Time and Everyday Life* (trans.) Stuart Elden & Gerald Moore (London: Continuum, 2004).
Lehman, B. H. *Carlyle's Theory of the Hero* (Durham: Duke University Press, 1928).
Leinwand, Theodore. 'Shakespeare, Coleridge, Intellecturition', *Studies in Romanticism*, 46, no. 1 (Spring 2007): 77–104.
Lele, V. K. (ed.) *Kavikanthabharana* (Delhi: Motilal Banarasidas, 1967).
Letwin, Shirley Robin 'Matthew Arnold: Enemy of Tradition' *Political Theory*, 10, no. 3 (Aug. 1982): 333–351.
Levy, Gayle A. *Refiguring the Muse* (New York: Peter Lang, 1999).
Lewes, George Henry. *Problems of Life and Mind* (London: Trübner, 1880).
Li, Wai-Yee. 'Between "Literary Mind" and "Carving Dragons": Order and Excess in *Wenxindiaolong*' in *A Chinese Literary Mind* (ed.) Zong-qi Cai (Stanford, Calif.: Stanford University Press, 2001), 193–225.
Lin, Shuen-fu. 'Liu Xie on Imagination', in *A Chinese Literary Mind* (ed.) Zong-qi Cai (Stanford, Calif.: Stanford University Press, 2001), 127–60.
Lipkowitz, Ina. 'Inspiration and the Poetic Imagination: Samuel Taylor Coleridge' *Studies in Romanticism*, 30, no. 4 (Winter, 1991): 605–31.

186 Bibliography

Liu, James J. Y. *Language-Paradox-Poetics: A Chinese Perspective* (Princeton, N.J.: Princeton University Press, 1988).

———. *Chinese Theories of Literature* (Chicago: University of Chicago Press, 1975).

Loewenstein, J. 'The Script in the Marketplace', *Representations* 12 (1985): 101–114.

Longxi, Zhang. *Unexpected Affinites: Reading Across Cultures* (Toronto: University of Toronto Press, 2007).

———. *Allegoresis: Reading Canonical Literature East and West* (Ithaca, N.Y.: Cornell University Press, 2005).

Lowry, Howard F. (ed.) *The Letters of Matthew Arnold to Arthur Hugh Clough* (London, 1932).

Mack, Michael. *Sidney's Poetics: Imitating Creation* (Washington, D.C.: The Catholic University of America Press, 2005).

Magnuson, Paul. *Coleridge's Nightmare Poetry* (Charlottesville: University of Virginia Press, 1974).

Makkreel, Rudolf A. *Imagination and Interpretation in Kant, The Hermeneutical Import of the Critique of Judgment* (Chicago: The University of Chicago Press, 1990).

Mall, James 'Le Neveu de Rameau and the Idea of Genius' *Eighteenth-Century Studies*, 11, no. 1 (Autumn 1977): 26–39.

Marotti, Arthur. 'All About Jonson's Poetry', *ELH* 39 (1972): 208–37.

———. *Manuscript, Print and the English Renaissance Lyric* (Ithaca, N.Y.: Cornell University Press, 1993).

Marsh, Robert. 'Shaftesbury's Theory of Poetry: The Importance of the "Inward Colloquy"' *ELH*, 28, no. 1 (Mar. 1961): 54–69.

Martin, Floyd W. 'Sir Joshua Reynolds's "Invention": Intellectual Activity as a Foundation of Art' *Art Education* 40, no. 6 (Reston, Va.: National Art Education Association 1987), 6–15.

Martindale, Charles. 'Ruins of Rome: T. S. Eliot and the Presence of the Past', *Arion*, Third Series, 3, no. 2/3 (Fall 1995-Winter 1996): 102–40.

Massumi, Brian. *Semblance and Event: Activist Philosophy and the Occurrent Arts* (Cambridge, Mass.: MIT Press, 2011).

Matar, Nabil. 'Alfārābī on Imagination: With a Translation of His "Treatise on Poetry"', *College Literature*, 23. no. 1 (Feb. 1996): 100–10.

Mattheissen, F. O. *The Achievement of T. S. Eliot: An Essay on the Nature of Poetry* (New York: Oxford University Press, 1947).

Mathews, Jackson (ed.) *Paul Valery: Collected Works* (London: 1964).

Maxwell, D. E. S. *The Poetry of T. S. Eliot* (London: Routledge, 1960).

Mcntyre, John P. 'Sidney's Golden World', *Comparative Literature*, 14, no. 4 (Autumn 1962): 356–65.

Meisemi, Julie Scott & Paul Starkey (ed.) *Encyclopedia of Arabic Literature* Vol. 1 (London: Routledge, 2004).

Miles, Rosalind. *Ben Jonson His Craft and Art* (Savage MD: Barnes and Nobles, 1990).

Mishra, R. C. (ed.) *Kavyadarsa* (Varanasi: ChowkhambaVidyabhavana, 1958).

Misra, Vidya Niwas. 'The Concept of *Sahrdaya*', in C. D. Narasimhaiah (ed.) *East West Poetics at Work* (New Delhi: Sahitya Academi, 1994), 48–56.

Mitra, R. (ed.), *Agnipurana* Vol. III (Calcutta: Asiatic Society of Bengal, 1879).

Mitra, Sourindra. *T. S. Eliot the Critic: A Study in Critical Ideology and Method* (New Delhi: Nataraj Books, 1985).

Moody, David. *Thomas Stearns Eliot: Poet* (Cambridge: Cambridge University Press, 1980).

Moore, Roger E. 'Sir Philip Sidney's Defence of Prophesizing', *Studies in English Literature* 1500–1900, 50, no. 1, (Winter 2010): 35–62.
Morrison, Keith. 'Educational Philosophy and the Challenge of Complexity Theory', *Educational Philosophy and Theory*, 40, 1, (2008): 19–34.
Murphy, John W. (ed.) *The World of Quantum Culture* (Westport, CT: Praeger, 2002).
Murray, Timothy. 'From Foul Sheets to Legitimate Model: Antitheater, Text, Ben Jonson', *New Literary History* 14, no. 13 (1983): 641–64.
Myrick, Kenneth O. *Sir Philip Sidney as a Literary Craftsman* (Cambridge, Mass.: Harvard University Press, 1935).
Nabokov, Vladimir. *Ada, or Ardor: A Family Chronicle* (New York: McGraw-Hill, 1969).
NaganathSastry, P.V. (ed.) *Kavyalankara* (New Delhi: Motilal Banarasidas, 1970).
Nancy, Jean-Luc. *The Muses* (trans.) Peggy Kamuf (Stanford: Stanford University Press, 1996).
Nandi, S. K. *Studies in Modern Indian Aesthetics* (Shimla: Indian Institute of Advanced Study, 1975).
Neel, Alexandra. '"A Something-Nothing Out of its Very Contrary": The Photography of Coleridge', *Victorian Studies*, 49, no. 2, (Winter 2007): 208–17.
Neff, Emery. *Carlyle and Mill: An Introduction to Victorian Thought* (New York: Columbia University Press, 1926).
Nelson, William. *Fact or Fiction: The Dilemma of the Renaissance Storyteller* (Cambridge, Mass.: Harvard University Press, 1973).
Nemoto, Hiroshi 'Who is a Proper Opponent? The Tibetan Buddhist Concept of phyirgol yang dag', *Journal of Indian Philosophy*, 41, no. 2 (April 2013): 151–65.
Newton, Richard. 'Jonson and the (Re)Invention of the Book', in *Classic and Cavalier: Essays on Jonson and the Sons of Ben* (eds.) Claude J. Summers & Ted-Larry Pebworth (Pittsburgh: University of Pittsburgh Press, 1982), 31–58.
Nicolson, Marjorie Hope. *Mountain Gloom and Mountain Glory: The Development of the Aesthetics of the Infinite* (Seattle: University of Washington Press, 1997).
Nietzsche, Friedrich. *Human All Too Human* (trans.) Marion Faber (Lincoln: University of Nebraska Press, 1984).
Nikolopoulou, Kalliopi. '"L'Art et les gens": Jean-Luc Nancy's Genealogical Aesthetics' *College Literature*, 30, no. 2 (Spring 2003): 174–93.
Noel-Todd, Jeremy. 'The Hero as Individual Talent: Thomas Carlyle, T. S. Eliot and the Prophecy of Modernism', *The Review of English Studies*, 64, issue 265, (2013): 475–91.
O'Flaherty, D. W. (trans.), *The Rig Veda* (New Delhi: Penguin, 1981).
Ouyang, Wen-chin. *Literary Criticism in Medieval Arabic-Islamic Culture: The Making of a Tradition* (Edinburgh: Edinburgh University Press, 1997).
Panofsky, E. *Idea: A Concept in Art Theory* (Leipzig and Berlin, 1924).
Payne, Paula H. 'Tracing Aristotle's "Rhetoric" in Sir Philip Sidney's Poetry and Prose', *Rhetoric Society Quarterly*, 20, no. 3 (Summer 1990): 241–50.
Perkins, David 'Johnson on Wit and Metaphysical poetry', *ELH*, XX (1953): 200–17.
Perry, Bliss. *Thomas Carlyle: How to Know Him* (Indianapolis: Bobbs-Merrill, 1915).
Perry, Seamus. *Coleridge and the Uses of Division* (Oxford: Clarendon Press, 1999).
Phillips, Mark Salber. *On Historical Distance* (New Haven: Yale University Press, 2013).
Plato, *Symposium* in *Collected Dialogues*: (eds.) Edith Hamilton & Huntington Cairns (New York: Pantheon Books, 1961).

Pound, Ezra. *The Spirit of Romance* (London: J. M Dent & Sons Ltd, 1910).
Pressly, William L. *The Artist as Original Genius: Shakespeare's "Fine Frenzy" in Late Eighteenth-century British Art* (Newark: University of Delaware Press, 2007).
Proust, Marcel. *The Captive/The Fugitive*, Vol. 5 of *In Search of Lost Time*, trans. C. K. Scott Moncrieff and Terence Kilmartin (London: Vintage, 1996).
Puttenham, George. *The Art of English Poesie*. https://tspace.library.utoronto.ca/bitstream/1807/4350/1160/displayprose59ec.html.
Quincey, Thomas De. *The Collected Writings of Thomas De Quincey* (ed.) D. Masson. 14 vols. (Edinburgh, 1896).
Quint, David. "Alexander the Pig": Shakespeare on History and Poetry', *boundary 2*, 10, no. 3 (Spring, 1982): 49–67.
Rabate, Jean Michel. 'Tradition and T S Eliot', in *Cambridge Companion to Eliot*, (ed.) A. David Moody (Cambridge: Cambridge University Press, 1994) 210–22.
Radhakantadeva, Raja. (ed.) *Sabdakalpradruma* (Delhi: Motilal Banarasidass, 1961).
Raiger, Michael. 'Sidney's Defence of Plato' *Religion & Literature*, 30, no. 2 (Summer, 1998): 21–57.
Ralli, Augustus. *Guide to Carlyle* Vol. 1, (London: G. Allen & Unwin Ltd., 1920).
Rand, Benjamin (ed.) *Second Characters of the Language of Forms* (Cambridge: Cambridge University Press, 1914).
Rapple, Brendan. 'Matthew Arnold and Comparative Education', *British Journal of Educational Studies*, 37, no. 1 (Feb. 1989): 54–71.
Ravaisson, Félix. *Of Habit* (Translation, Introduction and Commentary) Clare Carlisle and Mark Sinclair (London: Continuum, 2008).
Raysor, Thomas Middleton (ed.) *Samuel Taylor Coleridge: Shakespearean Criticism*, Vol. II (London: Dent, 1960).
Read, Herbert. *The True Voice of Feeling* (London: Faber and Faber, 1947).
Ribner, Irving 'Dryden's Shakespearean Criticism and the Neo-Classical Paradox', *The Shakespeare Association Bulletin*, 21, no. 4 (October, 1946): 168–71.
Rickett, Adele Austin (ed.) *Chinese Approaches to Literature from Confucius to Liang Ch'i-ch'ao* (Princeton, N.J.: Princeton University Press, 1978).
Robinson, Forest G. *The Shape of Things Known: Sidney's Apology in its Philosophical Tradition* (Cambridge, Mass.: Harvard University Press, 1972).
Roditi, Edouard. 'Paul Valery's Poetics as an Exact Science' *The Kenyon Review*, 6, no. 3 (Summer 1944): 398–408.
Roe, Nicholas. (ed.) *Samuel Taylor Coleridge and the Sciences of Life* (New York: Oxford University Press, 2001).
Ronell, A. *Stupidity* (Urbana, IL: University of Illinois Press, 2002).
Rowe, George E. 'Ben Jonson's Quarrel with Audience and its Renaissance Context', *Studies in Philology* 81, no.4 (1984): 438–60.
Rowe, Jr. George E. 'Interpretation, Sixteenth-Century Readers, and George Gascoigne's "The Adventures of Master F. J."', *ELH* 48, no. 2 (Summer, 1981): 271–89.
Rudrata. *Kavyalankara*, (ed.) Pt. Durgaprasada (Bombay: Nirnayasagar Press, 1928).
Russell, G. W. E. *Matthew Arnold* (New York: Haskell House Publishers Ltd, 1904).
Sastri, P.S. *Coleridge's Theory of Poetry* (New Delhi: S. Chand & Co., 1980).
Scanlon, Mary. 'Ethics and the Lyric', *College Literature*, 34, no. 1 (Winter 2007): 1–22.
Scheiner, Corinne. 'Teleiopoiesis, Telepoesis, and the Practice of Comparative Literature', *Comparative Literature*, 57, no. 3, (Summer 2005): 239–45.

Schulz, Max F. 'Coleridge Agonistes', *The Journal of English and Germanic Philology*, 61, no. 2 (1962): 268–77.
Semaan, Khalil I. H. 'T. S. Eliot's Influence on Arabic Poetry and Theater' *Comparative Literature Studies*, 6, no. 4 (1969): 472–89.
Sengupta, S. C. *An Introduction to Aristotle's Poetics* (Calcutta: N.M. Publishers, 1971).
Serres, Michel. *The Five Senses* (trans.) Margaret Sankey and Peter Cowley (London: Continuum, 2008).
Sethna, K. D. *Inspiration and Effort* (Waterfort CT: The Integral Life Foundation, 1995).
———. *Talks on Poetry* (Pondicherry: Sri Aurobindo International Centre of Education, 1989).
———. (ed.) *Overhead Poetry* (Pondicherry: SAICE, 1972).
———. *Sri Aurobindo: The Poet* (Pondicherry: Sri Aurobindo Ashram, 1970).
Shaftesbury, Anthony Ashley Cooper, Third Earl of, *Characteristics of Men, Manners, Opinions, Times*, etc., (ed.) John M. Robertson (London, 1900).
Shaheen, Muhammad. 'Eliot in Modern Arabic Poetry,' in *T. S. Eliot.: Man and Poet*, vol. 1, (ed.) Laura Cowan (Orono, Maine: National Poetry Foundation, 1990), 151–64.
Sharma, L. S. *Coleridge: His Contribution to English Criticism* (New Delhi: Arnold Publishers, 1993).
Shawcross, J. (ed.) *Biographia Literaria* (London: Oxford University Press, 1907).
Sherfan, Andrew Dib. *A Third Treasury of Kahlil Gibran* (Philosophical Library, 2011).
Sherwood, John C. 'Dryden and the Critical Theories of Tasso' *Comparative Literature*, 1, no. 4 (Autumn 1966): 351–59.
Shih, Vincent Yu-chung (trans. & annotated) *The Literary Mind and the Carving of Dragons* (Hong Kong: The Chinese University Press, 1983).
Shriramamurti P. (ed.) *Camatkaracandrika* (Waltair: Andhra University, 1969).
Shusterman, Richard 'T. S. Eliot on Reading: Pleasures, Games and Wisdom' *Philosophy and Literature*, 11, no. 1 (April 1987): 1–20.
Simmel, Georg. 'The Stranger', *The Sociology of Georg Simmel* (trans.) Kurt H. Wolff (Glencoe, Ill.: The Free Press, 1950): 402–8.
Simpson, Evelyn M. and George R. Potter, (ed.) *The Sermons of John Donne* 10 vols. (Berkeley: University of California Press, 1953–62).
Smith, Laurajane. *Uses of Heritage* (London: Routledge, 2006).
Soldo, John J. 'T. S. Eliot and Jules LaForgue', *American Literature*, 55, no. 2 (May 1983): 137–50.
Somekh, Sasson, (ed.) *Studies in Medieval Arabic and Hebrew Poetics* (Leiden: Brill, 1991).
Spender, Stephen. *The Making of a Poem* (London: Hamish Hamilton, 1955).
Spenser, Edmund. *The Faerie Queene* (ed.) Thomas P. Roche Jr. (New York: Penguin, 1979).
Spingarn, Joel. *A History of Literary Criticism in the Renaissance* (New York: Columbia University Press, 1908, reprinted 1963).
Stallybrass, Peter and Allon White, *The Politics and Poetics of Transgression* (London: Methuen, 1986).
Stange, G. Robert. *Matthew Arnold: The Poet as Humanist* (Princeton, N.J.: Princeton University Press, 1967).
Steinberg, M. P. (ed.) *Walter Benjamin and the Demands of History* (Ithaca, N.Y.: Cornell University Press, 1996).

Stevens, Wallace. 'Three Academic Pieces,' in *The Necessary Angel: Essays on Reality and the Imagination* (New York: Knopf, 1951), 69–90.
Stolnitz, Jerome. 'On the Significance of Lord Shaftesbury in Modern Aesthetic Theory' *The Philosophical Quarterly* 11, no. 43 (April 1961): 97–113.
Stone, Donald D. 'Matthew Arnold and the Pragmatics of Hebraism and Hellenism', *Poetics Today*, 19, no. 2 (Summer 1998): 179–98.
Strobach, Nico. *The Moment of Change: A Systematic History in the Philosophy of Space and Time* (Dordrecht: Springer, 1998).
Strozier, Robert M. 'Poetic Conception in Sir Philip Sidney's *An Apology for Poetry*', *The Yearbook of English Studies*, Vol. 2 (1972): 49–60.
Super, R. H. (ed.) *The Complete Prose Works of Matthew Arnold*, Vol. 5 (Ann Arbor: University of Michigan Press, 1962).
Tagore, Rabindranath. *Rabindra Rachanavali* Vol. 13, (Kolkata: Government of West Bengal, 1990).
———. *Sadhana* (Madras: Macmillan, 1979).
———. *The Religion of Man* (London: George Allen and Unwin Ltd., 1958).
———. *A Vision of India's History* (Calcutta: Visva Bharati Bookshop, 1951).
Thorne, J. P. 'A Ramistical Commentary on Sidney's "An Apologie for Poetrie"' *Modern Philology*, 54, no. 3 (Feb. 1957): 158–64.
Thorpe, Clarence Dewitt. 'Addison and Hutcheson on the Imagination', *ELH* 2, no. 3 (Nov. 1935): 215–34.
Tigerstedt, E. N. 'The Poet as Creator: Origins of a Metaphor' *Comparative Literature Studies*, 5, no. 4 (1968): 455–88.
Tillotson, Geoffrey & Brian Jenkins (ed.) *Samuel Johnson: The History of Rasselas* (Oxford: Oxford University Press, 1977).
Tomlinson, David. 'T. S. Eliot and the Cubists', *Twentieth Century Literature*, 26, no. 1 (Spring 1980): 64–81.
Townsend, Dabney 'Shaftesbury's Aesthetic Theory' *Journal of Aesthetics and Art Criticism*, 41, no. 2 (Winter 1982): 205–13.
Traill, H. D. (ed.) *On Heroes, Hero-Worship and the Heroic in History* (Centenary Edition; New York, 1897–1901).
Trela, D. J. & Rodger L. Tarr (eds.) *The Critical Response to Thomas Carlyle's Major Works* (Westport, Conn.: Greenwood Press, 1997).
Tripathi, R.S. (ed.), *Dhvanyaloka* (Delhi: MotilalBanarasidas, 1963).
Trowbridge, Hoyt. 'The Place of Rules in Dryden's Criticism', *Modern Philology*, 44, no. 2 (Nov., 1946): 84–96.
Vickers, Neil. 'Before Depression: Coleridge's Melancholia', *Studies in the Literary Imagination*, 44, no. 1 (Spring 2011): 85–98.
Virkar, P. N. 'Was *Sahrdaya* the name of the author of the Dhvanikarikas?' *Annals of the Bhandarkar Oriental Research Institute* 57, no. 1/4 (1976): 192–98.
Walker, Keith (ed.) *John Dryden the Major Works* (Oxford: Oxford University Press, 1987).
Wark, R. R. *Discourses on Art* (New Haven, Conn.: Yale University Press, 1975).
Weber, Samuel 'The Singular Historicity of Literary Understanding: "Still Ending ..."' *MLN*, 125, no. 3 (April 2010): 626–41.
Weil, Simone. *La Pesanteur et la grace*, Pocket (12 février 1993).
Weinberg, Bernard. *A History of Literary Criticism in the Italian Renaissance* (Chicago: University of Chicago Press, 1961).

Weinbrot, Howard D. 'The Reader, the General, and the Particular: Johnson and Imlac in Chapter Ten of Rasselas', *Eighteenth-Century Studies*, 5, no. 1 (Autumn 1971): 80–96.
Weitz, Morris. *Problems in Aesthetics* (New York: Macmillan, 1959).
Wesling, Donald. *Bakhtin and the Social Moorings of Poetry* (Lewisburg: Bucknell University Press, 2003).
Whalley, George. 'The Harvest on the Ground: Coleridge's Marginalia', *University of Toronto Quarterly*, 38, no. 3, (April 1969): 248–276.
White, Helen C. 'Matthew Arnold and Goethe', *PMLA* 36, no. 3 (Sep., 1921): 436–453.
White, Peter. 'Tradition and the Individual Talent' Revisited', *The Review of English Studies*, 58, no. 235 (Jun. 2007): 364–92.
Whitehead, Alfred North. *Process and Reality: An Essay in Cosmology* (ed.) D. R. Griffin and D. W. Sherburne (New York: Free Press, 1978).
———. *Adventures of Ideas* (New York: Free Press, 1967).
———. *Science and the Modern World* (New York: The Free Press, 1967).
———. *Modes of Thought* (New York: Macmillan and Cambridge University Press, 1938).
Will, Frederic 'Cousin and Coleridge: The Aesthetic Ideal' *Comparative Literature*, 8, no. 1, (1956): 63–77.
Williams, Louise Blakeney. *Modernism and the Ideology of History: Literature, Politics and the Past* (Cambridge: Cambridge University Press, 2002).
Wilson, Douglas B. 'The Dreaming Imagination: Coleridge, Keats and Wordsworth' in *Coleridge, Keats, and the Imagination* (ed.) J Robert Barth & John L. Mahoney (Columbia: University of Missouri Press, 1990), 59–62.
Woolf, Virginia. *The Common Reader* (London, 1932).
Worden, Blair 'Historians and Poets', *Huntington Library Quarterly*, 68, no. 1–2 (March 2005): 71–93.
Worden, Blair. *The Sound of Virtue: Philip Sidney's "Arcadia" and Elizabethan Politics* (New Haven: Yale University Press, 1996).
Yao, Steven G. 'The Unheimlich Maneuver; or the Gap, the Gradient, and the Spaces of Comparison' *Comparative Literature*, 57, no. 3 (2005): 246–55.
Yingping, Zhu. (ed.) *Wenxin diaolong suoyin* (Shanghai: Shanghai guji, 1987).
Young, Terri De. 'T. S. Eliot and Modem Arabic Poetry,' *Yearbook of Comparative and General Literature* 48 (2000): 3–21.
Youngquist, Paul. 'Rehabilitating Coleridge: Poetry, Philosophy, Excess', *ELH*, 66, 4 (1999): 885–909.
Youngren, William 'Dr. Johnson, Joseph Warton, and the "Theory of Particularity"', *Dispositio*, 4, no. 11/12, (Verano-Otoño 1979): 163–88.
———. 'Generality, Science and Poetic Language in the Restoration,' *ELH*, XXXV (1968): 158–87.
Zilcosky, John. 'Modern Monuments: T. S. Eliot, Nietzsche, and the Problem of History' *Journal of Modern Literature*, 29, no. 1 (Autumn 2005): 21–33.
Ziolkowski, Jan M. 'Incomparable: The Destiny of Comparative Literature, Globalization or Not' *The Global South*, 1, no. 2 (Fall 2007): 16–44.
Zoeren, Steven Van. *Poetry and Personality, Reading, Exegesis, and Hermeneutics in Traditional China* (Stanford, Calif.: Stanford University Press, 1991).

Index

Abhinavagupta 54–55, 128–130
Addison, Joseph 70–71, 80
Adorno, Theodore 15
Agamben, G. 12, 15
Akenside, Mark 67
Al-Askari, Abu Hilal 158
Al-Farabi, Abu Nasr 34
Al-Jurjani, Abd al-Qahir 33, 58
Al-Qartajanni, Hazim 34, 58
alterity 155
Anandavardhana 55, 128, 130, 133, 135
Andrade, Oswald de 154
An*tagonism* 4, 11, 43–46, 48, 50–53, 56, 58, 78, 83
Aquinas, Thomas 36
Arcadia 31, 38
Aristotle 22, 25–26, 28, 32, 35–37, 68, 71, 82, 129, 137, 162
Arnheim, Rudolf 94
Arnold, Matthew 166
As You Like It 32
Atharva Veda 114
Attridge, Derek 153
aucitya 136
auditory imagination 150
Auerbach, Eric 9
Augustine, St. 36, 91, 92

Bachelard, Gaston 97, 164
Badiou, Alain 9
Bakhtin, Mikhail 151
Barad, Karen 103
Barrett, Joseph 110
Bataille, G. 15
Baudelaire, Charles Pierre 167
Beach D. M. 25
Beardsley, Monroe 36
Benjamin, Walter 6
Bergson, Henri 152, 164, 168
Bhamaha 133, 139
Biran, Maine de 62
Blake, William 1, 95–96

Bouhours, Dominique 82
Bradley, F. H. 148–149
Brady, Jennifer 52
Brett, R. L. 66, 68
Browning, Robert 166
Bruno, Giordano 35
Buber, Martin 157
Burke, Edmund 68

Caciarri, Massimo 7
Cantarino, Vicente 33
Carlyle, Thomas 2–3, 164
Cassirer, Ernest 99
Chaucer, Geoffrey 129, 135
Christ, Carol 166
Clarke, Graham 162
Coleridge, S. T. 81, 140, 163, 165
complexity 8, 167
Confucius 48
Coste, Didier 44
Croce, Benedetto 133

daemonic 95–96
Daiches, David 25
Dandin 134, 137, 139
Dante 95, 115–117, 136
Delaura, David 111
Deleuze, Gilles 11, 167
Dennis, John 68–69, 72, 80
Derrida, Jacques 9
Descartes, Rene 3, 95
Dewey, John 3
Diderot, Denis 78–79
Dieckmann, Herbert 78
disinterestedness 64
Donne, John 50, 159
Driesch, Hans 150–151
Dryden, John 69–72, 78, 80, 140
Durakovic, Esad 157

Eliot, T. S. 4, 103
Ellman, Maud 149

Emerson, Ralph Waldo 3, 141
enargia 71–72, 83
Engells, James 80
Enthusiasm 67–68, 80
Eskin, Michael 151

Fabian, Bernard 80
Fakhreddine, Huda 57
Falmer, Norman 33
feign 29, 32, 34, 36
festina lente 15–16
Fichte, Johann Gottlieb 112
Fish, Stanley 51
flanuer 1
Flatley, Jonathan 15
Follet, Mary Parker 10
Ford, Andrew 21
Ford, Ford Madox 14
Foucault, Michel 157
Frendo, Maria 161
Freud, Sigmund 154

Gadamer, Hans Georg 2, 12, 167
Galvin, Rachel 154
Garrison, Jim 2
Gascoigne, George 27–28
generality 76–77
Genesis 22, 30
genius 78–83
Gerard, Albert 78–81
Ghose, Aurobindo 109–121, 134
Gibran, Kahlil 138
Gilpin, George 95
Goethe, J. W. V. 111, 118, 133, 140
golden 29, 31–32, 34, 37–38
Grassi, Ernesto 26
Greville, Fulke 32–33

habitus 9
Harington, J. 30
Harrold, Charles 112
Hayot, Eric 10
Hegel, G. W. F. 150, 155
Heidegger, Martin 9
Herder, Johann Gottfried 126
historical sense 147–148, 153, 155–157, 165–166
Hobbes, Thomas 66
Homer 136
Horatio 32
Hulme, T. E. 160
Hume, David 9
Hume, Robert 72, 98

Hutcheson, Francis 76
Hutchinson, Mary 148
hybridity 156
hybrid poetics 157

Idea 29
imagination 69–71, 74, 76, 78–83, 90–92, 96–103
imitation 28–30, 32, 34–37, 70–71, 81–82
Inada, Kenneth K. 153
indifference 10
instant 164–165
interruption 6
intra-active transculturality 9
invention 31

Jackson, Kenneth 154
Ja'far, Qudama Ibn 33
James, William 14
Jay, Gregory 150
Johnson, Samuel 73–80
Jones, Michel Alhadeff 8
Jonson, Ben 132
Joyce, Michael 90, 148

Kant, Immanuel 3, 4, 69, 98–100, 102, 151
Kaplan, Edward 97
Katona, Gabor 35
Keats, John 132, 137
Kenner, Hugh 148
Kermode, Frank 152
Khayyam, Omar 140
Kipperman, Mark 95
Kishler, Thomas 35
Ksemendra 136–137
"Kubla Khan" 93
Kui, Jiang 51
Kuntaka 134–135

LaForgue, Jules 148, 156
Lefebvre, Henri 16
Leibniz, G. H. 3
Letwin, Shirley 127
Lin, Shuen-Fu 96
listening 4, 156–157
Locke, John 66

Mack, Michael 29, 38
Mammata 130–131, 133
Marotti, Arthur 46
Marsh, Robert 63–64

Index   195

Martin, Floyd 75
Martindale, Charles 155
Massumi, Brian 14
Matar, Nabil 34
Matthiessen, Francis 161
McFarlane, James 163
McIntyre, John 31
Mencius 49, 53
Michelangelo 82, 127
Mill, John Stuart 67
Milton, John 135–136
Moore, Roger 23
Morrison, Keith 8
Murray, Timothy 45

Nancy, Jean Luc 9, 13
Neff, Emery 110
Neitzsche, Friedrich 12, 153–154
Nemoto, Hiroshi 5
Newton, Richard 45
Noel-Tod, Jeremy 164
Novalis 112, 155

Pater, Walter 166
Payne, Paula 37
Perry, Seamus 92, 95
Pierce, Charles 62
plagiarism 157, 158
Plato 1, 22, 29, 31–32, 62, 64–65, 67–68, 77, 96
Plotinus 29
Pontano, Giovanni 26
Pope, Alexander 70, 140
Pound, Ezra 159, 168
Puttenham, George 26–27, 32

Quint, David 26

Raabih, Ibn Abd 33
Raiger, Michael 22–23, 32
Rajasekhara 55, 117, 137
Ramus, Petrus 37
Ranciere, Jacques 17
rasa 54–55
Rashiq, Ibn 34, 158
Ravaisson, Felix 3
Rembrandt, Rijn van 82
Reynolds, Joshua 74–77, 80, 82–83
Richards, I. A. 140
Rig Veda 114
Ronnel, Avitor 16
Roupnel, Gaston 164
Rowe, George 46, 52

sahridaya 44, 53–57
Sartor Resartus 2
Saussure, Ferdinand de 6
Saussy, Haun 12
Scaliger, J. J. 23–24, 26, 29, 32
Schegel, A. 111
Schelling, F. W. J. 96, 102
Serres, Michael 1
Sethna, Kaikhosru 120
Shaftesbury, Third Earl of 63–66, 69–71, 76, 78–79, 81
Shakespeare, William 29, 55, 77–78, 91, 101, 115–118, 120, 130, 132, 164
Sherwood, John 72
Simmel, Georg 6, 7, 8
singularity 6, 152–153
Spender, Stephen 161
Spenser, Edmund 29
Staub, Susan 27
Stevens, Wallace 11
stranger 6, 7, 8
Strobach, Nico 5
stroll 7
Strozier, Robert 28
Sutherland, James 77

Tagore, Rabindranath 1, 14, 24–25, 129–131, 133–135, 139, 141
tarka 4–5
Tasso, Torquato 27, 32, 72
Temple, William 37
Tennyson, Alfred 166
Thorpe, Clarence 70–71
trans-habit 21, 26, 36, 38, 44, 48, 57, 62, 73, 78, 90–92, 94, 96, 100–101, 109, 121, 127–128, 141, 147–149, 151–152, 166, 168–169
Trowbridge, Hoyt 73

Valery, Paul 94, 162–163
Vamana 55, 134
Virgil 26, 159
Visvanatha 132

Wallas, Graham 94
Waller, Edmund 67
Warton, Joseph 77
Weber, Samuel 6
Wellek, Rene 76
Wesling, Donald 151
Whitehead, A. N. 12

Worden, Blair 25
Wordsworth, William 129, 135, 138, 140, 165

Xie, Lui 52, 56, 57, 96, 102

Yi, Cheng 49

Zai, Zhang 57
Zi, Zhuang 50
Zoeren, Steven Van 49

For Product Safety Concerns and Information please contact our EU
representative GPSR@taylorandfrancis.com
Taylor & Francis Verlag GmbH, Kaufingerstraße 24, 80331 München, Germany

www.ingramcontent.com/pod-product-compliance
Lightning Source LLC
Chambersburg PA
CBHW061446300426
44114CB00014B/1858